12 MORE ESSENTIAL SKILLS FOR SOFTWARE ARCHITECTS

12 MORE ESSENTIAL SKILLS FOR SOFTWARE ARCHITECTS

DAVE HENDRICKSEN

✦✦ Addison-Wesley

Upper Saddle River, NJ • Boston • Indianapolis • San Francisco
New York • Toronto • Montreal • London • Munich • Paris • Madrid
Capetown • Sydney • Tokyo • Singapore • Mexico City

For information about buying this title in bulk quantities, or for special sales opportunities (which may include electronic versions; custom cover designs; and content particular to your business, training goals, marketing focus, or branding interests), please contact our corporate sales department at corpsales@pearsoned.com or (800) 382-3419.

For government sales inquiries, please contact governmentsales@pearsoned.com.

For questions about sales outside the United States, please contact international@pearsoned.com.

Visit us on the Web: informit.com/aw

Library of Congress Cataloging-in-Publication Data

Hendricksen, Dave, 1964– author.
  12 more essential skills for software architects / Dave Hendricksen.
      pages cm
  Includes bibliographical references and index.
  ISBN 978-0-321-90947-3 (pbk. : alk. paper)
  1. Software architecture—Vocational guidance. 2. Computer software developers—Life skills guides. 3. Career development. I. Title. II. Title: Twelve more essential skills for software architects.
  QA76.76.D47H466 2015
  005.1'20023—dc23
                                      2014021582

ISBN-13: 978-0-321-90947-3
ISBN-10: 0-321-90947-X
Text printed in the United States on recycled paper at RR Donnelley in Crawfordsville, Indiana.
First printing, August 2014

To my wife, Jennifer, my son, Tim, and my daughter, Katie.

CONTENTS

Preface   xix

Acknowledgments   xxiii

About the Author   xxv

Part I: Project Skills   1

Chapter 1:   Partnership   5
  What Is a Partnership?   6
  What Are the Key Aspects of a Partnership?   6
  Alignment   6
    With Whom Do I Need to Be Partners?   7
    Finding the Thought Leaders   9
    Knowing the Influencers   10
    Establishing Trusted Adviser(s)   10
    Community Review (Architecture Review Board)   10
    Seeking Alignment before Making Key Decisions   11
    Alignment of a Shared Vision Enables Partnerships   11
  Trust   12
    Establishing Trust   12
    Establishing Open Disclosure   12
    Avoiding Getting Spread Too Thin (Overcommitting)   13
    How to Unwind after You Have Overcommitted   14
    Learning to Say No   15
    Trust Enables Transparency—the Lifeblood of Partnerships   16
  Context   17
    Realizing the Nature of the Partnership   17
    Being Aware of Your Business Context   18
    Technical Decisions Require Partnerships   18
    Key Point: Technical Decisions Are Political Decisions   19
    Presenting the Situation First (Give Context)   19
    Having Your Partners' Backs   20

Contributing to Your Partners' Successes	20
Safety in Numbers	21
Collaboration	21
Bringing Value to the Table	22
Becoming a Mentor	22
Seeking a Mentor	23
Partnerships Can Be a Source of Opportunity	24
Partnerships Are a Step toward Ideation	24
Collaboration Drives Stronger Partnerships	24
Relationships	25
Partnerships Are Not Just about Business	25
Making Deposits before You Start Withdrawing	25
External Partnerships	26
Bad Experiences in the Past?	26
Avoiding Caustic Members of the Organization	26
Summary	27
References	28
Chapter 2: Discovery	**29**
What Is Discovery?	30
The Keys to Discovery	30
Understanding the Customer	32
Partnering with Sales, Marketing, and New Product Development	32
Meeting with Customers	37
What Will Delight the Customer?	43
Understanding the Market	43
Learning about the Customers' Customers	46
Where Are the Customers Willing to Spend Money?	47
What Is the Competition Doing?	48
Listening to Themes across Customers	50
Understanding Your Business	51
Learning What Your Business Wants to Do	52
Personalizing Your Company's Strategic Goals	52
Developing a Business Context for Decision Making	52
Summary	53
References	53
Chapter 3: Conceptualization	**55**
Ideation	56
Getting Involved Early	57
Conceptualization: Bringing Ideas to Life	58

Concept Formation 59
  What Language Are They Speaking? 59
  What Problem Is Being Discussed? 60
  When Arriving Late to the Ideation Party, Be Cautious
    about Committing 62
  What Does This Concept Look Like? 63
Concept Reification 67
  Minimum Viable Product 67
  The Need for Experimentation 68
  Establishing Assumptions Can Help Harmonize the Vision 68
  Establishing Essential Capabilities and Customer Roles 69
  Reify with Customers 70
Concept Evolution 71
  Being a Student of History 71
  Embracing Multiple Perspectives 72
  Seeking Conceptual Integrity 73
  Recognizing Adjacent Opportunities 75
Summary 75
References 76

Chapter 4: Estimation 79
Estimates Overview 80
  What Is the Purpose of the Estimate? 80
  Is There an Established Project Context? 82
  What Is an Architectural Approach? 82
Understanding the Estimating Process 84
  Estimating Pipeline 84
  Types of Projects 85
  Alternative Ways of Financing Projects 86
  Understanding the Business Process 87
Developing the Architectural Approach 88
  Is This a Partnership or a Contractual Relationship? 88
  What Is the Business Rationale for the Project? 89
  What Is the Marketing Approach? 89
  Is This a Repeat Estimate? 90
  What Risks Have You Identified? Can You Mitigate Them? 91
  Are You Building a Platform? 93
  Are You Re-platforming? 93
  What Technologies Are in Play? 94
  What Is the Organizational Structure? 95
  Do You Need to Seek External Research? 96
  Have You Identified Leverageable Components? 96

Estimating Strategies 97
   Plan for Unknowns and Challenges 97
   Be Realistic: Don't Cave In Just to Get the Project 98
   Keep the Critical Things Close 98
   Develop Estimating Feedback Loops 98
   Minimize Organization Coupling and Cohesion 98
   PowerPoint as You Go 99
   Develop Checklists 99
   Gain Executive and Organization Buy-in Early 99
Estimating Principles 99
   Know the Hard Problem 100
   Provide Options 100
   Leave Design Decisions Open 100
   Know the Schedule 100
   Know What You Want 100
   Avoid Being Negative 100
   Seek Opportunities to Say Yes 100
   Bargain Hard Now, Not Later 101
   Don't Cave In 101
   Trust Your Gut Feeling 101
   Beware of Projects That Others Have Estimated 101
   Know the Business's Targeted Build Price 101
Bringing It All Together 102
   Knowing Your Timeline 102
   Who Is Involved with Estimating? 102
   Understanding Your Leverage Points 103
   Putting It All Together 103
   Engaging Executives 103
   Selling the Estimate 104
Summary 106
References 106

Chapter 5: Management 109
Architecture Management Defined 110
Areas of Architectural Responsibility 110
Striving toward Technology Excellence 111
   Establishing a Vision 112
   Raising Awareness of Technical Debt and
     Funding the Right Solution 112
   Keeping the Technical Environment Interesting 113
   Finding Potential Patents 114
   Seeking Data Center and Operations Support for
     Your Direction 114

Generalizing the Solution   115
Making It Strategic   115
Leveraging Solutions   115
Delivering Projects   116
    Partnering with the Project Manager   116
    Eliminating Dependencies Ruthlessly   116
    Managing Expectations   116
    Mastering the Development Process   117
    Being Where the Problems Are   118
    Being Aware of Nontransparency on Your Projects   118
    Limiting the Number of Contractors in Leadership
        Positions   119
    Providing Technical Management (Areas of Responsibility)   119
    Managing by Walking Around   120
Resolving Issues   121
    Asking the Tough Questions   121
    Dealing with Problems in the Moment   121
    Saying No, but with Options   122
    Striving to Be Consistent in Your Decisions   122
    Learning to Deal with Things Head-on, Cards Faceup
        on the Table   124
    Knowing What You Are Willing to Cave On When
        Negotiating   124
    Being Willing to Challenge Areas You Don't Agree with
        (Respectfully)   124
    Being Willing to Stand Your Ground   125
    Knowing What Is Not Your Problem   125
Partnering with Executives   125
    Managing Risk through Transparency   125
    Reviewing Estimates   126
    Limiting the Number of Boxes on Diagrams   126
    Raising Technology Awareness   126
    Having Your Boss's Back   127
    Avoiding Interrupting Executives When They Are Talking   127
    Being Confident   127
Managing Your Time   127
    Limiting the Number of Projects to Which You Commit   128
    Defining Your Role and Bounding It   128
    Prioritizing Where to Engage Your Time   128
    Learning to Make Decisions on Limited Data and
        with Limited Time   130
    Attending Meetings Only If You Are an Active Participant   130
    Getting a Deadline   130

Delegating to Those You Trust   130
Meeting in Person   131
Grooming Technical Talent   131
Having an Architecture Mentorship Program   131
Having a Technology Forum   132
Encouraging Members of Your Technical Team to
    Attend Local Conferences and User Groups   132
Hiring the Best People: Don't Just Fill a Position   133
Enhancing Your Skill Set   134
Sitting with Other Architects   134
Doing Something Technical Every Day   134
Focusing on What Scares You   135
Becoming an Expert in an Area   135
Looking for Projects Where You Can Grow Your Skills   135
Summary   136
References   136

Part II: Technology Skills   139

Chapter 6:   Platform Development   143
Platform Development Defined   144
The Elements of Platform Development   144
Capabilities   145
Defining the Set of Objectives   145
Defining the Set of Capabilities   146
Focusing on Leverageable Capabilities   146
Developing a Strong Conceptual Model   147
APIs Are the Keys to the Kingdom   147
Ecosystem   148
Platform Users   148
Platform Ownership   148
Platform Management   155
Platform Development   158
Acknowledging the Costs Associated with the Platform   161
Managing Platform Quality   162
Platform Integration   162
Scalability   164
Security   164
Guiding Principles   164
Seek Exceptional Quality   164

Seek Operational Excellence   164
Seek Configurability over Hard Coding   165
Seek Leverageability   165
Seek Redundant Architecture   165
Seek Linear Scalability   166
Avoid Platform Entanglement   166
Avoid Platform Sprawl   166
Keep Upgrading to Current Technologies   166
Summary   166
References   167

Chapter 7:   Architectural Perspective   169
Architectural Perspective Defined   170
Architectural Principles   170
The Principle of Least Surprise   170
The Principle of Least Knowledge (aka the Law of Demeter)   172
The Principle of Least Effort (aka Zipf's Law)   172
The Principle of Opportunity Cost   173
The Principle of Single Responsibility   175
The Principle of Parsimony (aka Occam's Razor or KISS)   175
The Principle of Last Responsible Moment
(aka Cost of Delay)   176
The Principle of Feedback   177
Architectural Concerns   177
Availability   178
Scalability   180
Extensibility   181
Repeatability   182
Compatibility   182
Sustainability   182
Security, Disaster Recovery, Business Continuity, and
Open-Source Licensing   183
Third-Party Integration   183
Architectural Communication   183
Domain Model   184
Process Diagram   184
Context Diagram   185
User Interface Mock-ups   186
Logical Architecture Diagram   186
Executive Overview Diagram   187
Hardware Environments Diagram   187
Risks, Assumptions, Issues, and Dependencies (RAID)   188

Bringing It All Together   191
Summary   192
References   192

Chapter 8:   Governance   193
Governance Defined   194
Governance Principles   194
    Avoid Vendor Lock-in   194
    Encourage Open-Source Usage   195
    Minimize the Cost of Disruption (aka Enable Business
        Continuity Planning and Disaster Recovery)   196
    Enable Loose Coupling between Business Units   198
    Leverage Common Capabilities   199
    Ensure Regulatory Compliance   200
    Ensure Security   201
    The Principle of Least Privilege (aka the Principle of
        Least Authority)   202
    Seek Unified Identity and Access Management   202
    Seek Data Portability (aka Avoid Data Lock-in)   203
    Seek Integration and Automation   203
Areas of Governance   203
    Estimates   204
    Management Concerns   205
    Architecture   206
    Design   208
    Building, Coding, Integrating, Deploying, Testing,
        and Monitoring   208
Governance and a Healthy Tension with Agile   209
Summary   210
References   210

Chapter 9:   Know-how   213
Know-how Defined   214
Developing Know-how   215
    Developing Know-how Relevance   215
    Developing Know-how Currency   218
    Developing Know-how Excellence   221
Know-how Synthesis   229
Know-how-Driven Architecture   230
Summary   231
References   232

Part III: Visionary Skills   233

Chapter 10:   Technology Innovation   237
Technology Innovation Defined   238
Trend Awareness   238
  Areas of Trend Awareness   240
  Applying Trend Awareness   241
Business Alignment   242
  Paying Attention to Trends on Customer Inquiries   242
  Getting Customer Feedback   242
  Analyzing Customer Feedback   243
  When to Be Cautious about Trends   243
  When to Embrace a Trend   245
Strategic Research   245
  Research Approaches   246
Technology Innovation Principles   247
  Seek Approved but Minimal Time and Funding to
    Explore   247
  Make Small Bets   248
  Use Technology Scouting to Scan and Track the
    Trends Regularly   248
  Have a Lab Area   249
  Use Rapid Experimentation with User Feedback Loops   250
  Show the Business and Customers Prototypes   250
  Introduce New Technologies at the Edge   250
Pragmatic Technology Innovation   252
Summary   253
References   254

Chapter 11:   Strategic Roadmapping   255
Strategic Roadmapping Defined   256
Elements of a Strategic Roadmap   257
  Strategically Focused   257
  Time Sequenced   257
  Organized by Swim Lanes   257
  Dependency Aware   257
  Visually Represented   258
  Collaborative in Nature   258
  Code Named   258
  Context Dependent (Personalized)   258
  Multidisciplinary and Specialized   258

Prioritized   259
Iterative in Nature   259
Updated   259
Published   259
Measurable   259
Roadmapping Strategies   260
Whiteboarding the Roadmap Using Sticky Notes   260
Starting with the End (aka Work Backward)   260
Holding Workshops   260
Thinking of Roadmapping as a Project   261
Capturing Underlying Guiding Principles   261
Roadmapping Principles   261
Keep It Simple   261
Partner with the Business   262
Get Moving   262
Have Fun   262
Strategies without Goals Are Pointless   262
Identify Areas That Require Research and Innovation   263
Identify Skill and Knowledge Gaps   263
Be Flexible on the Timing of Getting to the Destination   263
Be Willing to Take a New Route   263
It's Not about the Details; Focus on the Destination and
    Key Milestones   264
Follow What Energizes You   265
What Is an Architect's Role in Roadmapping?   265
Where Can You Use Roadmaps?   266
Roadmap Considerations   266
Roadmap Socialization   268
Celebrating Milestones Achieved   269
Summary   269
References   270

Chapter 12:   Entrepreneurial Execution   271
Entrepreneurial Execution Defined   272
Elements of Entrepreneurial Execution   272
Entrepreneurial Spirit   274
Calculated Risk Taking   275
Delivering Results   276
Entrepreneurial Execution Principles   276
Affordable Loss Principle   276
Lemonade Principle   276
Patchwork Quilt Principle   277

Bird-in-the-Hand Principle 277
Pilot-in-the-Plane Principle 277
Seize the Moment 278
Follow Your Passion 278
Learn to Pivot 279
Learn by Doing (Making Mistakes), but Do It
    Cost-Effectively 280
Seek Feedback 281
Seek Leverage 282
Architecting with Entrepreneurial Execution 283
Summary 284
References 284

Epilogue: Bringing It All Together 287
Thinking about Skill Development 288
Final Thought 289

Index 291

PREFACE

"Architecture is not a profession for the faint-hearted, the weak-willed, or the short-lived."

—Martin Filler

"Architecture and building is about how you get around the obstacles that are presented to you. That sometimes determines how successful you'll be: How good are you at going around obstacles?"

—Jeremy Renner

"Architecture is a service business. An architect is given a program, budget, place, and schedule. Sometimes the end product rises to art—or at least people call it that."

—Frank Gehry

"Architecture is invention."

—Oscar Niemeyer

"I loved logic, math, computer programming. I loved systems and logic approaches. And so I just figured architecture is this perfect combination."

—Maya Lin

"I think about architecture all the time. That's the problem. But I've always been like that. I dream it sometimes."

—Zaha Hadid

"The Internet is probably the most important technological advancement of my lifetime. Its strength lies in its open architecture and its ability to allow a framework where all voices can be heard."

—Adam Savage

BOOK MOTIVATION

This book and my first book (*12 Essential Skills for Software Architects*) focus on the skills needed to become a successful software architect.

Software architecture is about learning how to relate to people and learning how to think about things with an eye toward architecture. *12 Essential Skills for Software Architects* focused on soft skills; without these, the rest of the journey is nearly impossible.

Shortly after I completed my first book, I began receiving questions about the assumed technical skills (shown in Figure P.1) that are referred to but not discussed.

This book dives into the details of those assumed skills—the technical skills you need on a daily basis in the role of an architect. It is the combination of soft *and* technical skills that will enable you reach your goals.

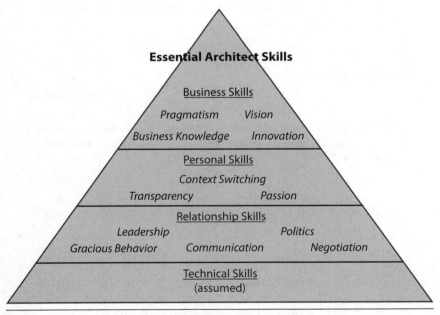

Figure P.1 Twelve essential skills for software architects

BOOK GOALS

My goals for this book are to

- Enable excellence in software architecture through skills development
- Enable architectural success in a business context
- Promote an architectural approach for thinking about the enterprise

BOOK ORGANIZATION

The format and style of this book are intended to help evoke critical thinking about your specific set of projects, your areas of architectural oversight, and your areas of direction-setting leadership. These take the form of project skills, technology skills, and vision skills.

These three areas are organized as follows:

- **Part I: Project Skills.** These skills enable you to drive projects from early ideation to project delivery through
  - Partnership (Chapter 1)
  - Discovery (Chapter 2)
  - Conceptualization (Chapter 3)
  - Estimation (Chapter 4)
  - Management (Chapter 5)
- **Part II: Technology Skills.** These skills ensure that the right technologies are built, bought, or leveraged through
  - Platform Development (Chapter 6)
  - Architectural Perspective (Chapter 7)
  - Governance (Chapter 8)
  - Know-how (Chapter 9)
- **Part III: Visionary Skills.** These skills enable the pursuit of the business's long-term competitive vision through
  - Technology Innovation (Chapter 10)
  - Strategic Roadmapping (Chapter 11)
  - Entrepreneurial Execution (Chapter 12)

The three parts can be thought of as a layered set of skills for software architects (see Figure P.2). Each layer is the basis for the layer above it.

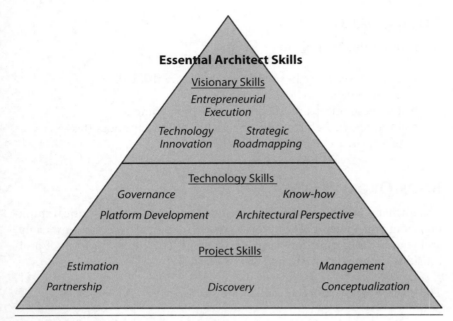

Figure P.2 Technical skills pyramid

Each of the chapters within the book is written to be read independently of the other chapters. This independence should enable you read the book in the order of your interests or needs.

I hope you enjoy reading the book and that you learn some new things that will enable you to become an excellent architect and better understand the role of an architect.

If you have any questions or comments, please feel free to contact me at dave@hendricksen.org.

ACKNOWLEDGMENTS

I would like to say thank you to the excellent staff at Addison-Wesley, specifically Olivia Basegio, Sheri Cain, Chris Guzikowski, Chuti Prasertsith, Kesel Wilson, and Barbara Wood. They have been absolutely fantastic to work with.

I would like to thank Brad Appleton, Kevin Bodie, Robert Maksimchuk, and one reviewer who chose to remain anonymous for reviewing my first draft of the book. They all gave me great feedback.

I would also like to thank the following reviewers from Thomson Reuters: Mick Atton, Dan Bennett, Cary Felbab, Scott Francis, Kevin Hakanson, Jesse Haraldson, James Jarvis, Andrew Lipstein, Andrew Martens, Lynn Meredith, Scott Post, Noah Pruzek, Chris Rowland, Bob Sturm, Bas Vellekoop, and Justin Wright. Each of them reviewed selected chapters in their areas of expertise.

In addition, I would like to say thank you to my wife, Jennifer, and son, Tim, for reviewing the book.

Finally, I would like to say thank you to my family and parents for their patience and support while I wrote this second book.

ACKNOWLEDGMENTS

ABOUT THE AUTHOR

"The most complicated skill is to be simple."

—Dejan Stojanović

"I strive for an architecture from which nothing can be taken away."

—Helmut Jahn

My name is Dave Hendricksen, and I am a Big Data architect for Thomson Reuters. These days I spend most of my time working on big data-related projects that span Thomson Reuters. I have also worked on WestLawNext (an online legal research tool), Optimus (a learning platform), and a wide variety of other projects, generally focused on new product development—I love to innovate. I also help run and organize an architecture mentorship program and a technology forum at Thomson Reuters.

Every day is busy and challenging; for me that equates to fun and engaging.

I have been married for 25 years to a beautiful lady. We have two great kids, one cat, one dog, and a *koi* pond. We have some lake property—it seems as if that's a requirement when you live in Minnesota, the Land of Ten Thousand Lakes. It is also the location of summertime building projects: trebuchet, go-cart, rain barrel water collection system, robotic lawn mower, and so on.

In a similar vein, I spend a fair amount of time mentoring the Eagan High School FIRST Robotics Team. We try to run our program like a small business—we need to raise money, market our team, build a product, and compete in tournaments.

Being the lead mentor for a large robotics team (more than 80 kids and more than 30 mentors) has many parallels to being an architect on large-scale development projects. There are a wide variety of opinions of what should be done, limited resources, limited time, and you need to deliver a successful product.

In short, I love to plan, research, organize, teach, mentor, architect, and build things.

PART I

PROJECT SKILLS

"I believe that architecture is a pragmatic art. To become art it must be built on a foundation of necessity. Freedom of expression, for me, consists in moving within a measured range that I assign to each of my undertakings. How instructive it is to remember Leonardo da Vinci's counsel that 'strength is born of constraint and dies from freedom.'"

—I. M. Pei

"I know the price of success: dedication, hard work, and an unremitting devotion to the things you want to see happen."

—Frank Lloyd Wright

"Architecture should speak of its time and place, but yearn for timelessness."

—Frank Gehry

"Make big plans; aim high in hope and work, remembering that a noble, logical diagram once recorded will not die."

—Daniel Burnham

"Not many architects have the luxury to reject significant things."

—Rem Koolhaas

Part I focuses on five essential project skills for an architect. These chapters focus on principles, strategies, and other areas related to project architecture oversight, such as dealing with drive-by estimates to help you become more effective in managing your architecture. These chapters are organized as follows:

- Chapter 1, "Partnership," will enable you to
    - Align with your business organization

- Establish mutual trust with your stakeholders
- Work within the business context
- Work collaboratively with your business colleagues
- Establish and maintain relationships throughout the business
- Chapter 2, "Discovery," will enable you to
  - Explore new areas with the business effectively
  - Gain a deep understanding of your customers, your business, and your marketplace
- Chapter 3, "Conceptualization," will enable you to
  - Help the business formulate product ideas and develop them into product concepts
  - Reify product concepts
  - Evolve product concepts into well-defined products with a solid architectural foundation
- Chapter 4, "Estimation," will enable you to
  - Lead technical groups in estimating projects
  - Identify project risks, assumptions, issues, and dependencies
  - Help communicate the estimates to project stakeholders, including executives
- Chapter 5, "Management," will enable you to
  - Manage the architectural areas of responsibility
  - Help drive projects from inception through customer delivery

Project skills comprise the foundational layer of skills needed to be an architect (see Figure PI.1).

The project skills are not necessarily sequenced. You need to learn the context of when to use them. Partnering with the business, discovering and conceptualizing new solutions to bring value to customers, and delivering the solutions are the foundations for the architectural life cycle of a project (see Figure PI.2) and the focus of Part I.

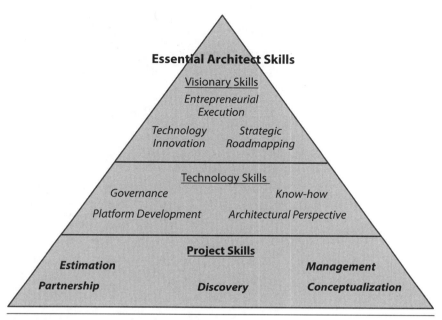

Figure PI.1 Essential architect skills (project skills)

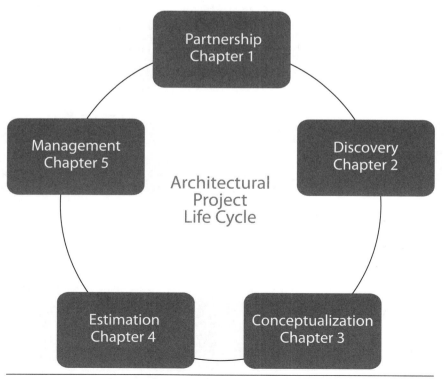

Figure PI.2 Architectural project life cycle

Chapter 1

PARTNERSHIP

"If we are together nothing is impossible. If we are divided all will fail."

—Winston Churchill

"In this new wave of technology, you can't do it all yourself, you have to form alliances."

—Carlos Slim Helú

"If you can run the company a bit more collaboratively, you get a better result, because you have more bandwidth and checking and balancing going on."

—Larry Page

"Keep away from people who belittle your ambitions. Small people always do that, but the really great make you feel that you too can become great."

—Mark Twain

Have you ever seen what appears to be a simple, straightforward technical decision unwind into political chaos? Conversely, have you ever seen what appears to be a politically charged decision just flow through without so much as a ripple of tension in the organization? In both cases, there seems to be a mystical force at work behind the scenes.

In the world of architecture, technical decisions need to be made every day. The needs of the business from both a short-term and a long-term perspective need to be considered. Your ability to determine the right direction and to convince those who need to implement it, to bear the operational costs, and to sell it will determine whether you are a success or a failure.

This chapter unveils one of the essential skills needed by a software architect: the ability to quickly form and establish partnerships.

Figure 1.1   Partnership success formula

WHAT IS A PARTNERSHIP?

A partnership is a relationship in which mutual trust is established. It is the willingness to stick together and pursue a goal even in the face of opposition. For an architect, forming partnerships is critical—it allows you to focus and present a common front when opposition comes.

Architecture is a social activity. The more buy-in you have, the more likely you are to succeed. Understand who your partners are; they will act as your guideposts (see Figure 1.1).

The ability to partner with others allows you to avoid being an island. In the world of technology, islands are easily defeated even when the goal or purpose is the right thing to do. On the other hand, a band of partners is not easily defeated.

WHAT ARE THE KEY ASPECTS OF A PARTNERSHIP?

The key elements of a partnership are alignment, trust, context, collaboration, and relationship (see Figure 1.2). Understanding each aspect is the focus of this chapter.

Taking the time and effort to build partnerships within both the business and technical communities is a time-proven formula for success.

ALIGNMENT

Establishing a community for the purpose of guiding the architecture of the software and services related to a business is essential to ensure that the business's near-term goals and the long-term vision are well aligned.

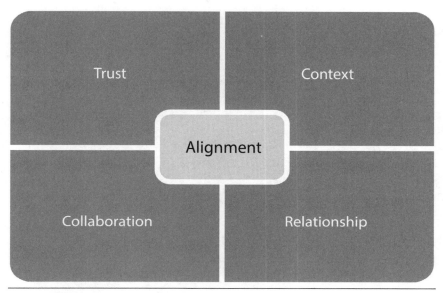

Figure 1.2 The elements of partnership

With Whom Do I Need to Be Partners?

The set of partnerships that you need to form is multidimensional (see Figure 1.3). You need to form partnerships with those above you (executives) within your business unit and potentially within other business units. You need to form partnerships with those who will be doing the work (managers, testers, coders, operations, etc.). You need to form partnerships with those who are your peers (other architects, directors). You may also need to form partnerships with those who are your integration partners (within your organization, across organizations, and potentially across companies). And finally, you need to form partnerships with the business (new product development, marketing, sales, finance, strategy, etc.)—those who fund technology efforts.

So, you might be saying to yourself, "It sounds like I need to be partners with everyone." The short answer is: to the greatest degree possible and to the extent that time allows it, yes. The time spent to collaborate with more people in making a decision (or, minimally, creating awareness of a decision) will serve you well. Not everyone will care passionately about the decision,

Figure 1.3 You and your partners form a circle of trust and transparency.

but all will appreciate being informed. As a practical matter, there is usually only a limited amount of time in which to make a decision, and you will need to decide who the critical stakeholders are before you execute. One really quick way to evaluate who these stakeholders are is to ask the following questions:

- Who will pay for the development costs? The licensing costs?
- Who will pay for the maintenance? The scaling costs? The safety costs?
- Who owns the assets being created?
- Who will pay for the migration costs?

- Who will pay for the reengineering costs? If the reengineering occurs within a year of the project's initial development, this may be an issue. If it occurs more than three years out, it most likely is a nonissue.
- Who will pay for the operational and legal costs?
- Who will develop the product? Test it?
- Who owns the resources for development? For operations?
- Who owns the intellectual property rights?
- Who owns the policies governing development?
- Who owns the deployment? Who determines where the product will be deployed? Are there regional, national, or international laws governing the deployment?
- Who owns the long-term strategy? Are you enabling it or disabling it?

The short answer is to start by following the money. Who will be financially impacted by the decision? Who is seeking what is best for the customer? These are your future partners. Their roles as business leaders, as well as yours, is to find ways to grow the business and ensure its future sustainability.

Finding the Thought Leaders

In every business, there are those individuals who have significant influence with respect to the technical directions that are considered acceptable and desired. They have the right contacts within the industry, they have a solid sense of what is happening throughout the industry, and they have a finger on the pulse of technology.

These are the individuals to whom you need to listen.

Even if it is from a distance, learning what they are interested in and watching the directions in which they are heading can give you a model to emulate. It can also give you a likely safe path for technology-related decisions in areas in which you are not an expert. If you follow their technology directions, you need to understand the rationale for them and ensure that they apply to your situation.

If these individuals work at your business, you may have the opportunity to meet with them occasionally and use them as a sounding board for any tougher situations that you encounter.

Knowing the Influencers

The influencers are the individuals who can accept, reject, override, or negatively influence the decisions being made. In the world of architecture, these are often other architects, directors, VPs, senior VPs, and CTOs.

These individuals may or may not be directly involved with your project, but they hold the attention of most individuals in management when it comes to making decisions in particular areas. If they are not on board with the decisions you make, they will either directly or indirectly exert their influence to negatively impact those decisions.

The key is to discover who the influencers are and what areas of expertise they have. When decisions about directions apply, you are usually best off seeking their opinion. This serves multiple purposes.

First, they usually are experts and have good insights into the pros and cons of heading in certain directions. It is unlikely that your situation is completely unique, and they may have encountered it before; they may have a good sense of what has or has not worked in the past. They may also have a sense of what direction the company or industry is heading in this area.

Second, as others within the organization come to them to get a sense of whether the decisions being made are reasonable, the experts have an opportunity to act as salespeople for you. They will understand your problem, the approach you are seeking to take, and the solutions that were or are under consideration.

They are now acting as partners instead of outside consultants.

Establishing Trusted Adviser(s)

As an architect, you need to establish a small advisory board of trusted individuals with whom you can share ideas and from whom you can get honest feedback. They can help identify gaps in the approach you are taking, risks that may be associated with the approach, other benefits of the approach that you may not have considered, or others you may want to consult.

Community Review (Architecture Review Board)

In some organizations, there is a process of community review of ideas, technical decisions, and approaches. This review is an opportunity to gather feedback about ideas at various stages. The process can be useful for a variety of reasons; most people will give you

- Honest feedback on their similar experiences from the past
- Suggestions for alternatives you may want to consider
- Ideas for others you may want to consult
- Agreement that the approach is reasonable (which can be useful later on, to show that the decision was not made in isolation)

The goal is to use the community to leverage other people's experiences and knowledge.

Seeking Alignment before Making Key Decisions

Architecture review boards can often derail the architectural directions you are trying to promote. To help prevent this, take the time to meet with key architects in advance of the board meeting to ensure that their concerns are addressed. This will help enable the architectural review to run smoothly for a couple of reasons. First, either key stumbling blocks have been removed or a better rationale for the decisions will have been created. Second, the group will require less education and you will likely now have allies who can help sell your architectural approach.

Unity helps drive consensus.

When there is a lack of unity, these meetings can turn into a feeding frenzy, even when the underlying architectural approach may have been reasonable.

Remember, you get only one shot at a first impression for the project you bring forward, and it will be a reflection on you. What type of impression do you want to leave?

Alignment of a Shared Vision Enables Partnerships

My personal experience has been that once you have alignment in a shared vision with strategic and noble aspirations, establishing partnerships is a natural outcome. Several years ago when I was working with new product development, we were trying to solve a challenging customer problem about how to quickly and easily access relevant information. The conversation continued over a series of weeks.

Over this time, we looked at every imaginable solution both inside the company and outside the company. The more we dove into the problem, the more key elements of the customer needs began to fall out. Our vision of where we needed to take the product line began to emerge. The technology to pursue this vision simply did not exist, but we could start to see a roadmap of how we might achieve the vision over the course of several projects and several years.

Our shared vision aligned our projects, architecture, and funding for the next three years, created new capabilities across multiple products, and resulted in a patent being issued.

TRUST

Partnerships are founded and flourish on the notion of mutual trust. Without it, they will slowly wither away.

Establishing Trust

When you are partnering with individuals, you need to develop a sense of trust. That is, you need to be very clear about the situations in which you are asking for help. If there are any risks, previous history about the situation, or stories behind the story, you should be open with this information.

Part of establishing trust is to disclose the good as well as the bad. Allowing the other person to make a decision about whether or not to support your idea is important. Eventually the facts will surface, and your disclosure, or lack of it, will become very obvious to those involved. Early disclosure is almost always the correct path to choose, even when it is to your disadvantage.

Listen to your partners' responses closely; they may identify risks, other solutions, or even better sales material.

Establishing Open Disclosure

When dealing with your partners, you need to operate in a manner of open disclosure. You may not be able to fully disclose all the information you are aware of due to constraints of confidentiality or the timing of public disclosure, but you, to the degree possible, should communicate openly.

Note

When you disclose information to your partners that they shouldn't have access to, you are letting them know that you do not honor the confidentiality of others and that you might distribute information that they provide to you in confidence to others. It is essential to maintain your integrity and act in a trustworthy manner.

As you are asking for guidance or approval, you need to be clear about the problem or solution that is being discussed. Giving the appropriate background information will ground your partners in what you are dealing with. This includes disclosing

- The context of the problem or solution (what project it is related to, who the customers are, what time frames you are dealing with, requirements, usage information, etc.)
- Previous history related to the problem or solution, especially within the organization for similar situations (are others using it and if so, why; if not, why not)
- Known risks associated with the problem or solution
- Previous attempts at solving this problem (successes and/or failures)
- Alternatives considered, including their pros and cons
- Cost-related information (development, operational, licensing)
- Scale or usability information
- Related licensing restrictions
- Pros and cons of what you are considering

The key here is to let the partners know that you have done your homework and due diligence in presenting the information. This will enable them to fully understand the lay of the land and to give you real feedback. Otherwise, you are just trying to get them to support a conclusion you have already made, and you are wasting their time and unnecessarily lowering their level of trust.

Avoiding Getting Spread Too Thin (Overcommitting)

The opportunities for distraction for an architect are extremely high. There are always new projects, new technologies, new areas that need help. The challenge is that there are only so many hours in a day. If you say yes to everything, you will need to work 25 hours a day. It's not possible.

The other challenge is that you may be asked to do something for one of your partners—one who may have just saved your back, and you may not even be aware of it—and you may have no spare time. You may have to say no, and saying no doesn't always come easily.

> **Note**
>
> If you commit, you need to follow through—no ifs, ands, or buts—no exceptions. Your word is your honor. If you commit and fail to follow through, you will at best lose trust; at worst you will lose your partner.

One of the best ways to combat this problem is to establish margin in your day; that is, purposely set aside time to act as a buffer. Guard this time closely; it will help keep you and your partners sane. Be cautious; the fact that you have a spare hour or two in your day doesn't mean you should take on another commitment.

Sometimes there are seasonalities that come into play when you know you are going to be unusually busy or unusually free of commitments. When these occur, you will know in advance to either guard your time with extra caution or be more available to help others.

How to Unwind after You Have Overcommitted

If you are like me, once or twice a year all of your projects seem to have major time commitments converging at the same time. To deal with this, you can pursue several options.

The first option is to simply work more. The challenge with this is that the work of architects is highly social. A significant portion of their time is spent working with other people, and this tends to be during core working hours. There is only so much work that can be shifted away from the core work hours.

A second option is to evaluate the work you are doing and determine if any of it can be delegated to others. On most projects, there are some tasks I like to reserve for myself, such as investigating new technologies. Usually when I start feeling overwhelmed by the amount of work I am doing, it is because I have chosen to take on too many tasks that I deem fun. In reality, I need to start delegating and allow others to do the fun work. It's a hard thing to do, but it gives others an opportunity to grow and learn.

A more drastic approach is to stop taking on new projects or assignments. Sometimes passing on that new and exciting project is the right thing to do; the project won't seem so exciting when you are swamped and are unable or barely able to keep pace with all of your commitments. In reality, this is effective only with the help of your manager. There are a very limited number of times you can do this, so proceed with this option cautiously.

If you are unable to avoid taking on new work, the best route is to simply let each of the projects know that you are being stretched thin and that you will be spending less time with them. Ask them to engage you specifically when they need your help. Clear communication about the situation will resonate with others and enable them to understand how to determine the times and situations when it is appropriate to engage you.

As an architect, you need to know your limitations. Often the reward for good work is more work. When this happens, it is up to you to recognize the situation, manage your time efficiently, avoid overcommitting, and definitely avoid underdelivering.

Learning to Say No

Managing your time so you don't get overwhelmed usually involves saying no. Learning to say no is essential to establishing trust.

When you are an architect, questions, requests, and consulting sessions can simply consume all of your time. The challenge is to figure out which ones you absolutely need to address yourself. In almost all circumstances, you need to listen for a while to figure out what the issue at hand is. If you don't have time to deal with it immediately, you may need to ask your colleagues to come back later or, if possible, redirect them to someone else on the team who can help them.

Once you have had a chance to listen to and hear what is being requested, you have to make a determination of whether you have time to deal with the request.

Realize that you are the easy answer if you take on the request. Others may simply be trying to optimize their time instead of investigating the issue on their own. Sometimes letting others struggle a bit is not a bad thing. It will enable them to learn how to research an issue and to work it through the organization. Sometimes people are looking to get out of trouble; they may be handing you a bad situation that they created because they don't want to deal with it themselves.

Most people have legitimate requests, but if you are swamped, you need to figure out if someone else on the project can take on a new request. On the other hand, if it turns out to be a critical issue that is likely to get raised up to senior management, you will want to drop everything you are doing and deal with it immediately.

Issues that involve senior management need to be managed very carefully. You do not want to let such issues be learning opportunities for the person making the request. Whenever senior management gets involved, the set of possible outcomes can vary dramatically. Now isn't the time to say no.

Before you say yes, understand the commitment (Is this really your problem?), the amount of time needed, and the amount of risk you are taking on if you say yes or no.

Often just giving people additional ideas about how they can move forward can get them off and running again. Are there others to whom they should talk, websites that have the information they need? Can they dig into the problem a little more deeply and then come back if they still haven't solved the problem?

Realize that the people you are dealing with are your partners. You are either adding value or removing value from the relationship, so be conscientious about how and when you say yes or no.

Remember, you may need their help in the future.

Trust Enables Transparency—the Lifeblood of Partnerships

Your ability to quickly and easily access information within your organization is critical to your success.

Recently, I had a chance to be included in an interview meeting with a customer about a new product area. The detailed information about the work the customer does illuminated the product ideas in a stunning fashion.

I am always amazed at how little I know about these new areas when this process starts and how much there is to know about the context of a customer for a new product area. I know that I need to immerse myself in the problem domain before I really begin to understand how to approach a reasonable solution to the customer's needs. It is always exciting to start a new journey into unknown territory.

I know trust has been established with my business partners when they are willing to include me in customer visits for their new areas of business innovation. This transparency about their business goals and direction enables me to make solid architectural decisions literally for years to come.

The customer visits usually give me more context about the business problem we are trying to solve than nearly any other experience I am likely to have. The experiences and the product conceptualization conversations that follow get indelibly etched into my mind and make for great projects.

The key is to remember that this journey doesn't start early unless trust has been established and maintained with business partners. They are not required to engage technologists when they interact with customers; it's a privilege to be included, not a right.

CONTEXT

Partnerships rely on operating in a particular context. This context helps frame the alignment, trust, collaboration, and relationship of the partnership.

Realizing the Nature of the Partnership

In life, context is critical to getting things right. Partnerships are no exception. Understanding the nature of the relationship with respect to your relative status within the organization is essential.

A person who is higher than you within the organization is likely hoping that you can provide a good sense of the current state of technology, what trends are occurring, and the success or lack of success a particular project is having.

A person who is more of a peer is likely looking to you as a sounding board for ideas, for help in an area where you have expertise, or for ideas on how to approach certain problems.

A person who is lower than you in the organization is likely looking for guidance on how to solve a problem, information about what opportunities may exist within the organization, or approval of a certain approach.

No matter whom you are interacting with, take the time to understand the context of the situation. This can help you determine how best to serve the person who is requesting your help.

Being Aware of Your Business Context

Architects need to be aware of their business context when advising partners on direction. The business context for an architect includes what markets the company is trying to enter or maintain and any specific policies
that are enforced with respect to security, open source, procurement, and
related areas.

The business context can help you quickly determine whether a particular
project is viable.

Embedded within the business context is an increasing need for architects
to understand the cultural and national differences of the various groups
with whom they interact. This is driven in part by the nature of many projects today that can span geographic regions, and in part because individual
teams that are involved in the projects include a wider diversity of people
with different cultural and national backgrounds.

Technical Decisions Require Partnerships

Technical decisions narrow the set of future options available to the business. If you choose to make a hack for the solution, you are committing the
business to future investment in that area if it needs to make a more strategic play. However, your hack may also enable the business to get to market more quickly and allow a refactor once the product has gained market
acceptance. Having others on board (partners) with the technical decisions
you make is essential to your future career health.

If the right parties were not involved with an earlier decision, they will have
no impetus to defend what was done even if it was the right thing to do. The
current thinking style and current development rules will be applied with
no regard to the past. If you were the lone wolf on this decision, you are
about to get sacrificed.

Take the time to gain key approvals anytime you are "hacking" the system or leveraging a legacy system that is scheduled for decommission. It is
almost always an easy answer if you are doing a strategic solution and the
business is willing to take on the cost.

The main point for seeking technical partnerships is to ensure that you are
capable of delivering the well-understood results for the price specified.
Coming back later to ask for more money is rarely well received.

Key Point: Technical Decisions Are Political Decisions

You might ask, "Why in the world is a technical decision a political decision, especially when I hate politics?" The answer is relatively straightforward: the decisions you make today will either limit or enable future options. You are in some very real sense putting handcuffs on the business. When the bill comes due, the business executives are likely to remember who made the decision. Of course, everyone wants to have all future options available, wants to be part of the decision making, wants to have the project cost a small amount, and wants to have it scale easily and inexpensively.

The larger the impact of the technical decision you are making (whether it be financial or strategic), the more carefully you will want to vet the solution, to ensure that you have the proper buy-in, and to know the scope of your decision. You will also want the business to understand the cost of making the decision as this will help drive the architecture and the decision process.

Presenting the Situation First (Give Context)

When presenting information, there is a tendency to want to dive into the problem, to quickly justify why your solution is correct, and to receive the praise of others on the brilliant solution you have devised.

The challenge is that most people do not have your context and need more background information to get to a point where they can reasonably evaluate what you are presenting.

One effective way to approach this is to use a process of presenting information called SCRAP (situation, complication, resolution, action, politeness) (see Figure 1.4). This is also occasionally referred to as SCQA (situation, complication, question, answer).

Figure 1.4   Context-driven selling: one of the easiest ways to get everyone on the same page when presenting a solution to a problem is to use SCRAP.

The idea is to

1. Start with the situation (nondisputable facts that everyone can agree upon)
2. Introduce the complication (the problem that needs to be solved)
3. Show possible solutions to the problem
4. Call the audience to action (how they can help)
5. End politely (thank everyone for their help and input)

This simple mechanism can be used to guide your partners to a solution without jarring them with low-level details and having the conversation be derailed. This technique is especially effective with executives. They need a clear, concise context for a situation before jumping in to help resolve it.

Having Your Partners' Backs

When you have taken the time to cultivate partnerships throughout the business, you need to guard those relationships carefully. Many conversations occur during the day. During these conversations, if someone is saying negative things about one of your partners, if possible you need to defend the person or correct the statements that are being made. Having your partners' backs and standing up for them is part of being a partner (see Figure 1.5).

If you don't defend them, silence is normally considered agreement. Worse yet, if you add fuel to the fire by disclosing information that puts them in a bad light, you are throwing them under the bus and thereby destroying a valuable relationship or, minimally, lowering its value. When this information gets back to the party involved (it usually does), it will take a significant amount of time and effort to undo the damage that was done.

Sometimes this is referred to as "keeping it in the family." Every family is dysfunctional at some level, and work is no exception. Present a united front and work out the differences offline.

Contributing to Your Partners' Successes

Find ways to help make your partners successful. When there is an opportunity to put in a good word for them, to help them out in areas that are not directly related to the projects you are currently working on, or to provide feedback on their other projects as a trusted adviser, take the time to invest in your partners' successes. Small things can go a long way toward helping bolster your partners' successes.

Figure 1.5   When your partners are being surrounded and attacked from many fronts, step in and help defend them. You will earn their trust.

Safety in Numbers

Whenever you are in architecture, you are in sales. You are typically selling a technology, a solution, an architecture, or some other key area. The broader the support you are able to build, the easier it will be to gain acceptance of the idea you are bringing forward.

Often within an organization, selling a solution isn't just about numbers; it is about having the right support. Knowing who the influencers are in your organization and gaining their support can make acceptance of an idea or direction much simpler.

COLLABORATION

In a business context, a partnership's success relies on the ability of those involved to work together toward common goals by contributing their best ideas in a cooperative environment. The spirit of collaboration can enable an open environment for conversations to occur and ideas to be reshaped and reformed. This reification of ideas is where innovation can spring to life.

Bringing Value to the Table

Most partnerships need to be more than a one-way street to information and guidance. You need to provide value in return for the information and guidance you receive. Often this means giving open feedback about information others may be seeking, ideas they may want to consider for projects they are working on, alternative approaches to solving problems they face. As you find information, websites, blogs, articles, or conferences they may be interested in, taking the time to forward this information to them can help balance the value of the partnership.

Becoming a Mentor

As an architect, you often encounter opportunities to mentor others. During the course of any given year, I typically work on mentoring a handful of individuals. Usually, they are individuals who are looking to get promoted at some point in the future.

The key to developing a successful mentorship relationship is to understand what the individuals are hoping to learn:

- Do they want to learn a specific skill?
- Do they want to learn what the role of an architect is?
- Do they simply want to do their current job better?

Once you understand the direction in which they want to go, you can work on finding reading materials, blogs, or potentially even project-related tasks that they can help you with. Often doing is the best way to learn.

Try to find a regular time when you can meet, whether once a week or once a month. Having a set regular time will help guarantee that you do in fact meet. Most mentoring relationships usually last about a year.

Sometimes formal mentoring programs are offered through a company or through local organizations. Sometimes the mentoring organizations are primarily for the purpose of bringing mentors and mentees together. Mentorship can take place as paired individuals or sometimes as a group activity.

Before you begin meeting, you should plan what you want to accomplish and tentatively put a plan together for how you are going to get there. The amount of preparation your mentees are willing to do in advance will be an indicator of how serious they are about working to improve themselves.

If you set an agenda in advance of each meeting and have whatever preparatory materials distributed and reviewed in advance, it will make the time you spend together much more productive.

At some point, giving feedback is essential. Mentees need to understand if they are on the right track or if there are other areas they may want to consider improving. One of the best pieces of feedback you can give is the strengths that you see; knowing that they are particularly good at something can help give them the confidence they need to pursue their goals. The areas where they need improvement may be very difficult to change, and many times the best they can do is minimize the impact of these areas.

Overall, seek to give mentees honest feedback and encourage them.

Seeking a Mentor

Over the years, I have had a series of mentors. I am always amazed at what they can see about me. They are able to quickly pick up on areas that I need to work on—areas that I thought I was actually good at—and, on the other hand, see strengths that I have that were not immediately obvious to me.

When seeking a mentor, you want someone who will give you a straight answer and tell you the things you need to hear, even when you don't want to hear them or may not agree with them. Often, these are things that are apparent to others, but not obvious to you.

I have had mentors both inside and outside of my organization. In general, the mentors inside the organization are better because they are aware of the organizational culture and politics. They have a much better sense of how to navigate the organization successfully.

You need to have a sense of what you want to get out of a mentoring relationship. You need to be clear with the mentor about what your goals are, what you are seeking to become, what you have tried to date, and what you are planning on doing in the future. Giving your mentor a sense of the books you like to read, the blogs you follow, and any training you may have sought or are seeking will help inform the mentor about where you are within your career.

Have a plan for how often to meet and the goals of each meeting. This is your time. You should drive the agenda, but listen for feedback and adjust based on that feedback.

The results of mentoring are usually not immediately obvious, but over the course of three to five years, you can see the changes that have occurred, and you may discover that some of the piercing words about things that you needed to work on were in fact true. Once you have a little more perspective, it is usually easier to see that these statements were accurate.

Partnerships Can Be a Source of Opportunity

Usually as new opportunities present themselves within the business, there is a certain lead time and limited revelation of the scope of the opportunity. Your network of partners will determine whether or not you are considered for the opportunity or even have a chance to hear about it.

When you do have a chance to hear about such opportunities, be willing to jump in and take a risk. If your partners are asking you to consider the opportunity, you usually already have their backing and support.

Normally, these types of opportunities do not present themselves on a regular basis. If you say no now, you may put yourself out of consideration the next time; so think quickly and be willing to jump even if you don't have all of the details.

Partnerships Are a Step toward Ideation

For architects, gaining the trust of the business and forming partnerships are essential. These partnerships eventually lead to the business being willing to draw you into the inner circle. It is inside this inner circle that the directions for the business are set. It is the place that will determine the future work and opportunities you will have. It is the home of ideation and discovery.

Collaboration Drives Stronger Partnerships

In today's world of fast-moving technology, collaboration is essential to provide competitive solutions. It is rare today that you have the ability to be the expert in all of the areas related to a solution for a customer. This collaboration needs to occur on multiple levels.

You need to collaborate with your customers to continually navigate toward high value. This may involve giving them early access to your pipeline of solutions to get critical feedback. You need to collaborate with your supply chain of technology providers to find solutions that will last and scale; this may take the form of proofs of concept, access to industry-leading experts for advising on technology selection, and specialized training.

My experience has been that the companies that are in the forefront of new technology areas, where the open-source community is beginning to thrive, have unique industry insights and are able to give expert guidance on the use of these new technologies.

These forms of collaboration both within the company and outside of the company will help solidify your community of partnerships and can provide significant value for all parties involved.

RELATIONSHIPS

Partnerships are established and maintained through relationships. These relationships both inside and outside an organization are essential for architects to be successful.

Partnerships Are Not Just about Business

As you develop partnerships, you need to develop and maintain the relationships. Although partnerships are critical to succeed in business, you need to cultivate them. Taking the time to get to know the people better—learning what they like to do for hobbies, who their kids are, what their kids like to do—will go a long way toward establishing a better partnership.

Find time to go out for lunch, get coffee, or just stop by to chat. You will find your days are more enjoyable. As with all things, be aware of what the cultural norms are to ensure that you are engaging with others in an appropriate manner.

Making Deposits before You Start Withdrawing

As with most relationships, there is a give-and-take to helping each other out. When one party makes continuous withdrawals, the interest level in maintaining the relationship becomes strained. Make sure you take the time to keep in touch and help out whenever possible; this will make it easier for you to ask for help in the future.

External Partnerships

Staying in contact with those who have changed business units or have left the company can be an excellent way to develop partners. In addition, being active in local user groups or conferences can also be an excellent way of keeping a broad network of people who can help advise on particular issues.

Knowing what other businesses are using for tools or what processes they are following can help inform you about what changes are occurring in the industry. They can also give you a sense of what types of projects local executives are approving.

A strong internal and external professional network is critical to maintaining success and also serves as a source of technical and business expertise that a single person would have difficulty developing and maintaining alone.

Bad Experiences in the Past?

Get over it. Suck it up. You need to make sure the right people are involved with decisions. If you don't, it will come back to haunt you.

For good or bad, whether you get along with someone or not, sometimes you need to get over your previous bad experiences with the person and draw him or her into a conversation. Learn to be polite, and ignore the past.

When you enter these situations, know what you want when you go in. Getting information that will help the business succeed is the right thing to do even if it's painful.

When you are finished, say thank you. The person may not even remember the previous event that is so fresh in your memory.

Avoiding Caustic Members of the Organization

There are always certain individuals in every organization who love to demean, destroy, and belittle others. They effectively establish fear in others and use that fear to their advantage. They are often caustic individuals and are generally politically aligned well enough that they are safe from being removed from the organization.

Although they may carry influence within the organization, it is usually best to avoid them. There is almost no good that can come out of interacting with them, and there is usually a large downside to interacting with them unless you enjoy a good fight.

If you do need to interact with them, it is usually best to let them speak their piece without interruption. Keep track of any points you wish to make, but make sure everything you say is well reasoned. The key is not to interrupt. Usually, this is not a conversation; it is more of a monologue.

SUMMARY

The road to partnerships begins with

- Establishing alignment
  - Finding the right partners
  - Finding the thought leaders
  - Knowing the influencers
  - Establishing trusted advisers
  - Leveraging community review
  - Aligning a shared vision
- Establishing trust
  - Establishing open disclosure
  - Avoiding overcommitment
  - Learning to occasionally say no
- Establishing context
  - Understanding the nature of the partnership
  - Being knowledgeable of the business context
  - Framing technical decisions with a partnership
  - Realizing that technical decisions are political decisions
  - Learning to sell with a context
  - Having your partners' backs
  - Realizing there is safety in numbers
- Establishing collaboration
  - Bringing value to the table
  - Being willing to be a mentor and knowing when to seek a mentor
  - Recognizing opportunities
  - Enabling ideation

- Establishing relationships
  - Being more than just about business
  - Making deposits before you begin withdrawing
  - Leveraging external relationships
  - Overcoming bad experiences from the past
  - Avoiding caustic members of the organization

For architects, establishing partnerships across multiple areas of the business is essential for survival. Architects live in a highly politicized world and are constantly being challenged for the decisions that they make.

You need senior executives, business partners, and others to understand and support the decisions that have been made. They can defend you when you aren't present. Without these partners, you will get the opportunity to view the underside of the organization as it drives over you.

REFERENCES

Bradberry, Travis, and Jean Greaves. 2009. *Emotional Intelligence 2.0.* TalentSmart.

Bruch, Heike, and Sumantra Ghoshal. 2002. "Beware the Busy Manager." *Harvard Business Review,* February.

Covey, Steven M. R., with Rebecca R. Merrill. 2008. *The SPEED of Trust: The One Thing That Changes Everything.* Thomas Nelson.

Gladwell, Malcolm. 2002. *The Tipping Point.* Back Bay Books.

Maxwell, John C. 2001. *The 17 Indisputable Laws of Teamwork: Embrace Them and Empower Your Team.* Thomas Nelson.

Patterson, Kerry, Joseph Grenny, Ron McMillan, and Al Switzler. 2011. *Crucial Conversations: Tools for Talking When Stakes Are High, Second Edition.* McGraw-Hill.

Schwartz, Tony, and Catherine McCarthy. 2007. "Manage Your Energy, Not Your Time." *Harvard Business Review,* October.

Chapter 2

DISCOVERY

"The real voyage of discovery consists not in seeking new landscapes but in having new eyes."

—Marcel Proust

"All truths are easy to understand once they are discovered; the point is to discover them."

—Galileo Galilei

"Mistakes are the portals of discovery."

—James Joyce

"Think different."

—Steve Jobs

Have you ever had the chance to go on customer visits and hear customers express their ideas? In comparison, have you ever had an internal customer representative express the same customer's ideas?

The two concepts have similarities, but often this can take on an aspect of the telephone game. This is the game where a story is told quietly to one person, and then quietly retold to the next person until it has traveled through multiple individuals.

The telling and retelling of the story from one person to another slowly introduces changes to the story. If you have ever played this game, it is amazing to hear the original version in comparison to the end version. The two are typically very different from one another.

By the time the story has been retold multiple times, significant changes have usually been introduced—not purposely; it is just the nature of communication.

In architecture, the need to clearly hear the voice of the customer is essential to delivering solutions that hit the mark. Customers' unique verbalization can often provide clarity to what they are seeking. The real problem is usually nuanced in their language.

By listening closely, you can often hear the problem they are facing and begin the journey toward simple and elegant solutions.

This need to hear the customer's voice is critical to the development process and emphasizes the need for architects and other development staff to know their internal and external customers. There is no substitute for direct customer feedback.

As an architect, you should meet with customers every chance you get. Extremely relevant information is exchanged on both sides.

This chapter unveils one of the essential skills needed by a software architect: the ability to hear the voice of your customers and discover their real needs. This is typically done in partnership with those who are closest to the customer—sales, marketing, and new product development.

WHAT IS DISCOVERY?

In software architecture, discovery is about venturing outside of technology and learning about the context of the customer. Sometimes this is easy because it relates to what you do. On the other hand, many of our customers live in a world that is quite different from what we do on a day-to-day basis. The more you know and understand who your customers are, what they do, how they do it, what their pain points are, what problems they face regularly, and the language they use to describe their world, the better you will be able to build systems that fit naturally into their space and to develop effective solutions (see Figure 2.1).

THE KEYS TO DISCOVERY

This chapter focuses on three key areas of discovery: understanding the customer, understanding the market, and understanding your business (see Figure 2.2).

Figure 2.1   Learn to venture out and discover new things.

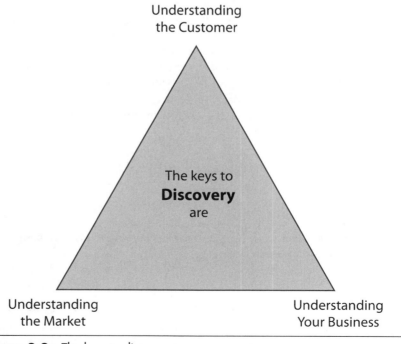

Figure 2.2   The keys to discovery

UNDERSTANDING THE CUSTOMER

One of the essential elements of understanding what products should be created is to understand the customers you have today as well as the customers you are seeking.

You want to learn what they do, but not necessarily how they do it or even what tools or products they use today. Once you learn what they are trying to do, you can find new and innovative ways of accomplishing it. You want to seek what they like and don't like, what seems natural versus awkward.

In some sense, learning the "what" is the easy part. For me, getting to actually meet customers is an extremely challenging problem. In a large organization, most people have narrowly defined roles. There is marketing and sales; their focus and language are different—their direct goals are meeting customer needs and generating revenue rather than bringing the architect along to learn about the customer.

The challenge is that unless the customers being served are well understood, there is little or no basis on which to judge the hundreds and thousands of micro technology decisions that impact the products that are produced. It is possible to determine what might cost more or less, what is technically better architected, or what risks might be involved, but in reality these really do not matter as much as knowing what provides value to the customer, what delights the customer, what drives product loyalty, or what makes your product essential. Given this kind of information, you and your partners can take a more holistic approach to decision making and move toward a common vision. This will give the overall product a stronger element of cohesiveness.

So whatever it takes, find ways to get out and meet your customers.

> **Note**
>
> It is essential to learn what your customers are trying to do and what their real goals and needs are.

Partnering with Sales, Marketing, and New Product Development

Typically, the only way to get out of the office and meet customers face-to-face is to partner with those who have an existing relationship with customers. These people are usually in sales, marketing, new product development (NPD), customer support, customer service, or customer training—basically anyone who interacts with your customers on a regular basis. Their jobs are aligned with knowing the types of customers, the variety of roles they fulfill, the value that your products bring to them, their vocabulary, their buying habits, and what is driving them to spend money on your products.

Take time to get to know the people in your organization who interact with your customers on a regular basis. Seek ways that you can "tag along" and interact with them.

Often these people will like having a technical expert along for the ride as it will give them someone to defer to if the conversation takes a technical turn. This happens more and more these days.

It will be an eye-opening experience to see the multiple perspectives that exist for the products that your business produces.

Meeting with New Product Development

In the world I work in, NPD is the group tasked with developing new, innovative products and solutions for customers. They are, in fact, a proxy for customers. They work with marketing and sales to gather feedback from the field (the land of the customer).

Long before projects ever see the light of day, a considerable amount of work has gone into the development and refinement of concepts for a product. Within the business, there is never-ending competition for the attention of those who allocate money to fund projects. The challenge is to find ideas that align with business goals and strategies. They need to be simple enough to be described in under two minutes and have a clear value proposition (revenue generation or protection opportunity).

In this space, architects have the opportunity to partner with the business to help develop and refine ideas for pitching to those who decide which projects to fund.

Architects also have the opportunity to act as a bridge between the business and technology. They typically have gained the domain knowledge of the business and a sense of what the capabilities of the technology organization are. With this background, they can help guide NPD into understanding what is possible, what is easy, and where less expensive alternatives exist.

Discovery with NPD

NPD has a language that is different from that of technology. They are business people from a broad set of backgrounds and with a wide variety of experience with respect to technology. Speaking to NPD in a nontechnical manner (avoiding terms of art, acronyms, etc.) will greatly improve your ability to communicate effectively.

There is an art to communicating with the business people; they control the money. Learning how to effectively communicate with NPD is an essential aspect of an architect's role within the technology organization.

You need to listen and hear the language NPD is using to describe what the customer is trying to accomplish or what problem the customer is facing.

> **Note**
>
> As you listen, try to use NPD's language when you are reflecting back what you hear.

NPD will care deeply about the "what" and not so much the "how" when it comes to solving the customer's problems. The "how" is your native language of technology but really has no place here. A key exception to this is when the costs are too high. In this particular case, NPD may quickly show a keen interest in learning your language to better understand the cost or risk drivers.

I know I have been adopted into a new product development group when they are willing to stop by at random times, sit down, talk about ideas they have, and begin navigating around concepts related to the idea.

This is one of the best chances to learn and help shape fledgling product concepts. Even if the business never pursues these ideas, it will give you a sense of where the business is trying to go. It can also help guide architectural and design decisions to ensure that those ideas are possible in the future. Without this knowledge, it is very easy to make design decisions that severely limit these new concepts or make them expensive to pursue.

Note

In the agile space, we often talk about refactoring code as if it were simple and inexpensive. When interacting with the business, try to remove the word *refactor* from your vocabulary. *Refactor* is often perceived as a code word for "This is going to be expensive," and as a result, it can derail productive conversations with the business and will likely be viewed as rework to a poor design.

Try to understand what is important to the business; often it is not the architecture, but rather the management of risk, cost, and maintainability. Learn not to take anything personally; often the business is pushing a different set of objectives.

The key is to tie the two areas (business and technology) together. This will help you to understand how to work together effectively and earn their trust.

Trust is critical and will lead to more opportunities than just about any other attribute.

Standing in the Shoes of the Customer (Learn to Look from the Outside In)

Initially, at least for externally facing applications, it may be hard if not impossible to actually get the sales team to drag some "crazy" architect along on a sales visit to meet with customers, but it can be done.

For internally facing applications, the stakeholders are likely the users and the management or executive management of the users. Access to these individuals may be simpler since you are likely to be able to meet with them directly.

In either case, whether external or internal, a better place to start looking from the outside in is to begin closer to home. Take the time to

- **Look at your product catalogs** or other internal forms of user documentation.
- **Watch, listen to, and read your marketing materials.** Think about
  - What is being said. Look for the capabilities that are being "advertised." It may be worth building a mind map of the capabilities that you discover.

- What is not being said. The goal here is not to infer that some form of deception is taking place or that you need to be a mind reader, but rather to try to think below the surface. What capabilities are essential for the application to be successful but are not necessarily visible, at least directly, to the user?
- How the materials change per market segment or user group. Why?
  Try to picture/understand the users. Put yourself in their shoes. What do they do at work? What do they do outside work?

- **Learn your product lines.** Why do these product lines exist? What is the rationale for their existence? It is important to understand the different segments of users and what value different product lines bring to them. How much configuration change is allowed? Why are these configuration changes valuable to the user?
- **Get access to your products.** Try using them; as you use them, think about these questions:
  - Is this the way you would want to work? Evaluate basic heuristics such as usability.
  - Why do these products exist?
  - What problems do they solve? The goal is to begin understanding how the users use the application and how your product fits into their overall flow of work. Why do the application boundaries exist? Are there problems that are not being addressed?
  - What are the customer's pain points in the workflow (not related to the systems being used)?
    The goal is to be able to think like your users. Understanding the nuances of the work they do will enable you to make better technical decisions.
- **Set up "interviews" with the product concept owners.** As you engage these business areas:
  - Be prepared with specific questions and areas that you want to learn more about.
  - Be prepared to describe what the uses of your products are and who uses them, even if you are just parroting the marketing materials. You want to show that you have done some homework.
- **See if you can listen in on some customer support calls.** Doing so will give you a chance to hear real customer voices and the problems they are running into. Think about these questions:
  - Why are these considered problems?
  - What could be done differently?
  - What is the root cause?
  - Is the product flawed?
  - Is the product not intuitive?

- What do customers praise the product for? Why? Find out what delights the customer and make a note of these things. Sometimes it is just the little things that can make the user delighted to be using your tools.
- Are new product ideas or improvements being suggested? The goal here is to find subtle areas of improvement that will help delight the customer. Are there simple changes that would eliminate the issue or make things more intuitive? These could range from training changes to documentation changes to application changes.

- **Consider signing up for customer training courses.** Think about these questions:
  - Why are these courses being offered? Are there different levels of training?
  - Is the training available online or is it available in a live classroom?
  - What is the stated purpose of the course?
  - Are there certifications?
  - Why are certifications required in this area? Safety? Security?
  - What product features are the training courses promoting? Why?
  - Is the message being delivered to the product user in these training courses different from the buyer/purchaser marketing message? Why?

    The goal is to discover why the training needs exist and if there are ways to increase the intuitiveness of the application. This may help improve the training and possibly minimize the need for training and enable the users to be more self-sufficient.

It is good to immerse your thinking in the context of the customer. It helps provide a constant source of guidance when making technical decisions as to which path is likely to need changes or which sets of options make the most sense together and provide the best user experience.

Meeting with Customers

Customer visits can take a variety of forms. They can be plant/facility tours, existing end user interviews, potential customer interviews, or product demonstrations, to name a few. As the interviews, demonstrations, or tours take place, find ways to capture the conversation—audio, video, note taking—whatever is appropriate and preapproved.

Be prepared to ask questions if the opportunity arises. If you were the customer, what questions would you ask?

When the customer responds to your or others' questions, let them go on rabbit trails; this is usually where the real value lies.

If you get the opportunity to go, be a good representative for your area. You want to allow others to have similar opportunities in the future; don't ruin it for them. Show value to the people who are hosting you; be gracious. You may be the first technical person they meet on the potential project, and you want to leave a good impression.

Another route to meeting customers is to consider what conferences they attend.

Customer service is also a great source of customer interaction. It can be stressful if the product is not performing properly, but their insights can be invaluable. A side benefit is that it can actually help defuse a bad situation as the customer will see the vendor putting some skin in the game if a senior technical person is part of the visit.

Regardless of the path, if you get a chance to meet with your customers, drop what you are doing, say yes, and go.

Preparing for Customer Visits

Before you visit, you should think about these issues:

- Are any nondisclosure agreements (NDAs) required? This is especially important if you are considering revealing new product ideas or approaches to external customers. You want to legally protect your company's ideas. The key is to do so in a tactful manner so as not to imply that the customers are not trustworthy.
- Can you visit them in person? If not, can you participate in a phone or video interview? Ideally you want to see their body language to find out where they really engage, what gets them excited, or what turns off their interest.
- Is there a script that will be used if you are doing interviews? The goal is to provide some level of consistency in how you approach obtaining the information.
- What are your competitors' products? Take time to review their websites and white papers.

If you are going to consume a sizable portion of a customer's time or elicit product feedback, consider sending a token of your appreciation.

Will you be traveling with the group that is making the customer visit? If the customer is close, carpooling with the others will give you a chance to talk. These conversations can dramatically improve your understanding of what is of true value to your customers. Ideally, travel in relatively small groups and with people from different areas of the business. They will give you unique perspectives and expose you to new ideas.

Express your gratitude; both the customers and your customer representatives are taking time out of their busy day to give you valuable information.

- **Let the business folks do most of the talking.** In most meetings with an external client, you are more of an observer.
- **Ask questions sparingly.** The goal is to let the customer talk and for you to listen and learn.
- **Build a mental map.** Discover cardinality; discover counts. You want to begin establishing models for the information that you are gathering. The more you can understand what the important entities of the user's environment are and the relationships these entities have with one another, the better you will understand what flexibility or constraints naturally need to exist.
- **Build a glossary of unique terms you hear.** You want to learn the customer's language and the nuances of the terms used.
- **Build scenarios around the problems or tasks your customers encounter**. This can help you understand the varied uses of the system.

If the customer uses your existing products, find out which ones, how they are used, and who uses them as well as any known issues with them.

If possible, try to meet prior to the visit with those who will be meeting with the customer. This will help enable the team to define roles, boundaries, planned outcomes, and scenarios. This can be extremely helpful based on the temperament of the customer. All customers are not created equal.

Meeting with Customers

When you think about your customers, consider the following:

- What are the customer roles? Listen for key sets of responsibilities from the customer's perspective and who is responsible for those tasks. Try to listen for how the customer's business is organized, and if any approvals are required for the customer's work. This can help identify the actors for the system.

- Why is the customer organized this way? Knowing this can help you understand the clustering of capabilities and why these capabilities need to be related to one another within the application.
- Does the size of the organization affect the way it is organized? Are there scale issues? Identifying organizational needs and scale considerations early on can make or break your application's ability to fit naturally into the organizational structure.
- Are there privacy issues? Understanding privacy concerns can help drive your security requirements and potentially the need for certain certifications.
- Do you understand the customer's workflow? How does this workflow add value or remove cost for the customer? Knowing how your product fits into the overall workflow can help determine if new/different capabilities are needed and can help raise the overall value of the product you deliver.
- What advantages exist for the customer to work this way? Customer workflows have usually been established over time, and there are natural efficiencies that have evolved. Try to understand the rationale for why the work might be done the way it is. It will help inform your decision making later on.
- Are there other systems that need to be interacted with or integrated with? Does your product naturally fit with other products? Are there natural partnerships that can or should be established with other companies due to their market leadership?
- Are notifications needed? Are there alerts or notifications that can bring essential information to the attention of the customer? Customers could save time if the system lets them know whether something is complete, something is about to fail, or some new information is available. Can the user configure this information?
- Does this information need to go anywhere? The answer to this question can help identify potential reporting or notification needs. What types of reports does the customer produce today? What needs to be tracked? Are there analytics about the workflow that could help drive efficiencies in the work or help improve quality?
- Has the customer identified any problems currently being faced? How are these problems handled today? Is the solution handled manually? Can it be automated?
- Are the customer's current systems satisfactory? What would make these systems better? Would the customer pay for improvements? If so, how much? Identify areas on which a customer is willing to spend money; these are real opportunities for your product to establish value.

- Does the customer currently have a budget for the product? Learning who controls the purchasing decisions is essential for your product needs. In the end, you need to show value not only to the person using your product, but also to the person who will approve the decision to purchase your product.
- Do your customers know of potentially competitive products? If so, what are they? Why are they or aren't they using them? What are the pros and cons? Are there other products that offer similar services but aren't considered competitors? The more information you can gather about the specific value the competing products offer, the more you can determine where your product may need to move to be competitive.
- Are there risks associated with solving the problem, such as legal, regulatory, or safety? Understanding the risks surrounding certain products can help you make a determination of what needs to be managed, tracked, or tested with respect to the products you are offering.

Near the close of the meeting, ask the customer for feedback and recap key learning from the visit to make sure you heard everything accurately. This can also help build a relationship.

Recapping the Customer Visit

Once you have had a chance to go on a customer visit, it is essential to summarize what you learned. It is interesting to see how this changes and morphs over time as you learn more about your customers.

If possible, try to talk to others who were also on the customer visit about the meeting. Discover what they heard, what they learned, and how it applies to your business.

What is different in what they are talking about compared to your preconceived notions or different from the thoughts you have had previously? Is it significant? Is it a different opportunity?

Capture your ideas electronically and store them in a good searchable area to enable you to find them later.

Circle back with product management for a review of the visit and impressions.

My experience has been that the recaps of the customer visits are the most valuable. It is fascinating to hear what others thought of the customer visit and to compare and contrast the perceived and real needs of the customer. Everyone has different insights. I have seen the initial thoughts about where there may be product opportunities completely change and new, more strategic opportunities emerge. It is in that newly gained deep understanding of customer needs where the real value lies. The insights that are gained in these customer visits leave a lasting impression on me and enable me to make better architectural decisions literally for years afterward.

Capturing the Voice of the Customer

As you begin to think about what the customers have said and how they have said it, try to use the language of the customer and the customer's customer in your domain modeling exercises.

Take the time to understand the nouns being mentioned. Listen carefully. Are there terms that conflict with the language you use? Were you talking past one another? Capturing these types of subtle details can save you dramatically by avoiding bad assumptions about what the customer was trying to communicate.

If you sense some subtle variances in what customers are saying and catch them early enough, ask questions to clarify what they really mean, not just what you thought they said.

Learning the language of the customer can also help with the development of marketing materials.

Listen First, Solutions Later

> "Man cannot discover new oceans unless he has the courage to lose sight of the shore."
>
> —André Gide

From a product concept point of view, it is really easy to dial into solutions before you have had a chance to digest what the customer has said and to consider the problems more broadly. Take the time to listen to carefully to customers and hear their stories (see Figure 2.3).

Before you jump into solutions, listen carefully to what the customer is really asking for; after you have a basic solution for the customer (the topic of the next chapter), seek feedback and repeat the cycle over and over.

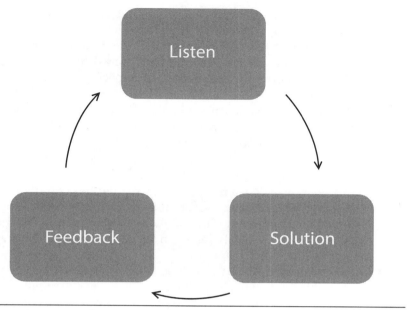

Figure 2.3   Listen first.

What Will Delight the Customer?

Customers will tell you a lot of things that they think they may need. What you want to find out is the following:

- What are their pain points?
- How can you make them more efficient?
- How can you fill a need?

If you can eliminate or greatly reduce a problem for potential customers, they will look to your product. Don't just solve their problems; seek to delight the customer.

UNDERSTANDING THE MARKET

After you begin to understand your customer, one of the next areas of focus is the overall market or markets that your product fits into. Consider:

- What markets does your product have an impact upon? Beginning to understand the variety of markets and industries where your product is used can help give you a sense of the diversity of needs to be considered, and if there is a need for product variances based on the markets being targeted.

- What is the overall market opportunity? Understanding where the largest amount of potential revenue is can help determine what features or capabilities are most important and help prioritize development efforts.

- Is this only a regional or national solution? Knowing what customers your product appeals to can help drive what features to focus on and also to begin getting a deeper knowledge of what drives sales. What is it about a particular region or a particular national alignment? Drive for the "why."

- Is this solution easy to replicate? Is it easy to do? It is critical to understand what your secret sauce that drives your value is. Typically, it is something that is not easy to replicate or easy to do. Finding areas that are uniquely yours can help drive market identity and adoption.

- Why hasn't anyone done this before? What is different now that enables this solution to be accomplished? What has changed? Understanding where the market is now and where it is in respect to near-future technology capabilities can help guide you toward areas to focus on.

- What is considered good enough? What is excellent? Working toward understanding what the minimal requirements to be competitive are and what requirements are needed to get in the door is essential. Ideally, moving beyond this and getting the features and functionality to delight the customer should be your desired end state.

- Are there any roadblocks to entry, such as certifications or licensing? Knowing the barriers to entry is important to help understand some of the base costs of doing business in this area.

- Are there required integrations? What tools are the users normally using together? Are there ways to make their work more seamless? Always be on the lookout for areas where you can simplify the customers' experience or save them time. These efficiencies can help drive sales.

- Are they similar types of customer activities? In different industries? In different areas of the business? The answer may suggest an approach to solving the challenges you run into.

- What is unique about what you bring to the table? Identifying key areas of differentiation and comparison is important to be able to stand out in the marketplace. Being just a copy of something else typically does not drive market value.

- What is the hard problem? Normally in any workflow there are problems that are intrinsically hard. Identify these as sources of risks and opportunities to be aware of. These may be areas that require human intervention if automation is not possible.
- Is there any natural tiering or grouping to the market? Knowing or developing a structure of how the overall market is grouped and personas that are associated with these groupings can help focus the set of features and functionality that are appropriate for each group both from a cost perspective as well as a capabilities perspective.
- What are the performance or scale requirements around this product? Knowing the volume of data, the expected response times, the acceptable downtimes, and the business criticality of the service or capability can significantly drive the overall approach and cost involved in creating solutions.
- Are there unique aspects to every customer? Do they require customization or specific configuration depending on the type of market that is being served? They may have expectations of being able to add custom functionality or modify existing functionality to meet their special needs. This may drive the need for a services organization to deal with the specialized needs of the customers in the market.
- What drives their decision making? Who is the decision maker for purchases? Sometimes it is the actual user of the product, but many times it is someone who specializes in purchasing or sourcing. If the decision maker isn't a user, who influences the purchasing decision? Understanding the purchaser's concerns and constraints on making a buy decision can affect how you package, bundle, or license the product.
- Do the customers act in a pack? In other words, do they all tend to follow one another? If so, who is the early adopter? Or do they act independently? Can or will the early adopters provide referrals?
- What influences customers to buy? Is the decision based on what other people in the industry are doing? Is it based on cost savings? Is it based on quality improvements? Knowing what adds perceived and real value can help drive which features are better investments and help with product development and roadmapping.
- Are you providing the entire solution or just a module or portion of the solution? Understanding what portion of the solution you are providing can help determine its overall value.
- What are the barriers to entry? Can you easily overcome them? If not, with whom could you partner to do so? If you do decide to

partner with someone, get the arrangement documented and signed early; life can take unusual twists along the way and invalidate your investment. I have seen a lack of early signed agreements hold a product hostage from release due to an inability to come to an agreement on terms late in the process.

One key consideration is to make it easy for your customers to do business with you; this will give you a better chance of making a sale. On the other hand, make it hard to purchase and you might as well not bother. The best product in the world has no value if no one buys it.

As you look at the overall market, look for opportunities, think out of the box, and look after your customers' best interests. There are usually opportunities everywhere.

Learning about the Customers' Customers

Taking a broader look at the notion of the market or markets in which your products operate is to consider who your customers' customers are. If you can understand the problems your customers are trying to solve for their customers, you have a much better chance of providing relevant solutions and potentially alternatives to how they approach their customers.

When you take this approach, you have the opportunity to become a valued partner with your customers and not just another expense they are trying to reduce. As you begin thinking about this approach, take time to consider the following:

- Who are your customers' customers? Think about what their customers' primary concerns are. What brings value to them?
- How does your product help your customers serve their customers?
- What is the nature of their relationship with their customers? Are they a partner with their customers? Are their customers repeat customers?
- How does your product impact their customers' needs? Learn how you bring value to the table.
- Are there other ways that you can help them serve their customers better?
- What is their sales model? Are they subscription based? Are they ancillary based? Is it a single purchase? Is their product consumable? Knowing how your customers make money can influence

what features they are interested in and if the features can justify a potentially higher price.

- How does your product enable your customers to make money? Are you an expense for them or do you raise their value as part of their overall value proposition?
- Will your product enable them to maintain market share? Whom are they competing against? How do they differentiate themselves? Being able to help your customers maintain and grow their market presence will help you grow your business.
- What competitive advantages does your product give them? How can your product help them maintain their competitive advantage? It is important to understand what value you bring to the table. Are there other areas you could expand into and bring more value to your customers?
- Will your product or new product features help save customers money? The more efficient you can make your customers, the more value you bring to the table and the better you are able to justify the financial arrangement your business has with them.

The key is to gain more and more context for the work you are doing and to understand the nature of the problems that your customers are encountering. You want them to view you as a partner in their business.

Where Are the Customers Willing to Spend Money?

By taking the time to learn who your customers' customers are, you can find the areas of highest value to your customers. This should in turn give you a sense of where your customers are willing to spend money (see Figure 2.4)—where real value exists.

There are always an endless number of features that can be added to a product, but the key is to find the features that add enough value that you are able to attract new customers, that you bring existing customers back to purchase more, and that your customers are willing to pay you more for the extra value you are adding.

Technology is continually improving, which means you need to factor changing table stakes into your business model.

The challenge with always adding new features is that at some point there are diminishing returns for customers. The additional cost does not justify the amount of time they will save or the complexity involved with training

Figure 2.4   Learn to understand what the customer values.

everyone on the new features. Simplicity is almost always an essential element in our willingness to adopt new things. There has to be enough of a gain to justify the pain of learning something new.

True value is expressed when customers are willing to part with their cash. Think about what makes you willing to spend your cash. We are all customers, so thinking about the product or service from their point of view will usually open some new perspectives (see Figure 2.4).

What Is the Competition Doing?

Look at your competitors and consider:

- What are the competing products in your field? Learning who your competitors are, what products they offer, and where they are making investments can help inform where your company needs to differentiate and compete in the marketplace.
- How do they describe their products? When they are marketing, what roles do they identify? What features do they deem valuable?

- Are they comparing or contrasting their products and yours? If so, how do they see themselves as different or better? Are they trying to compete on cost, quality, or ease of use? Knowing how your competition views your products can help suggest where investments are needed and also shed light on areas where the competition may be weak or vulnerable.

- What problems are they solving? Even though you may produce products that are nearly identical to those of your competition, understanding what they view as their value proposition can inform you about what kinds of customers they are trying draw in and may shed light on new market areas for your products.

- Are they trying to provide a premium product or service? Or are they trying to be a value provider, focusing more on the cost side of the equation? The way they are able to differentiate themselves from you can build perceived value in the eyes of their customers. It can also give you new and alternative ways of thinking about your products.

- Are there areas where the competition's products are not meeting the needs of their customers? Why are they not addressing these needs? Try to consider how their customers would view the absence of these capabilities.

- Are there table stakes—must-have features? Are these features required for every role? Knowing the minimum set of features to even be considered for purchase is a key element. If your customers can quickly eliminate you because you are not internationalized or you don't support a certain kind of user need, it makes their life easier. There are now fewer options, and you have given them an opportunity to look as if they have done adequate due diligence. If you are rejected for a particular bid, take time to find out what the rationale for not selecting your product was. The answer may help identify a set of capabilities that your product needs to have.

- Are there experts with whom you can partner? Do they exist in the industry and can they help guide your product decisions or approach? Often within an industry, there are experts who have a finger on the pulse of the overall market and can give you insights into how your products are perceived. They can provide feedback about what is missing or unnecessary in your product.

- Is your competition aware of emerging trends? Where is your competition trying to go? Should you be trying to go there or is there really no value in that direction based on your company's strategy? Read the blogs and books of industry leaders. Also, read articles in trade publications and organization websites.

- Can you be a fast follower? Sometimes this can be a great strategy and minimize the risk of investment.

When looking at the competition, ask yourself what product you would buy. Answer objectively. Your answer can tell you a lot about the product you are going to market with.

Your competition can provide a great sense of urgency for areas that need to be addressed and help spur investment in the products for which you are the architect. Your competition is likely not standing still even if they are looking to get out of a market.

By learning the nontechnical areas, you bring new value to the business. Instead of just bringing new technology approaches to the table, you can color the conversation with real business analysis to show how the new capabilities provide value to your customers and give your company an advantage over the competition.

Listening to Themes across Customers

If you are fortunate enough to meet with many of your customers in a relatively short amount of time and you listen carefully, you begin to hear common themes across those customers (see Figure 2.5).

As these themes develop:

- Can you formulate a recipe for solving the problems that are emerging? It is always interesting to hear two or three customers describe a similar problem they are facing and their ideas of what their needs are. A new approach for addressing the situation in a strategic manner can begin to appear. You begin to see where flexibility is needed in the solution.
- Are there needs for customization? Sometimes each customer truly has unique situations that need to be dealt with. Are you able to accommodate those needs?
- Does your solution apply to more than just the customers you are currently thinking about? The more generalized you can make the solution, the more likely it is that you can find a broader audience for the product or feature set to appeal to.
- Where else might your product be applicable? Does this solution simply apply to the problem at hand, or are there similar problems

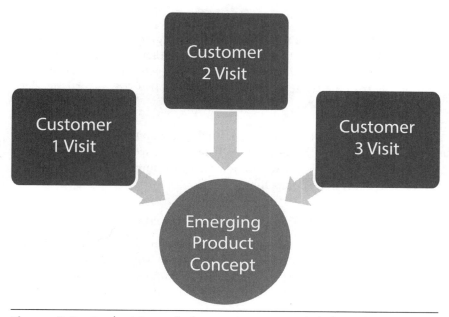

Figure 2.5   Synthesizing multiple customer visits can help bring focus to emerging product concepts.

that with minimal modifications the solution may be applied to as well?

- Where does it make sense to start? Determine what is of the highest value to the customer and what the biggest pain point is. Solving these areas will help drive interest in any solution you may be looking to provide.
- In what market does your solution make the most sense? Sometimes solutions apply to many different markets. Try picking one initially. This will allow you to hone the solution and work out any issues before venturing into too many areas.

UNDERSTANDING YOUR BUSINESS

Your business normally has a stated vision, mission statement, and goals. There is usually a key phrase or motto that captures the essence of what the company aspires to be. Learning the nuances of the stated purpose of the business and listening carefully to the vision being projected by the leaders of your business will help you align the solutions that you produce.

Learning What Your Business Wants to Do

The business you work in has goals and strategies for what it wants to accomplish. Take note of the strategic thinking that you hear your executives evangelizing; look for ways to align the projects and products you are considering to these strategic goals. What is the five-year plan? How does your product fit in?

Begin developing a story—an elevator pitch. How do the pieces fit together? As you begin telling others this story, listen to the feedback they give. Can you clarify or refine the story with new facts or information to improve the story and make it more compelling?

Personalizing Your Company's Strategic Goals

As you discover endless amounts of information about your customers, your industry, and your company's strategic goals, you need to boil it down to what is essential. For the purpose of what you are trying to accomplish, learn where to focus and separate the essentials from the noise.

For me, this is about following areas that I am passionate about.

During the early stages, you are still learning inordinate amounts of information. Be open to change; that's what discovery is all about.

Developing a Business Context for Decision Making

The point of all this is that later on when you are estimating, conceptualizing, and developing a system, you have the context to understand why one decision/design/approach may be significantly better than another. You will likely understand the areas that change frequently and what areas provide the most value; as a result, you will be able to prioritize one feature over another.

Be prepared for false starts; be open to change as you discover new information; be prepared for new independent opportunities—orthogonal opportunities.

Discovery will ultimately enable you to act as a better partner with the business. Always remember: it all starts and ends with the customer.

SUMMARY

The road to discovery begins with

- Understanding your customer
  - Partnering with sales, marketing, and new product development
  - Visualizing your products from the vantage point of the customer
  - Preparing for customer visits
  - Meeting with customers
  - Recapping information learned from customer visits
  - Focusing on capturing the voice of the customer
  - Seeking to delight the customer
- Understanding the market in which your products compete
  - Learning about your customers' customers
  - Discovering where your customers are willing to spend money
  - Keeping an eye on the competition
  - Listening for themes across customers
- Understanding your business
  - Learning what your business wants to do
  - Personalizing your company's goals
  - Developing a business context for decision making

The area of architecture I personally enjoy the most is discovery. It generates my most formative ideas about customers and the world they live in.

The models that get produced and the grounding in the business domain pay dividends for years and years. This is what enables me to be a better business partner and to be a contributor to the conversation and not just a service provider.

REFERENCES

Amabile, Teresa M., John Seely Brown, Martha Craumer, Peter F. Drucker, Constance N. Hadley, Steven J. Kramer, Theodore Levitt, Andrall E. Pearson, Ellen Peebles, and John D. Wolpert. 2003. *Harvard Business Review on the Innovative Enterprise.* Harvard Business School Press.

Christensen, Clayton M., and Michael E. Raynor. 2013. *The Innovator's Solution: Creating and Sustaining Successful Growth.* Harvard Business School Press.

Cooper, Robert G. 2001. *Winning at New Products: Accelerating the Process from Idea to Launch.* Basic Books.

————. 2011. *Winning at New Products: Creating Value through Innovation.* Basic Books.

Drucker, Peter. 2008. *The Five Most Important Questions You Will Ever Ask about Your Organization.* Jossey-Bass.

Hagadorn, Andrew. 2003. *How Breakthroughs Happen: The Surprising Truth about How Companies Innovate.* Harvard Business School Press.

Murphy, Kevin J. 1992. *Effective Listening: How to Profit by Tuning into the Ideas and Suggestions of Others.* ELI Press.

Porter, Michael E. 1988. *Competitive Advantage: Creating and Sustaining Superior Performance.* Free Press.

Chapter 3

CONCEPTUALIZATION

"An architect is the drawer of dreams."

—Grace McGarvie

"It is essential to an architect to know how to see: I mean, to see in such a way that the vision is not overpowered by rational analysis."

—Luis Barragán

"The great thing about being an architect is you can walk into your dreams."

—Harold E. Wagoner

"I claim that is where architecture starts, with the concept."

—Louis Kahn

Have you ever been listening to someone talk, and the ideas you hear begin coalescing into notions? These notions don't have names yet, but they are real, though a bit cloudy. As the conversation continues, these notions continue to evolve into ever more solid ideas. Eventually these ideas take on personalities and names of their own: you can draw them, name them, relate to them, and talk about them as if they were sitting right next to you. This process is known as *conceptualization*, *ideation*, or sometimes the *fuzzy front end*.

In the world of software development, the architect is typically one of the chief links between the business world and technology. Your ability to hear what the business wants, translate it into a high-level concept, and align it with the strategic needs of the business is a vital role.

This chapter unveils one of the essential skills needed by a software architect: the ability to conceptualize a client's or customer's notion into something implementable through ideation.

IDEATION

Ideation is a customer-centric solutions approach where the focus is finding new ways of solving customer problems. In a business setting, the focus is not simply solving new customer problems but adding value in a way that will ultimately drive revenue, reduce costs, or gain/maintain strategic advantage (see Figure 3.1).

Note

Ideation is not about programming language selection, platform selection, writing code, or purchasing hardware. It is not about technology; it *is* about the customer. Keep your focus there, at least for now.

Figure 3.1   Ideation is customer centric; contemplate a variety of alternatives to meet the customer's needs.

GETTING INVOLVED EARLY

Usually long before you begin ideating with someone, you begin forming a partnership.

Ideation is risky; you are exposing your dreams, you are vulnerable. If your partners don't like it, the idea may die before it gets a chance to grow wings and fly.

Ideation is fundamentally founded on the notion of trust: Will you help embellish the idea? Will you try to kill the idea (it's not yours)? Will you try to steal the idea (use it as your own as a vehicle for your own success)? Trust is an essential quality to establish in a partnership for the purpose of ideation.

Sometimes you have the time to slowly form a connection with the person or group. Other times you are thrust into a situation where trust may not yet be present. If it is not, you will need to start working on building it immediately.

Learning your role in the partnership is essential:

- Are you the leader?
- Is this your idea?
- Are you there to help crystallize the ideas?
- Are you there as more of a fly on the wall? (It's okay to listen, but you may not have earned speaking rights yet. It may be okay to ask questions in these situations, but wait and feel the situation out; it's not always clear.)

Over time, you may establish enough trust that your partners or customers will share not only their current ideas, but their ideas about the future, the big ones that can shape the future business and have a meaningful impact on others.

Typically, a place in the partnership is earned through hard work, socialization, and your ability to assimilate into the group.

If you are fortunate enough to win over their trust and demonstrate value early in the ideation process, your customers will eventually begin inviting you to the table for their earliest conversations and treat you like a full partner.

For more information on partnerships, see Chapter 1, "Partnership."

CONCEPTUALIZATION: BRINGING IDEAS TO LIFE

Conceptualization and ideation lead to some of the most exciting times in the product development life cycle:

- Your understanding of what the customer is seeking grows dramatically.
- The range of possible solutions explodes.
- How existing ideas and new ideas can be synthesized causes revolutionary thinking about your products.

This process of bringing concepts to life is one of the foundational elements of software architecture (see Figure 3.2). The conceptualization life cycle is rooted in seeking the essential.

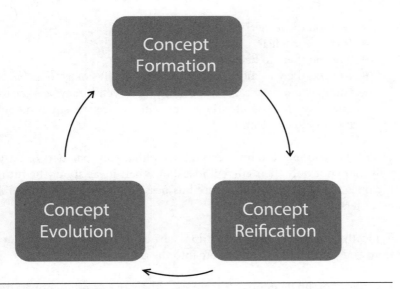

Figure 3.2   Concept life cycle

CONCEPT FORMATION

Concepts are formulated and reformulated many, many times during the product development life cycle. There are several key elements of building a foundation for these product concepts. These include forming a common language, understanding the context of the user, and developing visualizations of the concepts.

What Language Are They Speaking?

After you have begun working with a new group, customer, or partner, you begin to hear words being repeated; they have a distinct usage, pronunciation, and context. Your understanding of the subtleties of these words and their meaning is the beginning of your acceptance into the new tribe. This language enables your new tribe to communicate effectively, quickly, and precisely.

For me, capturing this language visually is the first cognitive form of understanding with the tribe. Until I am able to converse in their language and understand the meaning and interactions between the words they are using, I am not really part of the conversations that are taking place. It's like being dropped off in a foreign country: at first you are struggling to learn not just the basics, but the essentials—the equivalent of "Where is the bathroom?" "Where are the restaurants?" "Where are the hotels?"

The visual form this takes is usually a domain model. At first, I am simply trying to relate the words to something I already know and understand. If I can make the leap—for example, "This is just like a manufacturing process, this is just like a compiler," or some other process or system I am familiar with—I can establish a bridge to what is being conceived and can begin to have a high-level understanding of what is really being talked about.

Note

Many times, a word or phrase can have different meanings in different contexts. Oddly enough, sometimes this can happen even between groups that are colocated. They implicitly know the context switch in meaning. You need to be clear about your assumptions about what things mean.

Until you begin to understand these language nuances, you are doomed to poor decision making and forming assumptions that are simply wrong.

These are your future budget busters—the "Oh, I remember talking about that; you meant . . . ," and the reply, "I never said that; I said . . . ." The realization that you did in fact talk to each other but no real conversation occurred begins to emerge, and your opportunities for a smooth-sailing project diminish.

At this early point, I am just trying to understand the main concepts and the meaning of the words used:

- What is the "big picture"?
- Who are the stakeholders?
- What are the use cases?
- What are the key nouns?
- What are the key verbs?
- How do they relate (associate) to one another?
- What is their cardinality?
- Is there a hierarchical ("is a kind of") relationship and, if so, what is it? For example, this a vehicle; a Ford is a kind of vehicle; a vehicle has doors, sometimes two doors, sometimes four doors, . . .
- Are there any natural process flows that occur?

Although these initial models may be partially wrong, that's okay; they begin to give you a foundation for understanding what is being said around you. These models typically take the form of diagrams (simple boxes, nouns and connecting lines, verbs; see Figure 3.3).

> "Models are incredibly sticky—because they help people understand the world."
>
> —Olivia Mitchell

What Problem Is Being Discussed?

As you begin diving into business problems that need to be solved, whether for internal or external customers, you need to become familiar with these issues:

- What is the set of problems to be solved? Knowing and understanding the purpose of what you are doing will bring clarity to the product concept.

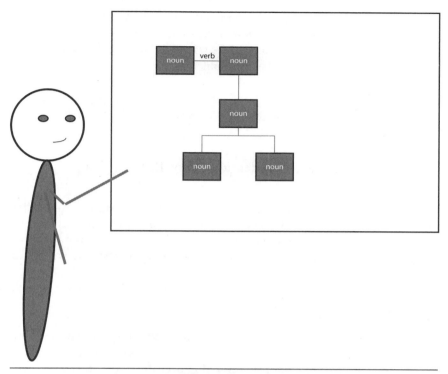

Figure 3.3 Domain models and a glossary of terms are effective tools for capturing the language of the customer.

- What are common practices for solving the problem today? Gaining a sense of how people solve a problem today can begin to suggest how the solution might be automated, what aspects may not be able to be addressed by a system, and what areas can be improved.
- What are the results the customers are hoping for? What is the value add? Why would customers want to spend money on this? How does it make their life better? Ideas are plentiful, but adding real value is the key to a successful product concept.
- What are the possible new ways of solving the problem? Coming in from the outside can be a good thing. It can enable you to think about how you would solve the problem from a fresh perspective and enable new, innovative ways to delight the customer.
- Is there a process to solving the problem? If so, can it be described? Some things are not simple tasks but require a sequence of steps. Capturing these steps can give you a place to start from and help you see where improvements or wholesale changes can be made.

- How is the customer going to earn money or save money?
- What is the value proposition of the solution for the customer?
- To whom will the end solution be targeted? Do the intended end users really think they have a problem?

Answering these questions with a domain model can help place the customer's problem in an understandable context and help drive the needed capabilities within the system.

When Arriving Late to the Ideation Party, Be Cautious about Committing

Sometimes when you enter a conversation, everyone else is miles and miles in front of you. They have worked together for years, they are "experts" in the area, and you are the new person on the block. You don't know a pothole from a pile of gold. The solution is already at hand and they are willing to commit.

Be cautious about what you commit to.

If you don't understand the problem and its context (even when everyone else does) and you are the new architect being thrown into the mix, let it be known that you are responsible for this decision and you will be held accountable—you are the architect. Do you know what you are committing to? If the answer is no, stop the train; now is the time for you to understand

- The domain
- The problem to be solved
- The context of the problem
- Alternative solutions
- Where the business is trying to go

One of the special rights you have as an architect is to say no. Be prepared to defend yourself and justify your answer, but you do have the ability to stop the train (see Figure 3.4).

Saying no is a very effective tool for putting things on pause and allowing further investigation or justification to occur.

- Would you at this very instant feel comfortable asking for money for this solution from an executive? If not, say no.

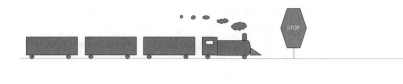

Figure 3.4   Learn to say no and stop the train if you are not confident you can reach the destination.

- Would you feel comfortable selling this solution to an investor or client? If not, say no.
- Are you reasonably confident that you have vetted this solution? If not, say no.

"Yes means nothing if you can't say no."

—Peter Block

Remember, your reputation, your relationships, and your future viability within the organization are at stake.

Bottom line is that architects need to get as many of the facts as possible and make an informed decision. It takes years and much success to build a great reputation, and it can crumble in an instant if a bad decision is made.

The goal is not to say no permanently, but long enough that reasonable options can be presented.

Taking the time to document the facts, assumptions, and risks that were known at the time of a decision can help calm the firestorm that may ensue later if things do not work out and executives are seeking an explanation.

What Does This Concept Look Like?

As you have been listening and engaging in the conversations about the problems being faced or the new opportunities that exist, you are likely to have started forming visual models of what the major components of a solution may look like (not detailed visualizations, but rough sketches—high-level boxes that begin encapsulating portions of the solution). These may be captured in a notebook, on a whiteboard, in an electronic solution (such as Visio or some other drawing tool)—it doesn't matter. The key is to begin capturing a variety of ideas about how the problem might be approached.

There are no right or wrong answers; you just want to begin playing around with the problem. Start to discover

- Where the real boundaries exist
- What the real requirements might be
- Who the real customers are
- What constraints exist
- What the main components of a solution are

You are working to discover as much about the problem and/or opportunity as you possibly can. Ideally, becoming involved in this process as early as possible is advantageous; doing so gives you the opportunity to

- Influence the solutions that will be considered
- Give the business a sense of the difficulty of solving the problem
- Give the business a sense of the cost of developing a solution for the problem
- Suggest alternatives that may solve part of the problem—but solve it with little or no cost (the low-hanging fruit)
- Find areas in which to partner with different groups and share the cost of developing a solution
- Find solutions or possible approaches from other domains
- Gain a better sense of where the business wants to go and potentially allow you to find a series of solutions that will get the business to the end state. (This may enable the potential for multiple business cases to incrementally fund the end state and reduce the overall risk.)

"The real voyage of discovery consists not in seeking new landscapes but in having new eyes."

—Marcel Proust

At this stage, developing context diagrams and conceptual diagrams will give you something to talk about as you discuss the problem and possible alternatives. Sometimes having several different diagrams can be helpful to show that this is not a fully baked solution but rather a series of alternatives to compare, contrast, and embellish.

Note

Getting involved early will give you the best chance to succeed. A project normally will follow the path where it starts. If you are able to get it off to a solid beginning, the rest will naturally follow.

Your ability to get involved at the very outset of ideation can have a dramatic impact on your ability to frame alternative approaches to how to deliver solutions. This context is invaluable later in the project or projects that are derived from this ideation.

Getting involved early fundamentally changes your role from being a solution provider/contractor to being a partner (one who sits at the table and contributes your best and brightest ideas). If you come into the process later, many of the boundaries for the concept have already been established and the willingness to rehash decisions may be limited.

Getting customers involved (finding out what problems they really have, where they will part with money, and how they deal with this problem today) can dramatically improve your ability to understand what products need to be produced and how they need to work.

If and when customers are involved, work hard to be at the table. Normally, businesses are terrified of the Dilbert effect that technologists bring to the conversation.

Early on, be cautious and work toward establishing trust; you need to demonstrate that you can be a good citizen in public before your influence can begin. Hearing a variety of customers react to the proposed concept can have a dramatic impact on its shape, size, and complexity. I have personally seen concepts that were radically more complex than the real needs of customers required.

The continual refinement of a concept with exposure to multiple customers (under NDA, of course, and paid for their time and efforts) can begin bringing clarity and understanding that simply never existed before. There begins to form a simple (nonessential elements removed) and elegant structure to the concept, one that may in the end require only a fraction of the cost to implement.

I have seen a case where the final solution was only 10% of the cost of the initial estimates for implementation due to early customer involvement, and where the solution was far more strategic in nature (it focused on at most a handful of essential things and delivered on them) and had applicability to many different business opportunities.

The key to success is to listen:

- Get the customers to talk.
- Ask questions.
- Record your conversations if the customers are willing to let you.
- Let them follow their own rabbit trails (that is usually where the gold is).

Remember, this is about the customer, not you:

- Let them talk.
- Don't interrupt.
- Be gracious.
- Be willing to change.
- Invite a variety of customer roles to be involved in the conversation; they usually have a wide range of views and insights into their world that they are happy to share if you give them the chance.
- Listen for legal concerns, human concerns, maintenance elements, and regulatory concerns that you may not have had knowledge of before.

The ideas, comments, and concerns that the customers express may very well be the keys to your delivering a solution that in the future will allow you to stand tall among your competitors.

As you speak to multiple customers, you will begin seeing new threads appear that you never perceived before. Having a small but limited team focus on the concept development can help establish trust and enable real conversations with the team to occur. Usually, allow one new member to travel along; that person's newness to the concept will help validate it from an outsider's perspective and ensure that you don't get so close to the concept that you can't see the big picture anymore.

Having to explain what you are thinking multiple times can help cement the ideas in your mind and bring clarity to languishing elements of the concept. You may hear comments such as

- "It would make my life so much better if . . ."
- "Really, what I would like is something that could . . ."

If so, capture them; they are the elements of your vision that will make your concept great.

When the opportunity arises to visit with customers, drop everything, even if the invitation to go somewhere occurs at the most inopportune time.

The important decisions usually require you to act immediately, with relatively little information and an unusually high level of distractions all coming to a head at the same time. Learn to listen to the small voice inside and follow your gut. Trusting your instincts and, if possible, consulting with trusted partners are usually good strategies.

CONCEPT REIFICATION

Concept reification is the process of making the product real, focusing on what is essential, assessing what is possible, and establishing essential characteristics of the system.

Minimum Viable Product

> *"My aim is to omit everything superfluous so that the essential is shown to the best possible advantage."*
>
> —Dieter Rams

From an architecture perspective, driving toward a minimum viable product (MVP)—the 20% of the functionality that people will use every day—should be the goal. The full list of features may eventually be required to dominate the market. But when you are trying to get a product out the door quickly and be the first to market, focus on MVP.

The MVP can be a challenge when working with customers or new product development. They typically want it all. By working with them closely, you can usually prioritize and distill the essential product features that need to be delivered first. Accomplishing this distillation will give you the opportunity to focus development resources on what is most important. It will also enable you to begin shipping usable software earlier and to start to generate a revenue stream. Live products have a much better survival rate than prolonged development activities that ship only at the end (they begin to look like money pits to executives).

One indicator that you are on the right track is that the system can be described on one page; it should be conceptually complete, and nothing more can be removed. When diagrammed, if there are any boxes with more than five lines coming out of them, you should evaluate the concept and verify that it is structured properly.

The Need for Experimentation

The area of experimentation is often a challenge for the business and technology in that it is often a nonfunded area of required research. There is often funding for doing the estimates, there is often funding for doing spikes once a project has been funded, but there is not always money to fund simple proofs of concept to determine the feasibility of projects or the lowest-cost approach, the simplest operational approach, or the best technical approach. A lack of funding for these experiments can cause high estimates to be produced in the space where there are many unknowns. This unintentionally causes the business to turn away from opportunities that may well have been great strategic opportunities, but the lack of ideation money causes the business to look elsewhere.

I have found that coming to the business with ideas is not sufficient. Ideas abound, even ideas with a great pitch. The best way to bring ideas forward is to produce simple proofs of concept. Working examples of code that demonstrate an idea—even in very crude, rudimentary forms—tend to have the highest impact and also have the highest likelihood of generating enough interest to get those who hold the financial purse strings to open the checkbooks and pursue formally estimating and authorizing projects (see Figure 3.5).

> **Note**
>
> As an architect, you live in the world of sales, and there is nothing like some working code to close the deal.

You will need every asset at your disposal to get the business hooked. I like to think of it as "A single proof of concept is worth a thousand estimates." It will engage the business in ways that almost nothing else will. As the old saying goes, "Seeing is believing." Without it, you may soon be doomed to an infinite loop of estimating. (My unfortunate personal record is 16 estimates for a project before it moved forward. In the end, the project was very successful, but I hope to never repeat this again: *death march estimating.*)

Establishing Assumptions Can Help Harmonize the Vision

Working with new product development to begin visualizing the system can bring a tremendous amount of clarity to everyone's thinking. It will quickly reveal major assumptions being made by new product development,

Figure 3.5 Find ways to experiment and perform proofs of concept—it's an effective way to build new solutions for the business.

marketing, sales, and technology. This emergence of assumptions is essential to begin harmonizing everyone's thinking about the product concept.

Establishing Essential Capabilities and Customer Roles

This visualization can also help with the emergence of customer roles within the new system. You will quickly be able to see what capabilities are possible and which are not. The conversations around this will begin the process of *concept reification*. Thus begins a virtuous cycle that can also include reengaging the end customers to validate the new thinking that has emerged. If they get it immediately, you are on the right track. If they don't, you need to evaluate what was wrong with the product concept:

- Was it pitched wrong? Different customers have different areas of concern and needs. Knowing a customer's particular situation and crafting the message to that situation can have a dramatic impact on the customer's acceptance of what is presented.
- Do the user roles make sense? Each customer may have a slightly different way of managing the problem. Have you captured user roles that easily map onto the way customers manage their businesses?

- Does the flow of tasks match how the customers work? Each customer may have tasks allocated differently based on specific needs. Is there enough flexibility with how you are approaching the problem to accommodate different needs?
- Are there missing capabilities? As you interact with customers and explain the different aspects of the system, are there areas that they can identify that are missing or don't really match their needs? If so, dive into these areas in more detail to better understand what their needs are and what would need to be done differently to accommodate them.
- Are the capabilities commingled and in need of restructuring? The key here is to find out if the granularity of the capabilities is at the level that they need to do their work or at the level at which they allocate work out to individuals. If they don't align well because they do too much or too little, it could be a barrier for the customer to adopt the system.
- Are nonessential items still present? Are you pursuing any capabilities that the customer simply does not need? If so, try to dig a little further to find out what is different about the situation or how the customer works that makes these capabilities unnecessary.

Based on these outcomes, consider asking customers to explain how your concept does or does not solve their *pain points*; you might be making the world worse for them. If you hear, "I would never do that," that is a warning signal that you may be on the wrong track, but at least the customer has identified a potential problem in your product concept.

Let your customers break your preconceived notions. Normally you are looking for validation and a stamp of approval on your thoughts; be open to change.

As you hear new requirements and ideas, there is a tendency to gold plate the ideas or concepts. Be cautious here. Avoid just looking for requirements to build the cool system you have been desperately hoping to build or use that new technology you just heard about. Focus on improving the concept, not embellishing it.

Reify with Customers

Keeping a regular rhythm of contact with key customers can help validate, provide feedback about, and enable new insights into the concepts that are emerging around their needs.

My ideation experience has been that most customers that we have gone out to visit and met face-to-face are more than happy to talk through in detail the work they do and the needs they have. If they are leaders in the area of work they do, they have already spent time thinking about how they can do things better. They are highly engaged, knowing that they are helping to craft the future. As the conversations with the customers and the post-analysis of those conversations continue, the cloudiness of the concepts gives way to clarity. With this clarity, the real product vision and roadmap begin to emerge.

This product navigation through reification helps identify and establish areas of high customer value.

CONCEPT EVOLUTION

The process of developing new products has one constant: change. This continuous change creates the need for continual refinement and evolution of product concepts.

Being a Student of History

At most businesses, many concepts have been around the block more than once. Critical thinking has been done about the problem and for some reason the concept didn't proceed, because of cost, timing, complexity, or any of a wide variety of reasons.

When you see yourself being drawn into what looks to be a repeat performance, take the time to understand what the previous concepts were. If you are lucky, there may be some documentation or survivors of the previous situation who can relay their war stories about what happened. As you dive into this in more detail:

- Listen carefully for the assumptions, risks, and requirements that drove the previous attempt. These can help give you insights into what may be different about the current proposal.
- Validate what you are hearing against what you have discovered to date. Note what you are finding; it can help when you eventually move into an estimating phase to have a deeper rationale behind what you are saying (and selling).
- Determine if anything has changed and, if so, what. Look at changes in the product concept, changes in the market, changes in the customer segmentation, and changes in technology. There are many factors that can influence the feasibility of a product.

- Has technology advanced? Is the technical approach that is under consideration different from what was previously conceived? This may be an opportunity to reduce the cost structure of the project.
- Has your customer base changed or adopted new technologies? Sometimes customer adoption of new technologies can enable different solutions and product concepts to be considered.
- Have your customers tried this solution before? If they have, how did it turn out? Why? Customers can be a great source of knowledge. They have seen and tried out a variety of solutions in the past and likely know where the pitfalls are as well as where they and others have had success.
- Beware of the naysayers. They failed at this, and they might be happier if you fail, too. Always filter what you hear. There are usually circumstances that were involved in previous situations that simply may not be in play now.
- Learn, but don't become infected with negative thinking. If you believe that you can't do something, you are usually right. You need to be open to what is possible based on your own analysis.

Being knowledgeable about your company's long-term and near-term history can be a great source of enabling decision making. This is especially true for projects that have failed or succeeded and also for projects that have only seen the light of estimation.

Embracing Multiple Perspectives

As you gather more and more feedback and work toward evolving a concept, consider different approaches for how the system might work, consider ways for how complexity might be reduced if certain assumptions were different, and consider what areas of the concept might have extensibility needs:

- Are you able to capture key aspects of events that occur within a customer's workflow? Are you able to see ways to automate the work that is being done based on these events? Can they be captured by a system? How common are these workflow events? Do they occur across multiple customers? Can you model these events into state transition diagrams?
- Are you able to recognize common or key customer tasks and their associated flow? The more customers you interact with, the more commonality you will be able to see in how they approach their work, what their typical problems are, and where they are unique.

- Are there critical dependencies between tasks? As you develop product concepts, there are dependencies that become clear with respect to other projects, customer infrastructure, and industry developments. Capture and document these dependencies; they will become essential as you try to move the product concept forward into the estimation and approval stages.
- What risks appear to be emerging? The more you are able to dive into a product concept, the more you are able to begin perceiving risks that are critical for others to be aware of as you move forward into an estimating phase. Capture and document these.
- Are there areas of concern that have been expressed? Try to dive below the surface to find out what the root causes of the concerns are. There may be no problems, or there may be a significant misunderstanding about the product concept being proposed.
- Are new capabilities emerging? If so, name them. Naming things has an amazing ability to bring them to life. Your ability to talk about them, relate them, and refine them increases dramatically.
- Are there patterns to the information you are gathering? If so, name them. Named patterns enable a significant amount of reuse and can act as a great point of leverage within the business. They can also assist with the development of domain-specific languages.

Your ability to synthesize these observations across multiple customers can have a dramatic impact on your ability to produce a strategic solution that has broad customer applicability versus simply a point solution.

For a deeper dive into the area of specific techniques and tools around this area, see the references at the end of this chapter.

Seeking Conceptual Integrity

As you evolve the concept, consider:

- How does this concept align with your other products? In most businesses, there is a suite of products that align with one another. How does your concept fit into this suite? Where does it overlap? Are there capabilities that you can leverage? Are these capabilities built in a way that can be leveraged? Are there areas of integration that should be considered? If the capabilities will be delivered in the near future, can you rely on the other product areas to deliver? If they miss, they may significantly impact your budget if they don't deliver or deliver in a way that doesn't meet your needs.

- How does this concept align with the customer base you are targeting? You need to understand how the concept applies to the various market segments and what sets of capabilities overlap and which ones are unique. It will help you understand what is absolutely critical to deliver from a business perspective as development priorities change.
- Can you describe the concept in under two minutes? Always be prepared to deliver an elevator speech. You need to have the core message down cold. You need to be prepared so that if you run into a senior executive you can nail the message of what the concept you are working on is, how it will help the customer, and how it will make the company money.
- Is the concept clear and concise? Do people get what you are saying quickly? If customers don't quickly grasp what you are proposing, your concept is most likely wrong or you are presenting it wrong. The customer is always right. You need to seriously look into what is missing or needs adjusting.
- Have the essential domain relationships been established? If you can identify key relationships within a domain model, it is likely that there is a natural way that certain capabilities need to function based on the relationships and their cardinality with one another. If you miss these, there will likely be natural impedances within your system that will make it feel unnatural to your end users.
- What are the two or three things that everything else revolves around? Get these areas right. Normally for most products there are a couple of key areas that are absolute must-have capabilities. Find out what these are and what makes them so essential. These are going to be the foundation upon which everything else is built.
- Are there similar concepts or patterns in other industries? Often there are similar capabilities in other industries that you may be able to leverage directly, leverage from a design perspective, or possibly leverage from an approach perspective. Be on the lookout for new and innovative approaches as you look for solutions.
- Can the concept be described on one page? If your concept cannot be distilled down to a single page as an executive overview, you need to take the time to work on the clarity of the concept. At this point, the concept needs to be clear, concise, and quickly understood by someone who is familiar with the area.

The goal is to sync the conceptual integrity of your product concept with the needs of the customer as well as with the needs of the company. The more synergies that can be applied, the more support you are likely to receive within your organization.

Recognizing Adjacent Opportunities

As you go through multiple cycles of product conceptualization, you often begin to hear and see use cases and different customer roles that don't cleanly align with one another. There is clearly something different about what they are doing and the goals they are trying to achieve. The customers may not have recognized these slight variances, but taking the time to distill these subtleties can potentially result in multiple products that share many of the same features but are marketed to different segments based on their differing needs.

Occasionally when you step back and look at the product concept from a more generic capabilities perspective, you are able to begin thinking about other areas where these capabilities could be applied. Sometimes there are adjacent markets that have more potential value than the current area that you are pursuing. For one concept that we were working on developing, the adjacent market opportunity turned out to be ten times larger than the original product concept.

This new market may have completely different performance and scale needs, but the market insights will give you critical information about the architectural needs of the product and likely future directions the business will want to pursue. The key is to be open to change and to be willing to expand your horizons.

SUMMARY

The road to conceptualization begins with

- Ideation with business partnerships
- Getting involved as early as possible in the process
- Concept formulation
  - Understanding the language of the customer
  - Developing domain models
  - Understanding the context of the customer
  - Committing cautiously when you are the new kid on the block
  - Visualizing the concept

- Concept reification
  - Developing a minimum viable product
  - Experimenting with prototypes
  - Establishing assumptions
  - Establishing essential capabilities and customer roles
  - Reifying with customers
- Concept evolution
  - Being a student of history
  - Embracing multiple perspectives
  - Recognizing adjacent opportunities

For technically inclined individuals like me who love to whiteboard and work with business partners to learn new problem domains and new challenges, seeking conceptual integrity makes every day exciting.

REFERENCES

Amabile, Teresa M., John Seely Brown, Martha Craumer, Peter F. Drucker, Constance N. Hadley, Steven J. Kramer, Theodore Levitt, Andrall E. Pearson, Ellen Peebles, and John D. Wolpert. 2003. *Harvard Business Review on the Innovative Enterprise*. Harvard Business School Press.

Brooks, Frederick P., Jr. 1995. *The Mythical Man-Month: Essays on Software Engineering, Anniversary Edition (Second Edition)*. Addison-Wesley.

Christensen, Clayton M., and Michael E. Raynor. 2003. *The Innovator's Solution: Creating and Sustaining Successful Growth*. Harvard Business School Press.

Cooper, Robert G. 2001. *Winning at New Products: Accelerating the Process from Idea to Launch*. Basic Books.

Cornish, Edward. 2004. *Futuring: The Exploration of the Future*. World Future Society.

De Bono, Edward. 1999. *Six Thinking Hats*. Back Bay Books.

Gray, Dave. 2010. *Gamestorming: A Playbook for Innovators, Rulebreakers, and Changemakers*. O'Reilly Media.

Hagadorn, Andrew. 2003. *How Breakthroughs Happen: The Surprising Truth about How Companies Innovate*. Harvard Business School Press.

Hohmann, Luke. 2006. *Innovation Games: Creating Breakthrough Products through Collaborative Play*. Addison-Wesley.

Ries, Eric. 2011. *The Lean Startup: How Today's Entrepreneurs Use Continuous Innovation to Create Radically Successful Businesses.* Crown Business.

Sibbet, David. 2010. *Visual Meetings: How Graphics, Sticky Notes and Idea Mapping Can Transform Group Productivity.* Wiley.

Von Oech, Roger. 2008. *A Whack on the Side of the Head: How You Can Be More Creative.* Business Plus.

Chapter 4

ESTIMATION

"There is no such thing as absolute value in this world. You can only estimate what a thing is worth to you."

—Charles Dudley Warner

"For me, every day is a new thing. I approach each project with a new insecurity, almost like the first project I ever did. And I get the sweats. I go in and start working, I'm not sure where I'm going. If I knew where I was going I wouldn't do it."

—Frank Gehry

"It's a simple approach. Sustainable architecture looks to the future by looking at the past."

—Stephen Gist

Have you ever had anyone stop by and ask, "I have an idea for a project; it looks a bit like this and has these high-level features. What will it cost?" Your mind begins to whir as you think about what this might entail. You begin asking questions for clarification. You begin considering where, when, and how this project will get used. You try to think of other projects that you have encountered that may be similar as you try to come up with a reasonable number. You begin thinking, "Wow, this is a cool project." Alternatively, "Am I going to be held to this number?"

Welcome to the world of estimation.

Long before a single line of code on a project is ever written, the business and senior technology will have been working closely together to secure the appropriate finances necessary to fund projects and keep the pipeline of revenue growth or cost savings alive and well.

The architect is one of the chief links between the business world and technology. Your ability to hear what the business wants, translate it into a high-level concept, align it with the strategic needs of the business, and frame the concept for technology is a vital role.

This chapter unveils one of the essential skills needed by a software architect: the ability both to provide rough estimates and to provide the context to enable business case estimates to be produced.

ESTIMATES OVERVIEW

Estimates are usually used by the business to help it obtain funding for a project. They enable the business to get a sense of

- What the cost of a project will be
- When the project can be delivered
- What risks are associated with the project
- What dependencies will potentially exist for the project
- What areas of the project are unknown
- What alternative approaches are possible
- What assumptions are being made about the project

Estimates come in all sizes and shapes, depending on what the needs of the business are. They will drive the associated costs, assumptions, risks, dependencies, and alternatives considered (see Figure 4.1).

What Is the Purpose of the Estimate?

When someone seeks an estimate from you, one of the very first things to do is to determine what kind of estimate the person is looking for:

- Is this just a quick sizing effort so that the person can get the information immediately (*a drive-by estimate*)?

    This type of estimate is best communicated verbally and not in an electronic format. It is usually used by the business to gauge what kind of investment is needed, to get some details about the nature of the development effort, and to determine if it is worthwhile diving into more detail. This kind of estimate may also be used to help the business pitch an idea to a product counsel.

    I usually let my manager and the associated program manager know about the potential project and the high-level number that I gave.

    This estimate has the potential to be off by an order of magnitude, up or down, given the lack of details that are typically exchanged

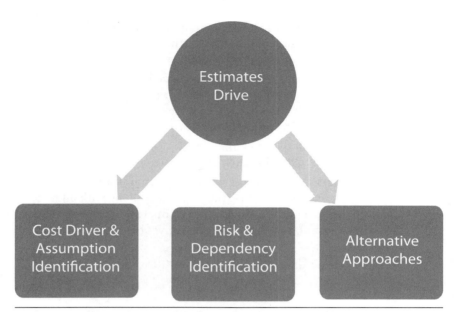

Figure 4.1   Estimates drive projects based on the value propositions they reveal.

and the amount of time spent on it (typically less than an hour, including the conversation with the requester).

- Is this a rough estimate on which the requester would like you to spend a day or two and to provide a little more detail (*a rough order of magnitude estimate*)?

This type of estimate normally takes on a little more formality. It is usually used by the business to gauge whether or not to move forward with a business case.

I usually work with the program manager to meet with the requester and develop an estimate. If necessary, we may include a handful of technology specialists if we are unsure about a particular area.

This type of estimate is usually formally communicated to the business and entered into an estimating repository along with any materials that were gathered and any high-level assumptions that went into the estimate. Again, I usually give my manager a heads-up about the potential project and the number that was delivered.

This estimate has the potential to be off by two or three times. Typically, for this type of estimate and for everyone included, try to spend less than eight hours.

- Is this something for which the requester wants a formal estimate—
  one that could be used to support a business case (*a business case
  estimate*)?

  This type of estimate is normally very formal. It is usually used by
  the business to make the actual request for money associated with
  a business case. It is also used to determine the groups, skills, and
  staffing needed for the project.

  I usually work with the program manager, the requester, and an
  estimating team to develop such an estimate.

  This type of estimate is usually formally communicated to the business and entered into an estimating repository along with all materials created as part of the estimate. The estimate will be reviewed by
  the estimators and their associated executives before being formally
  communicated.

  This estimate needs to be accurate within 10% and may take several
  weeks to produce.

With each of these types of estimates comes an increasing level of due diligence, documentation, and communication.

After the project has been approved and development has begun, there may
be *business case validation* estimates that are requested to verify that the
project is properly sized and scoped based on actual design details.

Is There an Established Project Context?

Ideally, by the time you are asked to help create an estimate for the business,
you will already have been involved working with your business partners
(refer to Chapter 1, "Partnership"), been involved in the discovery phase
(refer to Chapter 2, "Discovery"), and had the opportunity to help formulate the product concept (refer to Chapter 3, "Conceptualization").

If not, now is the time to deep-dive and learn everything you can about the
product being proposed.

Without having a solid understanding of what the business is asking for, it is
nearly impossible to develop an architectural approach and an estimate that
make sense for the business.

What Is an Architectural Approach?

The goal from an architecture perspective for any of these project-estimating
types is to develop an architectural approach. This will help set the bound-

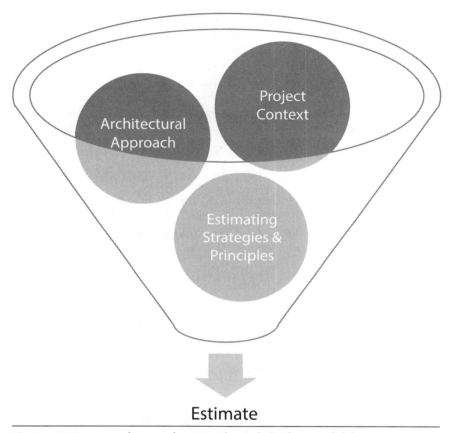

Figure 4.2 An architectural approach can help drive and deliver consistent and reliable estimates for the business.

aries to the estimate that is being produced and help frame what the project will potentially cost (see Figure 4.2).

The key elements of an architectural approach include

- Describing background information about the project.
- Showing how the approach meets the desired business requirements.
- Delivering key diagrams that pictorially tell the story of what is being built. These may need to vary depending on the audience to whom you are delivering (for example, data center operations, product operations, technology development, or product development).

- Identifying risks, assumptions, issues, outstanding questions, dependencies.
- Identifying at least one way to implement the project. This may not be the final approach, but it will help ground the estimating process.

Once you have the project context and the architectural approach and have applied the appropriate estimating strategies and principles, you and the estimating team can work to produce solid estimates for the business.

UNDERSTANDING THE ESTIMATING PROCESS

As an architect, becoming familiar with the estimating process of your organization is critical. This process will bound nearly all of the activities that are expected of you and others involved in producing estimates for the business and will define what success means.

Estimating Pipeline

Whether defined explicitly or implicitly, every organization has some form of process for funding projects. Often, this pipeline looks like the chevrons shown in Figure 4.3.

As you are familiarizing yourself with the pipeline process, take the time to consider these questions:

- What is the pipeline of work that is coming your way?
- Are all the resources fully filled? Will you need resources with specific skills?
- Is there a cadence to your estimating—quarterly, ad hoc?
- What is the prioritization of estimating? For me, it is my highest priority. I often drop nearly everything for several weeks when estimating occurs.
- How much money is allocated to estimating? (1% to 2% is normal.) Is it separately funded and tracked?

Figure 4.3   Knowing the funding process will lead to better insights into when to engage the business and when best to influence a project's direction.

- What do you do if you have three or four large projects that need to be estimated at the same time?
- What if your business partners are not picking up projects (what should the ratio of estimated to funded projects be)?
- Where do small features fit in? Where does maintenance fit in?
- Who will review the estimates? Make sure your senior management is familiar with the estimates before they are generally released.

Types of Projects

The type of project you are estimating can have a significant impact on the information gathered within your architectural approach. Getting an early understanding of the project type can help you formulate what considerations need to be taken into account. Normally there are five main types of projects:

- **Maintenance.** This type of project is usually a keep-the-lights-on type of project. It has fixed funding on a year-to-year basis; it does not have a lot of resources assigned to it, but it has a lot of defects to fix and minor enhancements to develop. There usually is not a lot of architectural activity in this area. An example of this type of project is an established product that needs a certain level of funding to stay current with technology or to stay competitive in the marketplace.
- **Migration.** This type of project is usually the result of a burning platform—the project needs to be migrated off the current platform and onto a different one. This may be due to legacy operating systems, software, or hardware that is going out of support or that is extremely expensive to maintain due to opportunistic vendors. The challenge with this type of project is that it typically has fixed features, fixed resources, and a flexible date. Unfortunately, the extent of the features or their usage is usually not fully known, leading to surprises (read: budget busters) later on. Since there may not be new revenue associated with this type of project, the business's interest in investing a lot will likely be limited. The challenge from an architectural perspective is determining how much change (reengineering) is warranted and helping to inform the business about the true cost of the migration (usually, not a popular message). An example of this type of project would be a move off of a mainframe.
- **New/enhancement.** This type of project is usually the result of market demand or potentially a new or adjacent market opportunity. These types of projects are usually fun and exciting, at least when they are starting out. The new product or new features may not

be clearly defined, but a vision exists of where the product owners want to go. The challenge from an architecture perspective is that the direction the product owners want to go may be somewhere the organization has never been before. An example of this type of project would be building solutions to fill a gap in your overall product portfolio or to expand your portfolio into a new high-growth area.

- **Integration.** This type of project usually arises when another product is a market leader in a particular area and your business wants to integrate with it to enable easier sales of your product. This type of project can be challenging due to a lack of appropriate interfaces for what you want to accomplish and minimal leverage with the other product. An example of this type of project would be integrating into an order-to-cash system or into a human resources system from your software.

- **Acquisition.** This type of project is a world unto itself. It is usually initiated when the business wants to buy its way into a particular portion of the market and buy either expertise or revenue. The challenges from an architecture perspective include figuring out what it would take to build these capabilities yourself and what it would take to integrate these capabilities into your existing suite of products while increasing the business's overall value. An example of this type of project would be purchasing a start-up to fill a gap in your overall product portfolio or to expand your portfolio into a new high-growth area.

Be cautious when you see a mix of these project types, such as Migration + New; the features are likely to not have been well thought out, and the requirements are likely to be "Make it just like the old system except for this handful of items." This type of mixed project is likely to go over budget and be completed well after the original planned release date.

If it is a truly large mixed project, the senior management leader is likely to not be with the company or have exited to another part of the organization before the project completes.

Alternative Ways of Financing Projects

There are typically two types of financing that are used to fund projects.

The first is a *spending envelope*. In this case, the business will likely ask for a yearly round of funding with a loose commitment to what will be accomplished. There may not be a specific return on investment (ROI) set for these funds. One of the advantages of this type of project is that if you don't get a feature done this year, it may not be a large issue since you may be able to simply complete it next year. Be cautious about underdelivering, though; it can cause issues that are hard to manage. The ability to reprioritize knowing that future funding is likely to be available enables the business to be more strategic about its decisions and allows technology to do more of the right things. In effect, the business acts as a property owner instead of a temporary resident. This type of financing also limits the business in terms of what types of efforts it can take on—it's fixed funding.

The second type of financing is *project centric*. This type is typically for a project that has a defined scope, a defined funding amount, a defined delivery date, and a specified ROI. One of the advantages of this type of project is that you can assemble a team that has the skill sets to address specific needs. This type of project typically requires that more tough decisions be made. Invariably, what the business wants to get done typically costs more than the available funds, which can lead to compromises in quality ("Let's do less testing") or fewer features ("This feature is too expensive or does not provide enough value").

In both cases, estimating plays a critical role in determining the success of the project. If you have sufficient funding and resources, you can get the project done on time and on budget; you will look very successful. If you have a budget overrun, you will look as if you have been involved in a mismanaged project. In reality, the only difference between the two was the estimate and the associated funding that was applied to both.

The challenge is to get the estimate "right" and have some margin for error.

Understanding the Business Process

Do you understand how the business goes about asking for and obtaining funds that enable the development process? It is not uncommon for corporations to have a waterfall business process and an agile development process. This allows them to maintain relatively tight control over and measurement of how and where the development dollars are invested.

Do you know when the business plans to ship the product? In many instances, it is the proposed ship date of the product when the financial clock starts, and it may be not at all related to the actual start date of the project. When estimating, you need to be clear about when the project will begin (avoid putting in specific dates when possible) and when it will be delivered (make this relative to the start date).

Many factors outside of your control can influence when a project might start. For example, there may be a hiring freeze or a contractor freeze that results in your project not being able to start until other projects have completed and existing resources are made available. Meanwhile, finance considers the funds to have been delivered whether they are in use or not, and the countdown to delivery is has begun. Once the funds have been delivered, how does finance track you to your numbers? Is there any kind of margin (plus or minus 10%)? If you go above the margin, how do you deal with exceptions? Knowing this kind of information can inform you about how tight your margins can be. If there is no room for error, your estimate needs to properly account for that.

DEVELOPING THE ARCHITECTURAL APPROACH

Architects are responsible for developing the architectural approach for a project during the estimation phase. This approach will serve as a backdrop for how the estimate will be formulated and will serve as an initial roadmap once the project begins.

Is This a Partnership or a Contractual Relationship?

Different business units operate in different fashions. Some will work with you as business partners and there will be open sharing of information in both directions. Others will work with you in more of a contractual manner, where the estimates you produce are fixed-bid estimates. They expect all of the features at the highest possible quality and delivered at or below the price specified. Knowing how a particular area of the business likes to operate can inform you about how you need to estimate and what contingencies you need to be prepared to account for in your estimate.

Depending on the nature of the relationship, you need to be prepared to defend your estimates at all times. You may be challenged by executives within the organization if they feel your solution is too expensive for what is perceived as gold plating. You may be challenged within your own organization if you provide a tactical solution to help the business meet a specific deadline. This tactical solution may be perceived as a hack that someone else will have to clean up, or it may introduce a scaling issue that unnecessarily uses up valuable resources. The key is to show you are being a good resident, and that there is a plan to address any technical debt that will be incurred.

Make sure as the creator of an estimate that there is ample backup material to make the estimate "real." Estimates are always challenged if they are seen as too low or too high.

Sometimes the relationship between the business and technology can be more political in nature. The business may use the estimating process to prove a political point.

In a large organization, managers often use estimates to justify getting more people (resource headcount) or maybe even creating new positions. To accomplish this, they may need to deprioritize or shut down some other effort in order to free up resources for this one.

What Is the Business Rationale for the Project?

Once you understand what the business is asking for, you need to get a sense of why the business wants to pursue this project:

- Is the purpose to drive cost savings?
- Is the purpose to grow revenue?
- Is there a strategic first-mover advantage that the business is seeking?
- Is this a competitive move to quickly catch up to the competition and be a fast follower?
- Is the business hoping for a quick win?
- Is this an exploratory project? Is the business just trying to test the waters?

Understanding the business rationale for pursuing the project can help drive a solution that will enable the business to meet and exceed its objectives. This rationale can provide some leading indication of what the ROI may be for a project or even the total cost of ownership (TCO) for certain types of projects, especially for build-versus-buy decisions.

What Is the Marketing Approach?

Understanding the marketing approach for your products can help guide your decisions about what architectural directions you need to take into account. As you gather this marketing information, consider:

- Do you understand the marketing side of the world?
- How is marketing going to sell this product?

- What customers are they going to approach?
- Do they have customer personas?
- Have they done customer research?
- Does the product apply to multiple customer segments? If not, what changes or skins would be necessary to make it apply to multiple customer groups?

Taking the time to understand how sales are made and how the product is presented to your customers can help you craft better solutions and prioritize decisions about the approaches being considered.

Is This a Repeat Estimate?

Often for technology, a project that needs to be estimated has been around the block before. If and when this occurs, consider why new product development keeps asking for the same project, but with minor twists. Are they searching for the combination that has the least cost with maximum profit (customer benefit)? Are the reestimates based on new insights from customer visits?

In nearly all cases, proceed cautiously when reestimating projects (see Figure 4.4).

Consider separating the features and making it more of a buffet-style estimate, one where the requesters can pick and choose the parts they want, including alternatives. When you do this, make sure that critical dependencies are noted. Some features may have dependencies on others, and you don't want selections to occur where there are hidden costs that were not accounted for. If there is a common core set of functionality among features, separate it out as a required portion of the estimate; this will help the requesters pick one of the alternatives or potentially both without under- or overcounting the effort needed.

> **Note**
>
> Having a matrix of options for the business to select from can usually help eliminate the need for repeat estimates.

The challenges are that giving a buffet-style estimate with multiple alternative options is expensive and potentially risky, can take a significant amount

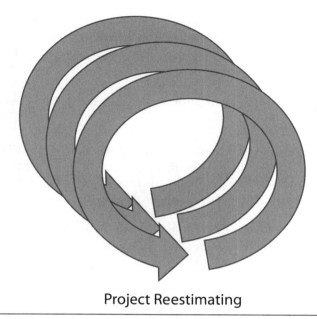

Project Reestimating

Figure 4.4 Proceed cautiously with projects that have been recycled and reestimated—understand why the project was not previously funded.

of time to produce, and may be challenging to present to the business in a simple manner. Ideally, it will fit on a PowerPoint slide.

What Risks Have You Identified? Can You Mitigate Them?

As you progress through the estimation process, the ability to identify and mitigate risk is one of the chief responsibilities of an architect. One of the best ways to mitigate risk in a new area is to do a proof of concept (POC). Testing the idea and validating the approach are invaluable if you have the time and funds. It has been my experience that doing a POC during estimating is nearly impossible. It is typically extremely hard to get POCs approved during, or prior to, estimating. The dollars are likely to not get approved unless there is "proof" of a reduction in cost savings or a growth in revenue or occasionally a strategic play. If at all possible, work with your technology management and business partners to look at funding these POC efforts. In the end, it is in their best interests to lower project risks and have projects succeed from a time, budget, and resource perspective.

The business typically has had the experience that most efficiency plays don't pan out. Great claims are made, but they don't materialize. The costs shift in other ways, and in the end, it looks like a shell game. You need to look at the total ownership costs.

As you estimate the development of the system, take time to consider these issues:

- Can you use virtual machines or cloud-based hardware when you will be first scaling/developing the system? In the long run, you need to be careful of what the real costs are—if your usage is high, you are probably better off with physical machines. You need to consider what the impacts will be on the overall ROI if you are forced to move to physical after initially selecting virtual machines or cloud-based hardware. Take the time to document what scenarios would cause you to make this course change. If one of these scenarios comes to fruition, you will be much better off having raised it as a risk.
- Do you understand the timelines of hardware needs? Given the normal slowness in bringing in new physical hardware, take the time to identify the critical dependencies for when the project kicks off.
- When do you need lower environments in place? Are there special hardware or software needs?
- Is operational development required (systems that have not been dealt with or set up before)?
- Do you understand where your customers will be located? Do you understand their potential latency?
- What kind of logging/diagnostic software do you plan to have in place? The ability to fully instrument your software can be a life-saver when things go wrong in production.
- What kind of caching concerns do you have?
- Are there areas of the application that will be sensitive to network latency?
- Is big data involved? Are you prepared to process the large volumes of data you may be gathering, and do you have a plan to put it to good use?
- Do you know what the key cost drivers are? What have you done to mitigate those?

Many times, people estimate work and see only the happy path. This presents issues when the business hears of this lower cost, not realizing that the estimate did not take into account the risks or all of the other support costs associated with a project.

The key to reducing risk is to first identify it; then you have a shot at addressing it and adjusting your estimate if needed.

Are You Building a Platform?

Building a platform versus an application requires a very different approach. If you are trying to build a platform:

- Have you considered multitenancy?
- Have you considered internationalization?
- Is there a need to integrate with multiple business systems?
- What types of analytic tools are needed? Do you need to integrate with more than one?
- What other third-party tools are required? What about licensing costs? How do these licensing costs change as your usage increases, number of users increases, number of installations increases?
- What about security? Encryption?
- Will you allow users to inject their own custom code? If so, how?
- Do you understand the partitioning rules?
- Do you understand the variance in presentation between different applications that may be hosted on your platform?
- Do you understand the common and unique data required for each application and potential applications?

Platform estimates are more complex, impact more people in an organization, and have the potential to go wrong in a very public manner. For more information on platforms, see Chapter 6, "Platform Development."

Are You Re-platforming?

Re-platforming an existing project can be a very challenging endeavor. Those holding the financial purse strings rarely want to hear the real cost and the effort involved to migrate to the new platform. When facing a re-platforming of a project, you will want to step back and take an innovative look at how you approach the problem:

- Can the new project be delivered in a manner such that it is a significant improvement over the existing product? If the improvements are dramatic enough, they can help justify an increase in revenue projections and help bolster the likelihood of obtaining approval of the project.

- Are there solutions that exist that you can leverage? Open source, cloud providers, and other alternative solutions may reduce the overall cost, shorten the delivery time, and minimize the maintenance costs of the new system.
- Are there ways to incrementally approach the problem? Being able to incrementally deliver value to your stakeholders through phasing will allow them to see positive results earlier and help mitigate financial risk. This may also allow those in charge of the finances to incrementally approve funding and adjust to market needs as time progresses.
- Are the stakeholders willing to reduce the overall requirements and simplify your product to areas that are essential and heavily used by your customers (the 20% that provides the greatest utility)?

Estimating a re-platforming project is one of the most difficult estimating efforts. Taking the time to consider and deliver multiple options for how to approach the overall effort can help mitigate the angst that typically surrounds these types of efforts.

What Technologies Are in Play?

The technologies that are selected during estimation can have a dramatic impact on nearly everyone's perceptions of the project. New technologies can garner significant excitement in the technology ranks, raise concern from your business partners, introduce a host of operational concerns, and open the door to a whole new set of capabilities that were previously unattainable.

The challenge is to introduce a limited set of new technologies that will demonstrate clear value to the business, minimize operational risks, and keep technology modernized to continue to attract talent to your organization.

As you craft a set of possible solutions for the estimating effort, do you have time to

- Perform small POCs to help validate the viability of the technologies that are of interest?
- Show the pros and cons of different technology solutions?
- Identify the risks, assumptions, issues, and dependencies for the different solutions?
- Identify required legacy system integrations? Identify financial system integrations?

- Identify different approaches to the problem? Can you use Hadoop to solve the problem? Can you use a NoSQL database?
- Determine the general appetite for change? If it is low, do you really want to be there?

When you take into account all of the technologies, deployment models, and technology stacks in play, consider the impacts on testing, operations, and support. All of these items have costs associated with them and can help you validate the viability of your technology choices.

What Is the Organizational Structure?

Conway's Law: "Any organization that designs a system (defined broadly) will produce a design whose structure is a copy of the organization's communication structure."

—Melvin Conway

Judging from my experience, the software being developed reflects the organizational structure of both the organization developing it as well as the organization that is receiving it.

What is your organizational structure?

In large software projects, the team is unlikely to be fully colocated in the same site. If it is in the same site, not everyone is likely to be on the same floor. If they are on the same floor, it is likely that not all of them are within 50 feet of one another. (This is the maximum distance for team members to be apart for collaboration to occur regularly, according to MIT's Tom Allen. This is less of an issue today with online collaboration tools, but close proximity definitely helps.)

As the architecture emerges and the key components become clear, consider the following:

- With whom within the area that is likely to receive the work can you review the approach?
- Who are your trusted partners?
- Are you assuming who will do the work? Things change.
- Do you have the ability to bring in contractors or contract out the work?
- Do you have the ability to colocate the team?

- If the team is not colocated, are they at least in the same time zone?
- Can you move the colocated team to an isolated area?
- Are there ways to minimize the number of dependencies with other organizations? Realize that coupling and cohesion are also factors in organizational structures.
- Can you eliminate all organizational dependencies and have complete control?
- Does the technology organization reflect the organization or market it is serving? If another area has a key skill that you need, it may be challenging to cross organizational boundaries to have that area do the work.

Do You Need to Seek External Research?

If you are moving into areas that your company has not previously dealt with on a regular basis, consider doing research on broader topics with companies like Gartner or Forrester Research. They can provide general industry direction and trends.

If you have something specific and more concrete, but still lack a level of expertise in an area, seek out firms (ideally, local) that specialize in what you are looking for.

Are there white papers? Websites? Blogs? Any information you can get to inform you is a good thing. Be cautious about investigating patents; that is legal's job, not yours.

Have You Identified Leverageable Components?

As you progress through an architectural approach, consider the following:

- Are there other projects whose work you can leverage?
- Are the leverageable components nearly complete?
- Is funding guaranteed to complete the components identified as leverageable?
- Can you depend on the implementation working for you?
- Can you feed requirements to the other project?
- Can you give them additional funding?
- Can you add to their source code if there are slight variations for your use cases? If not, can you take a copy?

If there are any dependencies that are not guaranteed to be delivered, you need to include the cost of the work you need plus the cost to finish and test that work to ensure that you obtain an appropriate level of funding.

I have had several projects where those who promised software failed to deliver. Usually their business did not want to pay for the strategic solution; they typically cared only about funding the absolute minimum that met their own business needs. In such a situation, the challenge is that, depending on the path the other business takes, you could be left empty-handed.

I have also seen situations where initially the business and technology promised support to develop the project strategically, took the money to do it strategically, but due to time constraints "hacked" the system.

Be very, very cautious about depending on other groups with loose or indirect ties to your project, especially when the work is not complete. If you do, clearly identify the dependencies in the estimate, and make sure that those at higher levels of the business are aware of what you are depending on and that there is an understanding of the dependencies, technical, political, and otherwise.

Generally speaking, if what you need is not in production, include the work to build the capability in your business case. If the other group delivers, you will have extra funds to cover other costs or maybe even additional features.

In general, treat the component supplier like an external vendor. This is not the time to let your guard down. A reasonable component supplier should welcome a formal agreement. It is a win-win for all sides.

ESTIMATING STRATEGIES

During the estimating process, there is a set of time-honored strategies to help the process run more smoothly, as described in the following sections.

Plan for Unknowns and Challenges

Make sure in your estimates that you include time for things to go wrong (for unknowns); nothing ever goes as planned. If you plan for things to go wrong, you will have sufficient resources to recover. If not, you are preparing yourself for a less-than-pleasant experience with the executives. They expect you to deliver regardless of what hurdles you encounter.

Be Realistic: Don't Cave In Just to Get the Project

If you can't get the numbers low enough for the business to be happy, it is okay for the project to go away. Being on a project that has half the money it needs (whether due to scope miscalculations or excessive hardware needs) is an awful experience.

Keep the Critical Things Close

Try to seek to delight the customer, and build a system in which you have most control in areas that are critical to your success and your business (this is likely what makes you special and differentiates your product from others). Don't build nonessential components; let someone else own and maintain them. When it comes to the maintenance cycle of nonessential components, it is not in your business's best interest to invest money in these areas either now or in the future.

Develop Estimating Feedback Loops

Developing feedback loops for the estimating process will help ensure that you are learning as you go and will help increase the speed and efficiency of the estimates that are produced. As you do this, consider the following:

- Do you have a consistent way of capturing estimates? Reviewing estimates? Improving estimates?
- Do you have a feedback loop for comparing estimates to actuals? Functionality requested to functionality delivered? If not, why not? If so, what improvements can you make?
- What value does what you are doing bring to the table?
- Can you eliminate anything from the process?

Refining your estimating processes through feedback loops allows you to stay up to date with new learned best practices in the industry and helps keep your estimates aligned with business needs.

Minimize Organization Coupling and Cohesion

Organizations are just like software components. Tight coupling between organizational units can cause many problems. Organizational units need to have the ability to flex and change without the rest of the organization having to change with them. In a similar vein, you should work to keep highly cohesive aspects of a project within organizational boundaries.

PowerPoint as You Go

When developing an architectural approach for an estimate, it is usually best to capture the information you are gathering directly into a PowerPoint presentation. You are going to be asked to present it many times, and Power-Pointing as you go naturally prepares you for impromptu requests to go over the status of the estimate.

The architectural approach is never fully complete. Deadlines will drive you to deliver what you have based on the timelines the business is seeking (which are normally very quick, usually a week or less for most of my projects).

Develop Checklists

One of the best ways to ensure consistent estimates is to develop and maintain checklists. As each estimate is delivered, take the time to go back and update your checklists to account for new learnings. The questions asked in this chapter may serve as a starting point.

Gain Executive and Organization Buy-in Early

As an architect, you are in sales. Before presenting the architectural approach you are about to roll out, you need to ensure that all parties have bought into it. This means you need to communicate early and gain buy-in with the executives and all dependent organizations that will be impacted by the approach you are recommending.

Remember
Executives and organizations do not like surprises.

If you fail to gain early buy-in and begin asking organizations to publicly commit to a direction during the estimating process without them having prior knowledge of that direction, you are almost always guaranteed to be faced with defensive posturing, a loss of trust, and a long estimating road.

ESTIMATING PRINCIPLES

During the estimating process, there are several principles to keep in mind.

Know the Hard Problem

This is the single factor that will determine the success or failure of a project. Take the time to find it and ensure that it is properly addressed or, minimally, properly documented.

Provide Options

When estimating, giving your business partners options will allow them to configure the project they want and compare the cost benefits of the options. They get to choose and feel as if they are in control. They are much more likely to be supportive of the decision going forward because they were the ones who made the decision.

Leave Design Decisions Open

Although you should understand at least one way of implementing a solution for the estimate, leave the final design decisions to when you are close to the problem; you and others may discover much better ways to address the problem.

Know the Schedule

When estimating a project, you need to have a sense of whether the desired deliverable date is achievable with a reasonable amount of staffing. If it is not, you need to communicate this immediately. Bad news early is much better than making commitments you are unable to keep and there is no time for an executive to step in and help remedy the situation.

Know What You Want

There are aspects of every project that you believe are critical to the integrity of the solution. Don't compromise on these areas.

Avoid Being Negative

There are many ways to respond to people. Avoid being negative when others are questioning your approach; they are trying to help.

Seek Opportunities to Say Yes

When possible, seek ways to give your business partners what they are looking for, and try to give the development staff opportunities to work on the areas that they perceive as interesting. They will naturally be engaged and deliver more than expected.

Bargain Hard Now, Not Later

The time to bargain hard is during the estimating process. You need to work out known issues instead of avoiding them. An open conversation early on can bring the real issues to the forefront and help maintain commitments from others well into a project when they know you have dealt with them fairly.

My experience has been that it is extremely hard to add technology-related items once the estimates have been reviewed and approved, even when they turn out to be of strategic importance.

Don't Cave In

Mild pain now; otherwise worse pain later. If you cave in on things that you are passionate about, your heart will not be in the project. You are far better off fighting for what you believe in and, if possible, fighting for the things others believe in. The road you travel will be much happier when it aligns with your convictions.

Trust Your Gut Feeling

If there is something that doesn't feel right during the estimating process, dive into the area and learn everything you can about it. Your gut feeling is almost always a good indicator of whether things are on the right path and sized correctly. If possible, back up your gut feeling with solid data-driven information. You will need this if you get challenged.

Beware of Projects That Others Have Estimated

When you take on a project that someone else has estimated, take a serious look at what you believe the approach should be. If the estimate is bad, you need to get that into the open before you begin working on the project. The longer you wait, the more you are communicating that you agreed with the assumptions that were in place when you took ownership of the project.

Know the Business's Targeted Build Price

The business rarely comes looking for an estimate without having given some serious thought to what it is willing to pay to build this product.

Often, the requesters have already polled or asked for revenue sign-up from the different marketing segments prior to beginning the estimating process. Ask for the target build price.

BRINGING IT ALL TOGETHER

Once you have the project context established, an architectural approach developed, and a solid understanding of the estimating strategies and principles, you are ready to begin engaging the estimating team(s) to develop the estimate that is being sought.

Knowing Your Timeline

Do you differentiate between effort and timeline? Does the timeline shift based on when resources are available? When does finance begin calculating ROI? Sometimes it is as soon as the project gets approved and the delivery date is set even though the estimating process took nine months and 15 iterations. (Oddly enough, this particular project was successful and highly liked by the users. For those involved in the estimating, though, it was grueling, tiring, and rotated through multiple sets of business partners.)

Who Is Involved with Estimating?

One of the key elements of getting a reasonable estimate is to have those who will be doing the work or have recently done similar work involved with producing the estimate. This is typically done by lead developers, those who are going to do the work or oversee it on a daily basis. If possible, try to avoid having managers or directors give estimates, and respectfully decline including VPs who offer up numbers.

Are there specialists in particular areas that you need to draw in? If they have estimated this type of work before, it is likely that they have standard estimates for the work being done (such as a certain number of days per style sheet). If you get estimates back from such specialists in something other than units of days, be very cautious; it is unlikely that they fully understand the scope of what is being requested.

Do those doing the estimate understand the likely ratio of contractors to employees? If not, again be cautious about the estimate; this is an area that can quickly bust a budget.

Understanding Your Leverage Points

Where does the functionality live within the organization? If you are trying to leverage work in another business unit, good luck. If the asset is built and owned by the other business unit, you will be at the bottom of their priority list when it comes to decisions. If it is built by the other business unit, but owned by the center (the corporation), you have a shot at sharing in prioritization and adding funding without ceding control.

> **Note**
> Look for leverage when there is an opportunity to have someone in a position of authority to be your advocate.

Typically, most business units do not work well together; they are incented to look good themselves. They do not want another business unit distracting from their need to meet revenue goals. Proceed in these areas with caution.

Putting It All Together

Can you put together a one-page picture of how the solution will work? Are there a couple of alternatives? What are the pros and cons?

What are the risks? What are the assumptions being made? What are the outstanding questions? What are the issues? What are the concerns? What are the key driving requirements? What is the history behind the project? What has changed? What is different?

Shoot for a ten-page deck (title, outline, ask for questions, and seven real pages). Think about the main message and key takeaways and actions you expect as a result of *how* you have presented the information.

Engaging Executives

Be prepared to be examined by the executives about

- Why the numbers are what they are
- The alternatives that were considered
- What risks have been mitigated
- What risks currently exist
- What dependencies exist

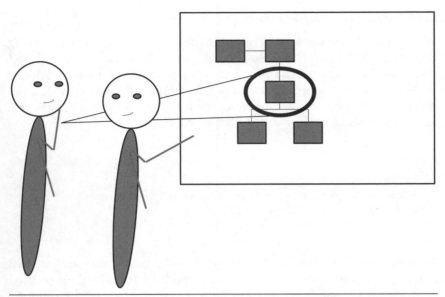

Figure 4.5 Executives like to deep-dive into specific areas where they sense weakness and will keep drilling down until they find it. Be prepared for this behavior.

- Whether there are other solutions
- Alternative requirements that could be used and still meet the business needs

Do your homework so you have all of the answers or at least an explanation of why you do not have an answer. Present the information at a very high level, but be prepared to speak to *at least two levels of detail deeper* than the level you are presenting at (see Figure 4.5).

Selling the Estimate

Make sure the leadership of the estimating team is in agreement, including your management. Make sure they are on board with the approach that is being recommended and that everything has been accounted for. In the right environment (you are truly partners with the business), it may be okay to give the business partners a sneak peek at the estimates; otherwise, don't publish the estimates until you have alignment with your leadership. Generally, be cautious with sneak peek estimates. Sometimes the recipient forgets that the estimate is just a sneak peek; that can be good or bad depending on whether the estimate is high or low. Before distributing the estimate, validate the following:

- Have you cross-checked all of the numbers?
- Are there gaps/overlaps in testing?
- Are there gaps/overlaps in hardware?
- Are other groups' assumptions that work is being done actually accounted for? Do those groups know they are doing the work?
- Are you assuming that another group is doing work but not explicitly funding it?
- Do you have an explicit agreement that the other group is in fact willing to do the work?
- Does this agreement come from a more senior-level person (director or above)? If so, do you have a commitment on the timing?
- Is the other group reengineering their system or in a major project? These commitments are not likely to be met, and you are a lower priority.
- Have you included time for user experience (UX) testing, for operations, for deployment, for fit and finish? Architect, project management (PM) time, scale testing? Hardware? Licensing costs? Should you consider an enterprise licensing agreement?
- Do you understand the system characteristics (concurrency, locking, caching, security, etc.)?
- Do you know the major components (persistence, user interface, batch, extract-transform-load [ETL], warehouse, operating system, business systems, etc.)?
- Are there internationalization needs?
- Are there reporting needs?
- What kind of service-level agreements (SLAs) are involved?
- Are there any safety concerns? Does the system in any way affect humans?
- What are the performance concerns? Availability concerns? Scalability concerns?
- Are there natural coupling and cohesion of major logical components?
- Is the business willing to incrementally fund this?
- Are there regulatory concerns (U.S. or international)?
- Does the placement of information/servers matter?
- Can you implement this out in the cloud?
- Are standard languages required? Is there flexibility?

- Are there unknown areas? Things that you have not implemented before? Are the unknowns simply unknown to your area? To your company? To the industry? To the world?
- Are there quick spikes that could be done to remove the unknowns?
- Can this be staged?
- Does the business partner have a budget in mind?
- Has the architect group or chief architect signed off?

If you follow the process, you are unlikely to have too many issues. You are going to be challenged as people try to understand the architecture you are proposing, but as long as you have detailed information and reasoned thinking behind your decisions, it's all good.

Just remember, you are a service provider: give accurate answers and, if you make a mistake, admit it. Give context; the business drivers and assumptions may have legitimately changed.

SUMMARY

The road to estimation begins with

- Understanding the purpose of the estimate being sought
- Understanding the project context
- Understanding the estimating process
- Developing an architectural approach
- Knowing the estimating strategies and principles
- Knowing how to bring it all together

For me, estimating is one of the more challenging aspects of being an architect. It is fun and exciting to learn new things, but being given a relatively short amount of time in which to develop an architectural approach and being prepared to defend it to everyone in the organization is challenging and forces you to think on your feet.

REFERENCES

Cohn, Mike. 2004. *User Stories Applied: For Agile Software Development.* Addison-Wesley.

———. 2005. *Agile Estimating and Planning.* Prentice Hall.

Hunt, Andrew, and David Thomas. 2007. *The Pragmatic Programmer: From Journeyman to Master.* Addison-Wesley.

Leffingwell, Dean. 2007. *Scaling Software Agility: Best Practices for Large Enterprises.* Addison-Wesley.

————. 2011. *Agile Software Requirements: Lean Requirements Practices for Teams, Programs, and the Enterprise.* Addison-Wesley.

McConnell, Steve. 1977. *Software Project Survival Guide.* Microsoft Press.

Chapter 5

MANAGEMENT

"People think focus means saying yes to the thing you've got to focus on. But that's not what it means at all. It means saying no to the hundred other good ideas that there are. You have to pick carefully. I'm actually as proud of the things we haven't done as the things I have done. Innovation is saying no to 1,000 things."

—Steve Jobs

"Be willing to make decisions. That's the most important quality in a good leader. Don't fall victim to what I call the 'ready—aim—aim—aim—aim syndrome.' You must be willing to fire."

—T. Boone Pickens

"Boundary setting is really a huge part of time management."

—Jim Loehr

"People who don't take risks generally make about two big mistakes a year. People who do take risks generally make about two big mistakes a year."

—Peter F. Drucker

"Your work is going to fill a large part of your life, and the only way to be truly satisfied is to do what you believe is great work. And the only way to do great work is to love what you do. If you haven't found it yet, keep looking. Don't settle. As with all matters of the heart, you'll know when you find it."

—Steve Jobs

Have you ever asked an architect if he or she aspires to be a "manager"? *Management* is not a word that inspires most architects, nor is it something that most architects aspire to.

In most organizations, the exact role of an architect is usually not well defined. It is a position that clearly owns the technical responsibility for projects, but it is also partially responsible for nearly all other aspects of projects. The challenge is that the depth to which an architect needs to step in on the other areas of a project is dependent on who the other members of the team are. This is why architects many times are referred to as glue: they fill in where they need to.

This chapter unveils one of the essential skills needed by a software architect: the ability to manage the wide diversity of responsibilities that are placed upon them.

ARCHITECTURE MANAGEMENT DEFINED

First, the bad news: architects are usually considered part of "management."

Management is the active oversight of the areas for which you are directly responsible and the areas for which others perceive you to be responsible; basically, the things you are going to get called into the office of a VP to explain when something doesn't work as expected.

The role of architect has a broad and diverse range of responsibilities within the organization (see Figure 5.1).

AREAS OF ARCHITECTURAL RESPONSIBILITY

Management from an architecture perspective is about

- Striving toward technology excellence
- Delivering projects
- Resolving issues
- Partnering with executives
- Managing your time
- Grooming technical talent
- Enhancing your skill set

These areas of management for architects are always in contention with one another. Change is a constant within these areas; the key is to learn to balance and prioritize these conflicting forces.

Figure 5.1   Key areas of architectural responsibility

STRIVING TOWARD TECHNOLOGY EXCELLENCE

Architects are the gatekeepers of technology for a business. Striving toward technology excellence can enable the technology organization to deliver new capabilities quicker, deliver them at a lower cost, enable scale as the business grows, and keep down maintenance costs. From a political standpoint, this may be more easily approached as technology sustainability when interacting with executives.

Establishing a Vision

Early on in a project or ideally before a project begins, work toward establishing an architectural vision of where you are trying to go. Even if it's wrong, it can help guide projects and give a sense of coherence to the direction that is being pursued.

Being able to articulate this vision will help to guide not only this project, but potentially an entire suite of projects. Each project on its own may not be able to deliver the entire vision, but each may be able to help move the overall product or product suite toward an ideal end state.

Raising Awareness of Technical Debt and Funding the Right Solution

Architecture is an active responsibility within a project. You don't just set the direction and stand back. Architects need to be actively engaged to help balance the immediate needs of the business (usually, getting it done quickly) with the long-term awareness of the investments being made (doing it right) (see Figure 5.2).

Most projects start out with strategic intentions but, due to deadlines and budgetary constraints, consider less strategic options as the project moves closer to delivery. This pragmatic balancing of what options are to be seriously considered is crucial not only for delivering projects on time and on budget, but also for the ability of the projects to create leverageable assets for the next set of projects. As a project progresses, the key is to avoid design decisions that will unnecessarily limit known or likely next phases for a project or product.

The goal should nearly always be enabling technical excellence.

You need to be aware that the more broken windows you allow in the architectural neighborhood, the more it will set a precedent that broken windows are acceptable.

If there are valid reasons for not taking the right technical approach, the decision needs to be made transparently. It enables key stakeholders to buy into the direction being taken and level-set expectations for everyone involved about the work and the funding that will be required to do both a short-term and a long-term solution. Do your best to avoid leaving technical debt with an unfunded path to fix it.

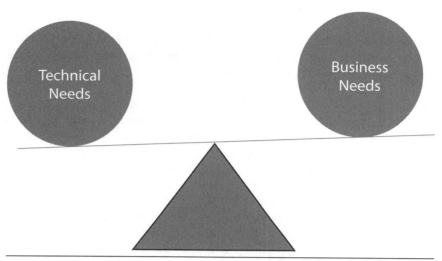

Figure 5.2 Balance the needs of technology and the needs of business.

Keeping the Technical Environment Interesting

Keeping the technical staff engaged and learning is one of the best ways to help with retention. Although they most likely do not report to you, finding ways to incorporate new technologies and approaches in a non-disruptive fashion will naturally keep up the level of engagement for most technologists.

The challenge in most of this is timing. There are natural spots within most projects to incorporate new things (usually near the beginning of the project or the start of a new release). The key is to ensure that you have a sufficient amount of time to recover from any unexpected issues and to limit the number of changes that are introduced at one time. If too many things are changing, it can be very challenging to figure out the root causes of issues that are surfacing.

As always, being transparent about what you are doing will help keep everyone on the same page and help to avoid future conflicts.

Finding Potential Patents

Have you engaged the legal department about any interesting ideas that you are pursuing for your design? Are there patents that should be filed? Are there provisional patents that should be applied for?

Protecting your business's key technology assets can create a strategic advantage over your competitors. As new projects come into your portfolio of architecture work, meet quarterly to semiannually with the patent attorneys to review new ideas and approaches. They will usually have a sense of whether your novel design approach is patentable and if the idea is in an area where the company wants to invest in patent protection.

The best approach I have found is to simply sit down on a regular basis with the patent attorneys and describe the projects I am working on. They usually are familiar with the overall patent portfolio and have a sense of what is interesting and unique. If they show interest in a particular area, we will dive into more detail. If they run into something truly interesting, they will usually go off for a few weeks and return if they want to consider filing a patent for it. The key is to have these conversations before the details of the technology approach are broadly known. Once the attorneys have decided to move forward, I usually spend many hours reviewing the documents and all of the details to ensure that the appropriate scope, language, and diagrams are in place for the patent. It's always interesting to see how lawyers describe the work you are doing or have done.

Seeking Data Center and Operations Support for Your Direction

As you seek to inject new technologies and capabilities into the organization, you need to ensure that the end product is operationally ready. Taking the time to work with data center and operations teams early on and letting them know the direction you are taking can establish a partnership for finding the right solution and for ensuring that the right tools and training are in place for them to do their work.

For instance, does the new database technology you are looking to introduce support the multisite, multimaster replication that your architectural style is dependent on? Do the new tools and technologies have the appropriate logging, monitoring, and alerting features to enable the operations team to quickly diagnose where there are issues in the middle of the night (or do you want to get that call and be on a pager)?

This partnership with operations can help identify issues that may help drive vendor decisions, vendor support, vendor product changes, and configuration standards before you are rushing toward a release. Partnering early on with the operations team can help vet issues that may ultimately determine if your project is successful.

Generalizing the Solution

There is often a more general form of a solution that can be created. If this is possible and there are other likely scenarios that leverage the more generalized solution, strongly consider this as the implementation path. Generalized solutions can help save the company money in the long term by reducing the amount of software that needs to be created and subsequently maintained.

Making It Strategic

If there is a clear strategic solution, you should work hard to put that solution in place. It is rare that the dates that are being bandied about for delivery are as real as they are portrayed. Sometimes just taking that extra time and putting in the right solution can save you from a massive refactor later on and let you be done with the capability instead of adding technical debt.

If it simply is not possible to put the strategic solution in place, take the time to think through the approach you would take for the strategic solution and try to avoid putting in unnecessary roadblocks to implementing it in the future.

Leveraging Solutions

It is rare in the software community that something hasn't been done before. Take the time to investigate what existing solutions are available. Is the business willing to adjust its requirements to match an existing solution if there is an opportunity to save money?

Leveraging solutions may not always be the cool or fun thing to do, but it will raise the business's level of trust in you and enable the business to invest the money saved in other ways.

DELIVERING PROJECTS

Projects are the lifeblood of any technology organization. The organization's ability to deliver projects in a timely and cost-effective manner is essential for its success.

Partnering with the Project Manager

One of the best ways to successfully drive projects is to partner with the project manager. Project managers are usually in charge of delivering the official communications with respect to the project, coordinating resources across multiple areas, and overseeing the schedule of the work that needs to be accomplished.

By partnering with the project manager, you can join forces to ensure that

- The messages that are being delivered to the stakeholders are consistent with your communication, especially when issues arise
- The work on the project is prioritized according to key dependencies
- The right people are working on your projects at the right time

Eliminating Dependencies Ruthlessly

One of the hardest things to manage on any project is dependencies. As you encounter dependencies in your architecture, your projects, and your code, learn to attack them ruthlessly. The fewer dependencies you have, the better shot you have at being in control of your own destiny (see Figure 5.3).

However, there are times when dependencies make sense, for instance, when

- The investment to eliminate the dependency is much higher than incurring the time, budget, or resource hit necessary to keep it
- The functionality or capability that the dependency brings is essential to the project, and no reasonable alternatives exist

Managing Expectations

From a technology perspective, it is easy to get caught up in all of the great qualities that surround new technologies and new approaches. The challenge is that it is easy to overhype and overpromise what adding these things to a project will accomplish.

As an architect, you need to manage expectations and ensure that as you sell certain technology solutions you have left room in the project for things to

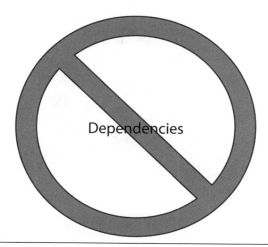

Figure 5.3 Be ruthless about eliminating dependencies; they often constrain your ability to deliver projects.

go wrong. In addition, you need to ensure that you will have enough time and resources to work through and deliver all of the great value that you promised.

Mastering the Development Process

Although architects may not be developing code every day on a project, there is an expectation of mastery of the overall development process. (For the development process cycle, see Figure 5.4.)

Architects should be involved with determining

- What methodology will be used—agile, Lean, Kanban, something else
- What development tools will be used
- How the system will be built, deployed, and tested
- What development teams will be involved during estimating, build, and testing
- What the core use cases (epics) of the system should be

Architects should be actively involved in determining the overall software development life cycle, its associated tools, and its execution. By being actively involved, technology will be able to be better aligned with the needs of the business and better aligned for overall success.

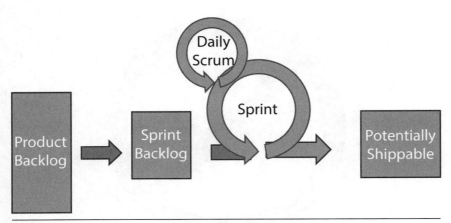

Figure 5.4   Scrum: find a process that is effective for both technology and the business.

Being Where the Problems Are

Generally speaking, as an architect, if things are going well in a certain area of the project, you are usually not as critical to that area. In contrast, the areas of the project that are struggling or having significant issues can benefit from your leadership and problem-solving skills. By jumping in and working in the areas that have the most problems, you can help remove roadblocks, provide alternative approaches, and connect the team with others who are experts in the areas where they are having issues.

If truly project-threatening issues are being encountered, you will have first-hand knowledge of the situation when the executives want to dive in and learn more about what is going wrong.

Being Aware of Nontransparency on Your Projects

As an architect, you can't be everywhere at once. At some point, you have no choice but to trust what others are doing. The challenge is that decisions are being made all the time that are directly or indirectly your responsibility, and even if you are not there, you will be held responsible.

As these decisions are being made, it is usually not an issue if you learn about them in a reasonably timely manner. You at least have an opportunity to correct course or have enough wiggle room to adjust course if things go south. However, some people really want to make the decisions and won't like the decision you are likely to make. They may choose to make a decision without your involvement and include you only when they get in over their heads. This may or may not become an issue, but if you have to routinely correct or jump in and rescue certain tech leads' decisions, you need to address this first with the individuals. If that is not effective, you need to engage their management. If you let these situations slide, your reputation is potentially at stake.

Limiting the Number of Contractors in Leadership Positions

Contractors are great resources to help staff projects with skills that are missing, to help fill a bubble in the amount of work needed on a project, and to help get a project moving quickly. The challenge is that contractors eventually leave and move on. If you have contractors in key leadership positions, when they leave, you may have a void in your long-term knowledge of that area, may encounter a lack of understanding as to why certain decisions were made, and may be left with a system that is unnecessarily biased toward the latest and greatest technologies due to the contractors' needing to prep for their next gig.

Most contractors do an excellent job, but having employees in leadership positions on a project helps

- Train the employees on why certain design decisions were made
- Balance business domain needs with technology decisions
- Maintain the long-term continuity of the project as the number of contractors ebbs and flows

I have seen projects (fortunately not mine) with over 75% contractors, including many in leadership positions. Those projects didn't turn out well. I usually like to have 10% to 20% of the staff on a project be contractors. They typically bring in a different perspective on technology approaches, have a broader set of experiences, may have skill sets that you don't have, and generally have a lack of fear of jumping into unknown areas.

Providing Technical Management (Areas of Responsibility)

Architects are responsible for the technical aspects of projects and platforms. Some of the chief areas of responsibility for architects are

- Managing and communicating technical direction and architectural approach
- Managing and communicating system boundaries

- Managing technical intergroup dependencies
- Working with the data center on hardware acquisition and configuration
- Working with procurement and sourcing on licensing and other vending needs
- Reviewing and helping develop business case estimates
- Helping identify and manage project risks and issues
- Establishing the big architectural rules/principles
- Overseeing contractors and possibly other architects
- Communicating architecture-related items to executives and other management
- Working closely with both the business and technology
- Working closely with development teams
- Ensuring proper project governance and oversight, including standards, guidelines, reviews, design principles, and design qualities
- Ensuring the privacy and security of user data
- Ensuring that system "-ilities" (nonfunctional requirements) are properly addressed
- Ensuring proper development life-cycle adherence
- Leading spikes and other technical investigations
- Working with project management to work through budgets, schedules, timelines, and resource needs
- Leading software and hardware selection for projects
- Working closely with the testing organization for various testing needs

The goal of architects is to provide technical management for projects and ensure that the software aligns with business goals and an appropriate level of technical excellence.

Managing by Walking Around

One of the best ways to successfully deliver projects is to manage by walking around. This simple act of meeting people and dealing with items in the moment not only keeps things moving quickly within the project, but it gives you a better sense of the real items that need to be addressed immediately within a project.

In a one-on-one setting, nearly everyone feels comfortable expressing concerns or asking questions, whereas they may not feel comfortable within a group. This short-circuiting of information needs helps keep both you and your team highly effective.

Managing by walking around includes stopping by and talking to everyone related to the project, including executives, on a regular basis. For me, just stopping by without an appointment and talking helps build good relationships and gives a much better sense of the heartbeat of the project than nearly anything else I can do.

Managing by walking around is a great way to fill in some of the time between meetings or when I just need to get away from my desk for a while. This movement helps me get past roadblocks that I may be encountering or helps me quickly track down answers that could take hours or days if they were dealt with through e-mail.

RESOLVING ISSUES

One of the chief responsibilities of an architect on a daily basis is to resolve issues on projects.

Asking the Tough Questions

On every project, there are always areas that everyone wants to shy away from due to either the political environment or a desire for conflict avoidance. As an architect, you are responsible for asking the tough questions and raising the issues so that they can be dealt with.

As you address issues, avoid making statements; instead, craft what you are seeking as a series of questions. This approach allows you to avoid presuming information to be factual and allows for a discussion to begin. Take time to qualify the questions with the context of why you are asking them. It can help defuse some of the political tensions. The questions can also lead the people who are involved with the discussion to open up to other alternatives that they may not have considered in the past.

The goal is to clear a path so that obstacles can be removed and transparency can exist throughout the project. This won't always make everyone comfortable, but it will enable people to do excellent work and level-set expectations for everyone on the project.

Dealing with Problems in the Moment

Architects need to jump in and address the elephant in the room when no one else is willing to. You either get to deal with it now or it will surface later; and later on, it will likely be more painful to deal with.

Architects are expected to get down into the details.

Learning to deal with problems in the moment helps in two key ways. One, the backlog of things to deal with stays short. Two, no one will take inaction as your indirect approval for the direction or course that things are on. It also sends a clear message that issues will get dealt with promptly.

Dealing with conflicts in the moment will force you to have thick skin.

Saying No, but with Options

No one likes to hear "no" in answer to a request. A better approach, if possible, is to say, "Here are the acceptable alternatives" (see Figure 5.5). This allows the other party to have some control over and say in the direction that is chosen. It also naturally helps with buy-in. The person may not get his or her first choice but at least was able to participate.

This puts more work on you, but it also forces you to work through the real issues with a request and determine what other alternatives are plausible that can achieve the same or similar objectives. If alternatives are not possible, it at least makes for a more in-depth conversation as to the rationale behind the decision and allows you to explain what alternatives were considered and why they won't work.

The options may also be a way to introduce a better overall option. It may take some convincing, but it is best to keep the door open to some dialogue as opposed to alienating someone you are likely to need to work with in the future.

Most people are willing to accept detailed and conscientious thought behind a response. If not, and you are challenged, you should have a defensible position.

Striving to Be Consistent in Your Decisions

The decisions you make as an architect affect many people. It usually takes time to ensure that everyone understands what the architectural approach is for a project, what the assumptions are, and what the risks and dependencies are.

Invariably as the project progresses, you learn new information about the project, information that if you knew it at the outset would have caused you to pick a slightly different path.

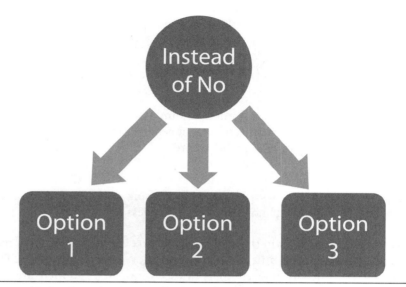

Figure 5.5 Don't just say no; give options.

The challenge as an architect is to weigh a change in direction very carefully. If the current direction meets the business needs and changing direction will be costly in real terms or in terms of communication and alteration of existing plans, it is usually best to keep the current course.

Think about what you could have done to learn this information earlier. No matter what you do and no matter what process you follow, there is only so much information available at any given time, and you need to make the best decision you can and execute.

If you do have to change direction, ensure that the executives and those in leadership who are affected by the change are on board.

Remember

Executives hate surprises. Don't let someone else inform them of changes in direction you are making. Tell the executives yourself and ensure that they are on board.

Using executive validation as a decision gate will help keep you from waffling on your decisions.

Learning to Deal with Things Head-on, Cards Faceup on the Table

Architects usually have very limited amounts of time. When it comes to dealing with issues, negotiating, selling, or general problem solving, the best approach is normally to be straightforward.

Putting your cards on the table faceup gives you a lot of flexibility. The person you are interacting with knows what is going on, knows that you are acting in good faith, and knows you mean business.

When you learn to work in this manner, you don't have to worry about having told different people different stories; your story is always the same. This gives you a distinct advantage: others can see your cards and there are only so many ways to play the hand. They also know that you know there are only so many ways they can play their hand.

Since you have acted in good faith to begin with, they are more likely to operate in a similar manner.

Act with integrity, and you will earn the respect of others.

Knowing What You Are Willing to Cave On When Negotiating

Architects have to learn to negotiate early on; it is essential to success to be able to give and take on a project. The key is to know what is critically important to you and what is less important. As you negotiate with the business or with other business units, you have to know what areas are non-negotiable. On the other hand, if you absolutely have to give on one item, you need to know in advance what you are willing to give up to reach consensus on a decision.

Being Willing to Challenge Areas You Don't Agree with (Respectfully)

During meetings when you are working toward a solution in a particular area, you need to be willing to challenge decisions that are about to be made when you don't agree with them. You may be surprised that many others share your concerns but are being cautious about voicing dissent. You owe it to the business to make your concerns known—not to derail the conversation, but to make sure that the right decisions are made.

You are almost always better off asking the tough questions within your group first because when the solution is reviewed by executives, you can be assured that they will ask the same questions. If you don't have a solid answer as to why some option wasn't considered, you will have some very unhappy executives on your hands. This lack of thoroughness will erode the trust executives have in you and your team.

Being Willing to Stand Your Ground

As an architect, if you truly believe that something is the wrong direction or the right direction, you need to stand your ground and fight for what you believe in, even if it's just a gut feeling. Others need to be able to adequately argue their positions well enough to convince you to change. If you need to raise the issue up to management to get a tie-breaking vote, that is an acceptable path, although in my experience, you are better off resolving it among yourselves. You will rarely be happy with the executive's decision.

Knowing What Is Not Your Problem

There are times when the fight that is being fought is not your fight. Although you may have an opinion on the matter, if it is truly not your issue and the others have not invited you into the debate, letting them work it out themselves is usually the right path. If they want your opinion, they will ask for it.

PARTNERING WITH EXECUTIVES

Executives play a critical role within any organization. They thrive on trust and have a strong need to have a finger on the pulse of the organization. One of the best ways for you to ensure success for both you and the executives is to become partners.

Managing Risk through Transparency

One of the best ways to manage risk on a project is to approach the risks with complete transparency to executives. Before a project begins and throughout its life cycle, keeping executives up to speed on risks is critical to your success.

As soon as you know about a major new risk or a change to a known risk, you need to bring it to the attention of the executives. This will give them the maximum amount of time to react and "help" if they think it is necessary.

Giving executives late notice of a risk when there is little or no chance of changing the outcome will not be dealt with positively and will reduce their trust in you.

Reviewing Estimates

Before estimates for a project are widely distributed to the organization, make sure that the executives over your area have had a chance to weigh in on them. They may know of other factors, assumptions, and risks that need to be considered for the project that is being proposed.

By reviewing the estimates with the executives in advance, you give them a chance to ensure that the project is aligned with the organization's goals and any recent developments that you may be unaware of. Projects are a commitment of resources by the organization, and they need to be aligned with the executives' thought processes.

As always, the last thing you want to do is publicly surprise executives with information (i.e., the details of the estimate) that they were unaware of, especially when they begin to get questions about the estimate for clarification.

Limiting the Number of Boxes on Diagrams

When presenting architectures to executives, you are usually better off leaving out the details of architectural diagrams and giving an extremely high-level view of the architecture, ideally keeping it to four or five boxes on the diagram. A simplified diagram will give them a sense of the key components. If they want more detail, they can always ask for it.

Think of this diagram as an *architectural elevator speech*—something that can be explained in less than two minutes.

Raising Technology Awareness

Part of your job as an architect is to keep executives and management briefed on technology. This is more about where the industry is going, what key trends are occurring, and how you are using technology that relates to key trends that would be mentioned in the CIO Hype Cycles or trade magazines.

You also want to keep the management staff up to speed on what other groups are doing with respect to technology advancement. Once another group introduces new technologies, the odds of being able to introduce the same technologies in your area can increase significantly because the operational aspects of the technology have already been addressed.

Having Your Boss's Back

In nearly every situation, you should work toward advocating for your boss's positions in terms of direction and boundaries. If someone is challenging your boss's choices, you need to come to your boss's defense. You may not always agree 100% with your boss, but when he or she is not present, you need to maintain your mutual trust. If you have issues with your boss's positions, you should take them up with your boss directly. If you fail to change his or her mind, you need to suck it up and be an advocate for the boss's position. Doing so will also let others know that you act with integrity with respect to your organization's wishes.

Avoiding Interrupting Executives When They Are Talking

Most executives are highly sensitive to being interrupted when they are talking. Wait a little past their normal pauses when they are speaking. It will make for a smoother conversation if they feel they have been listened to and have had the chance to fully express their thoughts.

Being Confident

Most executives have a sixth sense about areas in which you lack confidence and are likely to delve into those areas. They are likely to perceive your lack of confidence during a conversation as an area that contains an abundance of risk and will want to focus on that area, when in reality, you may just be nervous about interacting with an executive. Learn to sit up straight, keep your shoulders back, keep your feet directly under you when you are sitting, and look at the executive directly when you are talking. If there are areas of risk, bring those up early on in the conversation. It will make them more confident in you and help establish trust.

MANAGING YOUR TIME

For most architects, there are more projects, more estimating, more consulting to work on than there is time in which to do the work. Fortunately and unfortunately, there are only 24 hours in the day. The limited amount of time you have forces you to be highly effective in your time management.

Limiting the Number of Projects to Which You Commit

There always seem to be more projects than there are architects to oversee the work. As an architect, you need to be selective about the projects to which you commit. You need to ensure that, first and foremost, you have enough time to commit to truly owning a project before you take it on.

If you already have several projects that are consuming the majority of your time, you are not doing anyone a favor by taking on yet another project.

If the business has committed to doing a project, it needs to ensure that there is enough technical staff to execute the project; the business may simply be looking to you as an architect to be an insurance policy if things go wrong.

Your reputation is on the line for every project to which you commit. Make sure that you are willing and able to commit for the long haul and have the time to ensure that the project is delivered and delivered right.

Defining Your Role and Bounding It

Architects have wide and varying roles within an organization depending on the needs of a particular project. Given this fluidity, architects need to clearly define their role and their responsibilities. Limiting your responsibilities can help ensure that you have sufficient capacity to deal with the many demands of multiple concurrent projects.

Prioritizing Where to Engage Your Time

Deciding where to engage and not engage among multiple conflicting projects can be challenging. When it comes to conflicting meetings, consider the following:

- Who is attending the meetings? Generally speaking, if people from outside your company are attending and you are expected to be an active participant, attending should be one of your top priorities. Next, are members from outside your business unit attending the meeting? After this, consider which meeting includes the highest-ranking executive. The goal is to be in the right place at the right time (it's not always clear). Ensuring that you are delivering a positive image and brand to external entities and to executives is critical.

- Can the meeting be rescheduled? If so, ask people in your own business unit to reschedule first. You likely work with them on a regular basis and can more easily work through scheduling conflicts with them.
- Is this a regularly scheduled meeting? If this is not a regularly scheduled meeting, and there are key issues or decisions that need to be made, this meeting generally should be considered a higher priority.
- Do these regularly scheduled meetings have conflicts? If so, consider alternating between them or even attending the first half of one meeting and the last half of the other meeting.
- Do you really need to attend? If there are people with whom you feel comfortable making decisions for you at the meeting, you may not need to attend. Be cautious with letting others represent your views. Make sure you interact with any individuals to whom you are delegating responsibility. In the end, you are still responsible.

Above all, make sure you are communicating clearly to the organizers of the meetings whether or not you will attend and if not, who will represent you. If you cannot attend a meeting, ask for a summary of key meeting items, key decisions, and any action items. This information will allow you to follow up with others as needed and allow you to know the context of the next meeting if there is one.

One of your most effective tools in time management is simply to say no. If you do not have the time to deal with something and you cannot easily adjust your current commitments, simply letting others know that you cannot take on additional work is very effective.

You need to be careful about saying no. Sometimes the additional work could be an opportunity to do something that you really want to do. The key is to avoid spreading yourself too thin and having all of the balls you have up in the air come crashing down.

Although architecture is a very important aspect of the lives of architects, there are many other important areas of life as well, including family time. Being engaged in other activities outside work helps keep you more interesting and helps put into perspective some of the daily decisions that need to be made.

As a general rule of thumb, try to pick a reasonable time to leave every day. It is okay to work on things later in the evening, but try to have a consistent off time (there may be exceptions to this such as when an important release is coming up). If you don't get away, you have a real chance of burning out.

Learning to Make Decisions on Limited Data and with Limited Time

As an architect, you rarely get a chance to get all of the information you would like for a decision. The best you can normally do is to time-box the research or investigation. If possible, consult with others who have encountered similar situations.

When the time is up, you need to make a decision.

Sometimes, making a decision simply comes down to trusting your gut feeling. It doesn't necessarily give you a great amount of comfort, but in most situations, making a decision in a timely manner is more important than trying to make the perfect decision.

Long decision cycles are often met with false expectations and can also make management feel as if the project is dragging on.

Attending Meetings Only If You Are an Active Participant

For nearly any meeting, unless you are going to be an active participant and take the time to engage in the conversation, it is not worth your time to attend. Learn to either speak up or leave.

Getting a Deadline

When I get a request to do something, before I agree to do it, one of the first things I consider is when it is due, and if I have the time available to actually deliver what is being requested of me. If I don't feel I have sufficient time to deal with what is being requested, I will say no or request a date that enables me to ensure that I can deliver it.

Delegating to Those You Trust

To help manage the many demands on your time during the course of a day, try to find members of the team in whom you have a high level of trust and who can represent your views if you are not present. These are the individuals to whom you can delegate responsibility on a project and let them grow in the amount of responsibility they have. It will give them an opportunity to build their skills, and it will give you some additional time in your busy schedule.

Meeting in Person

One of the best ways to quickly resolve issues and gain consensus on a direction is to simply meet in person. If you can't meet in person, try to meet by some form of virtual means so that you can see each other face-to-face. The ability to see how a person is reacting to what you are saying can enable you to quickly adjust the direction of the conversation and avoid any misunderstandings.

If possible, avoid e-mail except for communicating the decisions and consensus agreed upon.

Meeting in person can save you a significant amount of time in the long run even though it may be a bigger commitment up front.

GROOMING TECHNICAL TALENT

Part of the responsibility of an architect is to help groom the technical staff for moving up in the organization and to help maintain a solid base of technologists within an organization to enable great software to be created.

Having an Architecture Mentorship Program

At Thomson Reuters, I help run an architecture mentorship program. This program includes architects, technical leads, and others who have an interest in the area of architecture. The program focuses on three core areas:

- **Broadening business knowledge.** In this area, we focus on bringing in speakers from different areas of the business (finance, marketing, strategy, and other areas). The goal is to give the technical staff a sense of the broad range of what is going on within the business outside of technology.
- **Introducing emerging and core technologies.** In this area, we focus on bringing in new or core technology experts who can broaden the solution tool set and help make new technology connections for emerging technologists. This can include bringing in

people from the data center, research and development, and other areas.

- **Architecture panel discussions.** In this area, we focus on discussing common or current architectural issues in a panel setting. This allows for an open conversation about how different architects are thinking about and approaching different issues.

The goal with the architecture mentorship program is to develop a sense of architectural community that invites up-and-coming technologists to learn and develop the skills to move into an architecture role. It also helps other architects to see different ways of thinking about projects and to share their experiences.

For me, mentoring is a great way to give back to the organization and help build up the next generation of talent. I usually end up learning at least as much as if not more than the mentee, and helping out others tends to be a highly rewarding experience.

Having a Technology Forum

At Thomson Reuters, I also run a tech forum series. This program is a place to help raise technical awareness in the organization. It serves multiple purposes:

- To let up-and-coming technical talent get up in front of a large group and show off cool technologies
- To give everyone in the business unit a chance to see live coding and help raise awareness of what technologies are currently in use and how they are being used
- To promote your area as a cool place to work and attract others within the larger organization to want to work in your area
- To expose up-and-coming technical talent to the executives and senior management

Encouraging Members of Your Technical Team to Attend Local Conferences and User Groups

You want to encourage the technical members of the teams you work with to be active in the local technical community. It will allow them to keep their skills current and help them grow the network of technical people they know. It will also help establish your company as an active development community and should help attract others to your company as a place to work.

Hiring the Best People: Don't Just Fill a Position

Hiring the right people is critical for your current projects and more importantly for your future projects. When interviewing, take the time to look for

- **Candidates who can whiteboard.** You want people who can get up to the whiteboard and coherently draw a solution they have previously helped create. They should be able to answer detailed questions as to why it is structured the way it is and what other alternatives were considered. You want to get a sense of how they solve problems and how well they can describe the solution. You also want to get a sense of whether they can think on their feet. How well did they sell their solution? Does it seem believable?
- **Candidates who can articulate why and when to use technologies.** This includes being able to explain the pros and cons of the technologies they use, when to consider using them, and when to avoid them. People in technology should have very distinct opinions about technologies. They should know the current versions of the software they use and the key features that have recently been added. You want to know that they know more than just the keywords that were in the job posting.
- **Candidates who are sociable.** Interacting with others is a daily activity for every developer. If candidates cannot reasonably socialize with you, you have to question how well they will be able to rise within the organization (building relationships quickly and easily is essential).
- **Candidates who can explain how they go about solving problems.** They should be able to describe what some of their worst problems in technology have been and explain in detail how they worked their way out of them. Listen closely for the language they use and the depth of detail provided.
- **Candidates who can describe what your business does and how it makes money.** You want someone who can do at least basic research.
- **Candidates who can describe how they interact with management.** They should be able to describe what their thoughts are about being questioned about the approach they took to a particular problem (architects get questioned about their approach all the time).

Are they defensive or do they shoot straight and get to the point quickly? Getting defensive is definitely a warning sign.

▪ **Candidates who can describe how they stay current with technology.** Ideally, the answer is they like to play around with technology in their spare time and have evidence of that.

Your ability to hire and attract developers who are passionate about software development is critical for keeping your business technologically current and the workplace a fun place.

ENHANCING YOUR SKILL SET

As an architect, it is easy to get caught up in the endless demands of others on your time. If you are not careful, they will consume every last second of every day and leave you no time to maintain and enhance your own skill set.

Sitting with Other Architects

Regardless of the size of your organization, you may want to consider locating your cube near other architects. Having the opportunity to overhear and become involved in architecturally related conversations during the course of the day can help you to keep current with what other areas of the business are encountering. This will help enable you to hear common problems, and to start formulating new capabilities that may be shareable across different projects or products. It will also enable you to hear about technologies that are being contemplated in other areas.

Sitting with other architects is a cheap and efficient way to help you stay current with the business and with technology.

Doing Something Technical Every Day

Take some time every day to do something technical. Usually early in the morning or later in the afternoon when the core of meetings, stand-ups, and impromptu questions end is a great time to dive in and do some research or try out some new technology that you are not familiar with. If worse comes to worst, take some time later in the evening to play around with something new.

Go to a conference; watch a webinar; read a blog; read an online magazine. All of these things will help keep you up to speed with what is going on in the industry and keep your technical skills sharp.

Staying up on technology is one of the best ways to ensure that you do not become obsolete.

Focusing on What Scares You

During the course of projects, some areas rise up that create a certain level of uncertainty for you. Take the time to investigate and play around in these areas enough that you are comfortable and have a base level of knowledge about them.

Becoming an Expert in an Area

As an architect, you will develop a brand for what you are good at and for areas where you are weak. Consider what brand you want to project within your business and within the industry where you work. Once you have a sense of how you want to be branded, work toward crafting this brand by becoming an expert in that area.

Consider writing a blog or giving presentations at conferences in this area as a way to help reinforce the brand you are trying to promote.

Looking for Projects Where You Can Grow Your Skills

Architects need to be constantly honing their skill sets. As you see projects that are coming down the pipeline at work, have a sense of what projects will enable you to grow, and actively lobby to be on those projects. If the projects at work are not able to provide you with the growth you are looking for, there are almost always projects outside of work that can use your passion and expertise.

There are often open-source projects or volunteer opportunities where people and organizations will be thrilled to have you dive in and help them solve their technology problems. You will get a chance to learn, and they will get some much-needed help on technology challenges.

SUMMARY

The road to management begins with

- Striving toward technology excellence
- Delivering projects
- Resolving issues
- Partnering with executives
- Managing your time
- Grooming technical talent
- Enhancing your skill set

In the end, *management* may not be an aspirational word in your vocabulary, but it is an essential function for you to deliver on the responsibilities with which you are entrusted.

REFERENCES

Anderson, David J. 2010. *Kanban: Successful Evolutionary Change for Your Technology Business.* Blue Hole Press.

Appelo, Jurgen. 2011. *Management 3.0: Leading Agile Developers, Developing Agile Leaders.* Addison-Wesley.

Berkun, Scott. 2008. *Making Things Happen: Mastering Project Management.* O'Reilly Media.

Duvall, Paul M., Steve Matyas, and Andrew Glover. 2007. *Continuous Integration: Improving Software Quality and Reducing Risk.* Addison-Wesley.

Humble, Jez, and David Farley. 2010. *Continuous Delivery: Reliable Software Releases through Build, Test, and Deployment Automation.* Addison-Wesley.

Hunt, Andrew, and David Thomas. 2007. *The Pragmatic Programmer: From Journeyman to Master.* Addison-Wesley.

Nygard, Michael T. 2007. *Release It!: Design and Deploy Production-Ready Software.* Pragmatic Bookshelf.

Leffingwell, Dean. 2007. *Scaling Software Agility: Best Practices for Large Enterprises.* Addison-Wesley.

Rasmusson, Jonathan. 2010. *The Agile Samurai: How Agile Masters Deliver Great Software.* Pragmatic Bookshelf.

Rothman, Johanna. 2007. *Manage It!: Your Guide to Modern, Pragmatic Project Management.* Pragmatic Bookshelf.

Rothman, Johanna, and Esther Derby. 2005. *Behind Closed Doors: Secrets of Great Management.* Pragmatic Bookshelf.

Rubin, Kenneth S. 2012. *Essential Scrum: A Practical Guide to the Most Popular Agile Process.* Addison-Wesley.

PART II

TECHNOLOGY SKILLS

"Architecture is easy: you just stare at the paper until droplets of blood appear on your forehead."

—Unknown

"No architecture is so haughty as that which is simple."

—John Ruskin

"What people want, above all, is order."

—Stephen Gardiner

"Architects have made architecture too complex. We need to simplify it and use a language that everyone can understand."

—Toyo Ito

"Architecture doesn't come from theory."

—Arthur Erickson

This part focuses on the four essential technology skills of an architect. These chapters focus on principles, strategies, and other areas to help you become more effective in managing your architecture. The chapters are organized as follows:

- Chapter 6, "Platform Development," will enable you to
  - Build leverageable capabilities across multiple applications
  - Create an ecosystem for platform development to thrive in
  - Establish and adhere to guiding principles for the platform
- Chapter 7, "Architectural Perspective," will enable you to
  - Guide the architecture via well-established architectural principles

- Ensure that nonfunctional architectural concerns are addressed
- Communicate your architectural perspective in an effective manner
- Chapter 8, "Governance," will enable you to
  - Provide principle-based architectural governance for the areas you are responsible for
  - Provide architectural governance for agile projects
- Chapter 9, "Know-how," will enable you to
  - Develop relevant architectural know-how
  - Build and maintain currency with your architectural know-how
  - Develop excellence with respect to architectural know-how

Technology skills are the second layer of skills needed to be an architect (see Figure PII.1).

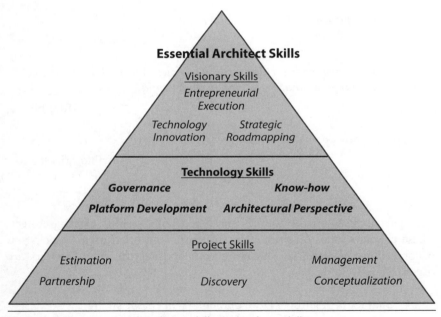

Figure PII.1   Essential architect skills (technology skills)

Technology skills can be thought of in three dimensions: technology leverage, technology oversight, and technology knowledge management (see Figure PII.2).

These three dimensions of technology skills are critical for architects to master. They will enable you to drive your organization toward its goals and objectives with a solid foundation in technology.

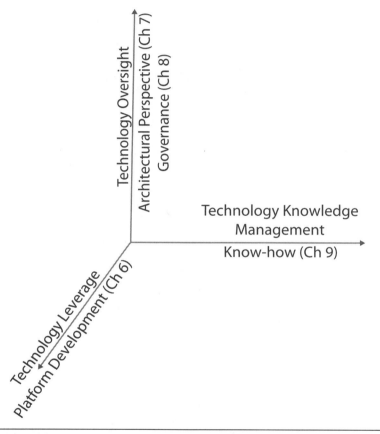

Figure PII.2 Technology skill dimensions

Chapter 6

PLATFORM DEVELOPMENT

"A 'platform' is a system that can be programmed and therefore customized by outside developers—users—and in that way, adapted to countless needs and niches that the platform's original developers could not have possibly contemplated, much less had time to accommodate."

—Marc Andreessen

"A product is useless without a platform, or more precisely and accurately, a platform-less product will always be replaced by an equivalent platform-ized product."

—Steve Yegge

"For the first time we're allowing developers who don't work at Facebook to develop applications just as if they were. That's a big deal because it means that all developers have a new way of doing business if they choose to take advantage of it. There are whole companies that are forming whose only product is a Facebook Platform application."

—Mark Zuckerberg

"One of the things I like about the computer that I use is that I can write a program on it or I can download a program on to it and run it. That's kind of important to me, and that's also kind of important to the whole future of the internet. . . . obviously a closed platform is a serious brake on innovation."

—Tim Berners-Lee

Architects are tasked with seeking solutions to business problems every day. The challenge is to find low-cost alternatives that provide the maximum strategic advantage.

Despite the initial cost of development, building and leveraging platforms can serve as one of the best investments companies can make to maximize their dollars spent.

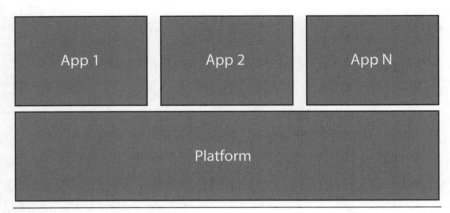

Figure 6.1   Platform development

This chapter focuses on the key skills and considerations needed by a software architect to construct or transform systems into platforms.

PLATFORM DEVELOPMENT DEFINED

Platform development is the process of transforming an application or concept into a base set of shared capabilities and ecosystems that can be leveraged by multiple applications or solutions concurrently (see Figure 6.1). Platforms enable common capabilities across multiple applications or solutions.

THE ELEMENTS OF PLATFORM DEVELOPMENT

Platform development can have a dramatic impact on your ability to produce applications quickly as well as to support customers in new and integrated ways. The challenge is how to manage the platform development in a manner that is not dramatically more expensive or more complex.

There are three key elements of platform development (see Figure 6.2):

- **Capabilities.** These are the functionalities delivered by the platform that basically tell you what the platform can do.
- **Ecosystem.** This is the environment in which the platform operates. It deals with everything that surrounds the platform.
- **Guiding principles.** This is the set of principles used to guide and direct the development and architecture of the platform.

These elements define the essence of the platform.

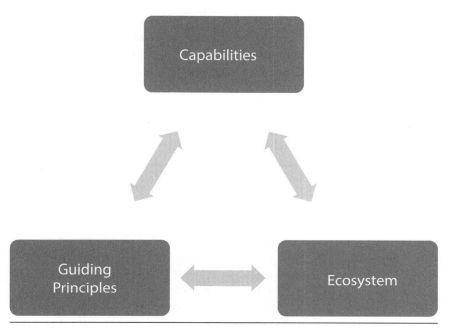

Figure 6.2 Platform development is made up of three key elements: capabilities, ecosystem, and guiding principles.

The approach taken to platform development can be dramatically different depending on where you are starting. Are you designing a platform up front in a mostly greenfield development exercise, or are you backing into the platform from an existing application? The end state may be the same for both, but the considerations and costs for how to get there may be extremely different.

CAPABILITIES

The core value of a platform is based on the defined set of capabilities it provides. These capabilities usually emerge from an application or a set of applications. With time, it is recognized that these capabilities are leverageable across a wide variety of applications. The challenge is how to package and distribute these capabilities to a wider audience.

Defining the Set of Objectives

Before diving into the set of capabilities for a platform, start working with the business to define the purpose and key objectives of the platform. That is, what will the platform help the business accomplish? This description usually contains three to five key objectives followed by a bulleted list that starts with words like *enable, provide, broaden, adhere,* and *partner.* These may seem like "mom and apple pie"–type statements, but they do help bound the scope and focus of the platform development.

Defining the Set of Capabilities

Normally, when I start thinking about the capabilities of a platform, I think about the high-level actions that the platform can perform, usually high above the API level that a developer would access. These actions, however, are relatively close to what a business person would think of with respect to the platform.

Ideally, as the capabilities are enumerated, the terms selected are from the domain of the user or at least terms to which users would quickly and unambiguously relate. This is usually the beginning of the logical architecture for the platform and typically represents the groups of services that the platform will support. If there are more than seven to ten services, consider providing a higher level of grouping for those services to help make the platform easier to conceptualize for users who are new to it.

Although your business partners may not be accustomed to thinking in terms of services or capabilities, it is worthwhile to partner with them and ensure that the names and words being used make sense to them. It will also help with the long-term advocacy of the platform if your business partners have been part of its inception and shaping.

I have had a fair amount of success by simply getting business partners in a room and whiteboarding the capabilities. The benefit of this style of interaction is that you can come up with an agreed-upon vocabulary for the capabilities.

Focusing on Leverageable Capabilities

When first starting to define the capabilities for a platform, it is tempting to include everything that you can think of and be all-inclusive. The goal should be to include only the capabilities that are known to be leverageable by more than one application or what may be leverageable in the future by other applications. If the capability is application specific, the application can provide the capability itself.

Be diligent about what is included in the platform; it should have a relatively narrow focus in the beginning and do a small number of things well.

Developing a Strong Conceptual Model

The platform capabilities are typically grouped into sets of related capabilities. These groupings embody the conceptual model of the platform and should naturally cluster together to form a cohesive unit.

APIs Are the Keys to the Kingdom

APIs unlock the value of the platform (see Figure 6.3). They give developers the ability to manage and access the platform. When designing the APIs into the platform, many crosscutting concerns need to be taken into account:

- What are the security concerns? Clearly defining identity management and access control in a platform is absolutely essential to ensure that the platform is a "safe" place for your partners to store and manage their data.
- What is the granularity of information that is transferred? Is it fine grained? Does the interface need to support large batch capabilities?
- Is the data model explicitly defined in the APIs? Or is the data access more generic where the information is not known to the system but is accessed mostly from a key perspective?
- What types of protocols and supported content types need to be established? Is this simply HTTP/REST with JSON? Or is this JMS?
- Where does service orchestration belong? Does it belong in the calling application or does it belong in the platform? Is there related workflow? What types of events need to be supported?
- Does the platform support inversion of control? If so, what types of configuration are required to support it?
- Do you have an API versioning strategy? It is unlikely that your interfaces are going to be perfect right out of the gate. The key is to get them reasonably close and allow for the platform to grow and mature as you learn more about the real usage and needs of the platform.
- How do you plan to deprecate APIs? As the interface definitions mature, old interfaces need to go away. Giving your partners a signal that certain interfaces are deprecated allows them to make necessary upgrades before removing interfaces.

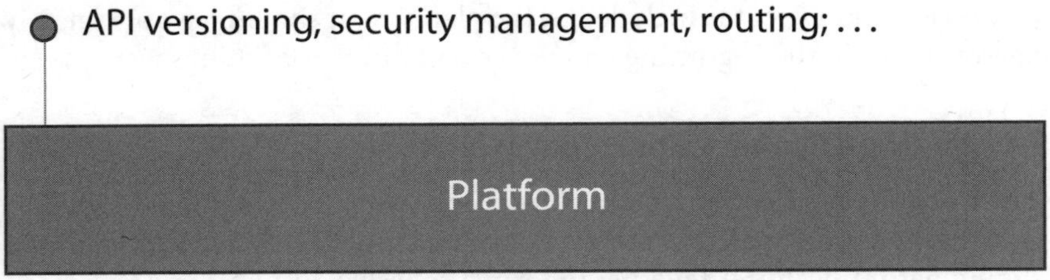

● API versioning, security management, routing; . . .

Platform

Figure 6.3 Managing the platform's interface is critical to the applications that will be built upon it; they simply expect it to work correctly every time.

ECOSYSTEM

The ecosystem (users, ownership, management, development, costs, quality, integration, scalability, and security) that surrounds the platform is nearly as critical as the platform itself.

Platform Users

Knowing and understanding the users of the platform are essential to knowing how the platform needs to be owned, architected, marketed, and developed. Key aspects of knowing the platform users include the following:

- What is the nature of the customers? Are they internal to your company or external to your company or both? Are they administrators or users? Are they revenue generating versus internal versus free? Understanding the nature of the customer can help drive your SLAs, your security approach, your disaster recovery approach, and what features are essential.
- If the platform is internal, is the service being offered within a business unit or across business units? Negotiating across business units gets tricky, not as much from a technical perspective but from both a political and a financial perspective.

Having this knowledge can drive how you need to seek funding, how you oversee the platform, and how you manage platform-related projects.

Platform Ownership

There are many subtle outcomes to the decisions that are made for a platform depending on who within the organization is the owner. The owner of the platform needs to guide funding, oversight, pre-engagement materials, project intake and requirements management, on-boarding, and awareness and acceptance.

Platform Funding

One of the more challenging aspects of developing a platform is not only to get the necessary support to fund development work, but to get it funded at a level that supports the strategic nature of the platform. It often takes more time to develop, test, and maintain flexible, multitenant platforms than single-purpose applications with limited capabilities.

Funding a platform requires you to manage and determine the following:

- Who funds the work? Typically, there is funding from each of the business units that is leveraging the platform, possibly from a central technology group, or potentially from other business partners.
- What do you do with those who want it for free? There are always those who want to come in and use the platform for free or for very low cost. This can be possible once the platform is more established, if they don't require development changes and their utilization of system resources is relatively low.
- How much of the development can occur for a platform partner without their contributing funding? The answer to this is usually very little unless the features they need are being funded by someone else or being funded by central strategic development dollars.
- Do you allow others to make decisions about strategic direction without funding commitments? The groups you want involved in helping make strategic decisions are those that have some skin in the game and are willing to commit financial resources to building and supporting the platform. They will have a natural alignment to making wise decisions with the limited funding resources.
- How do you fund bug fixes? There needs to be some form of support funding built into the maintenance of the platform. This often takes place as some form of charge-back to the business units that are leveraging the platform.
- How do you balance the needs of partners who have a lot of money versus the little guy who doesn't have as much funding to contribute? Platforms need to account for everyone who is at the table. If only the one group with a lot of funding gets all of the resources and attention, you destroy the sense of platform community and the sense of fairness that need to exist. Having some form of voting or

agreement mechanism that takes all of the core financial contributors into account typically works well.

- How do you ensure equitable investments? If there are multiple areas that can leverage a capability, how do you allocate the cost? Most of the time, it is first to market that pays; the others that follow typically get close to a free ride. This type of model limits the capabilities of the platform unnecessarily when they may be broadly needed. If possible, look for ways to broker a shared allocation of the costs. This is where the value of a platform truly comes into play; everyone gets a chance to benefit from the development dollars that others are contributing, and the amount everyone needs to contribute in the end is less.
- How do you allocate ongoing costs? For internal users, do you have a charge-back model in place as usage and scale increase? For external users, do you have a usage-based model for charging?
- Is this an external platform? Relationships with other businesses need to be worked through very carefully from both a development perspective and an operations perspective, but also from a legal perspective.

Funding platform development can be challenging, but the rewards can be significant.

One of the keys to successful funding is to have an evangelist on the business side, someone who can articulate the vision and business value of building, supporting, and moving to the platform.

When this is working well, you are able to collaborate across multiple partners in the development of new features. This enables partners to come in and create a new feature that they will leverage and pay for. Later, this development is further enhanced and paid for by a second business unit. Since these new features are developed within the platform, the new enhanced capabilities are now also available to the group that helped define the original feature at little or no cost.

This type of leapfrog funding helps create a sense of community around the platform development. Everyone is able to chip in a little to help get things built, and everyone is able to leverage the work that others add to the platform.

Platform Oversight (Steering Committee/Advisory Board)

The oversight of a platform is usually some combination of technology (including architecture) and representatives of the various business units that have an active stake in utilizing and improving the platform to meet their needs.

There is always a wide range of political issues that arise in determining the following:

- Who decides what work gets done? Ideally, each of the contributing business units has the opportunity to "vote" in some manner on which capabilities are addressed first, and that in turn allows them to help prioritize and negotiate for the platform capabilities that are most important to them.
- What level of the organization "owns" the assets? If one business unit "owns" the platform, the owning business unit usually appears to be getting an unfair advantage and access to the development team. One way this is typically addressed organizationally is to have a central development team that is not a part of any business unit own the platform.
- What is an equitable means of allocating work? Some organizations may not be able to commit the same level of funding or resources to the development of the platform. The key is to ensure that those who are at the table determining what should and should not get worked on have committed some funds to the game.
- Do you allow other groups to contribute work to the platform? Most platform teams are strapped for resources (time and people). If you allow others to work on the platform, you need to ensure that proper measures are in place to guarantee that the work being done is leverageable by all parties and not just a hack to meet one area's needs. One way to accomplish this is to have a limited number of committers to the code base.
- Can you open-source the platform? Depending on the nature of the platform, you may be able to open-source its development and let a truly wide set of developers have access to improving it. If, on the other hand, the platform is considered an internal strategic asset, you may not have an option to open-source it externally, but you may be able to open-source it within the corporation. If it is internal, you still need to work out the funding issue in terms of how people allocate their time when they are working on the platform.

- How will you demonstrate business value? A platform may not directly generate revenue for the business, but there needs to be an awareness of how the platform contributes to other applications and in turn enables them to generate revenue. If you don't generate revenue or contribute to generating revenue, you will be perceived as an expense. Finance folks don't like expenses.

Having a solid model for platform oversight is critical for the long-term success of the platform. It can enable the changing needs of the business to be incorporated into the platform and, as a result, increase the platform's long-term relevance to the business.

Platform Pre-engagement Materials

Having a good set of pre-engagement materials ready for new potential partners can help get many of the early questions taken care of and prepare the partners to have more on-point questions that will make your first meetings much more engaging for both parties. These pre-engagement materials usually include

- **Prerecorded product overview presentations.** These will give the partners a sense of the capabilities of the new platform and begin to prepare them to understand potential gaps and potential early wins for their applications.
- **White papers.** From these, new partners can get a sense of what and how other applications that have integrated with the platform have been deployed, what uses of the platform have already been put in place, what kinds of business services have been integrated with, and other basic information about the platform and its future direction.
- **FAQs.** A set of frequently asked questions will answer common initial questions that nearly everyone asks when first approaching the platform team.

The more prepared you are for new partners to come onto the platform, the easier it will be for both you and the partners to get a quick jump start to actual use of the platform.

Platform Project Intake and Requirements Management

Developing a solid mechanism for ingesting new platform requirements, change requests, and defects is central to the long-term health of the platform. Some of the key aspects of successful project intake include the following:

- **Providing timely feedback.** When new features or changes are requested of the platform, getting back to the requester in a timely fashion (measured in days) is a best practice. Respond nearly immediately as an acknowledgment of the request. Estimates should be responded to within a handful of weeks. Most estimating requests come in with some sense of urgency and need to be sized quickly to enable the requesting party to make investment decisions in a timely fashion. For an architect, there is usually a very limited amount of time in which to determine the appropriate solution for most requests. Ideally for newer areas, a quick POC or two can help significantly improve the confidence level of the estimate that is provided.

- **Dealing with conflicting requirements with an eye toward operations.** Often when multiple requests are made of the platform, there are conflicts between the different requests and potentially conflicts with the platform's long-term objectives. The challenge is balancing all of these needs. In some very true sense, you are managing to the common good while maintaining operational excellence.

- **Aligning with company goals.** As a platform team, your allegiance is not to a specific business unit but to the greater good of the overall company. Knowing and understanding the company's strategic goals are critical to helping guide architectural platform decisions.

- **Realizing that you are at least one step removed from the end customers.** For most platform development, you and your team are not directly interacting with the end customers. There is normally another group, business unit, or application that is interacting with the "real" customer. Take the time to meet with the requester to try to gain a deeper understanding of what is really being requested, to determine what alternatives may be acceptable, and to get a sense of the priority of the different aspects of the request. Try to develop and maintain customer focus even if you are a few steps removed.

Managing project intake with excellence is essential to keeping a platform thriving in the ever-changing world of technology.

Platform On-boarding

Getting new partners up and running quickly on the platform is an easy and early win that can pay great dividends with respect to goodwill and a positive trajectory with your new partners. Taking the time to prepare for a smooth on-boarding experience will help with both the management staff and the technical staff of the new partners. A good on-board experience usually includes having

- **Architectural overviews.** These will give the new partners a solid conceptual and technical understanding of how the platform works, how it is structured, and what is on the roadmap for future development.
- **Scripted live demos.** Anyone on the platform team can create these.
- **Trained staff assigned to new customers.** Staff can take care of any questions the customers may have and ensure that questions are answered promptly. Early on in the process these tasks can be handled by the architects, but with an increasing number of clients they need to be handled by others to ensure good customer service as the platform demand grows.
- **Rich reference implementations of common platform uses.** These should be easy to download and run in a handful of minutes. This will help enable a quick and smooth "Hello, Platform!" experience for your partners. You want this to be easy and painless.
- **An API explorer.** This enables the development staff to play around with the platform in order to get a sense of the conceptual model that surrounds it and to give them a quicker start on developing on or against the platform.

Platform Awareness and Acceptance

Once you have started to develop a platform, creating awareness of it throughout the company or industry can be a challenge:

- How do you make others aware of your platform? How do you make people aware that the platform exists and let them know what is possible? Internally, having an executive sponsor can be an excellent way to get the message out. A sponsor typically has the connections to reach across the various business units to get things moving. Alternatively, going on road shows to the different business units is also another way to develop a buzz within the company. Externally, this is really the job of marketing and sales. However, anything you can do to have demos, training, and white papers prepared can help simplify their job.
- Do you have a roadmap of features and their timing? How do you determine what is on the roadmap? Is it demand based? The ability to tell the story of where you are and where you are planning to go will help give your potential partners or customers the confidence that if they make the commitment to move onto your platform, they will have a solid set of new features to give to their customers. It also gives them the opportunity to let you know of any gaps you may

have and gives you a better sense of any adjustments you may need to make.

- Are you aligned with industry trends? Showing that you are aligned with trends within your industry or potentially adjacent industries will help both you and your customers keep up with the competition and ideally stay at least one step ahead of them.
- What is unique about what you are doing? Where is your value? Is that something other areas are willing to pay for? You need to know what your key value proposition is. What is the special sauce you bring to the table that makes you stand out against the competition? You need to be able to differentiate yourself.
- Do you enable quick application development? The ability for users to get up and running quickly on a platform is essential, and having default configurations of the most likely chosen options can help your customers do this. They can customize things later once they have had a chance to play around and get comfortable with the system. You need to get to "Hello, Platform!" with little or no configuration necessary. The ability to support self-service with appropriate documentation can go a long way toward enabling customers to get up and running quickly and help minimize your customer support costs.

  The lack of simple reference applications demonstrating the use of the platform can be an impediment to platform adoption.

- Is it possible to start with a small set of core passionate customers? Ideally, you have the opportunity to hold off on having a broad customer base until the core of the platform is solid; otherwise, you will deal with mass operational issues and concerns and may destroy the brand you have worked so hard to develop.
- What is your name, brand, slogan, iconography, and so on? Who you are and the image you want to project need to be crisp and clear. Everything you do needs to be tied together and present a common brand. Working early toward having branding standards is critical. Anything that doesn't align with the brand you are trying to project simply raises questions about what you are doing, either consciously or subconsciously.

Platform Management

Having a clear understanding of how the platform will be managed is important for clear direction setting and the stability of the platform as a whole.

- Who is in control of the capabilities of the platform? From an overall company perspective, picking the right group to own and manage the platform is important. You want to ensure that they will have their customers' best interests at heart and not just represent the interests of the business unit in which the platform resides.

- Is there a central person who acts as the benevolent dictator of the platform, or is there a community process that manages the capabilities? Sometimes having a single person who can oversee, guide, and direct a platform can work out well. The key is that this person needs to have a great business as well as technology acumen. He or she needs to have the ability to sell the platform and to know how to drive development of the platform in a way that will best benefit the business as a whole. Alternatively, having a steering group perform this function can also work if its members agree on the overall vision they are shooting for.

- How do you share capabilities? From a platform perspective, you need to understand what the model is for people to leverage capabilities. Are you looking to implement a multitenant environment where there are common instances of the software that understand how to run in the context of a user on every thread, or do customers host their own versions?

- Where are other platforms going? Ideally, the platforms that are being developed throughout the company are following common standards, patterns, and guidelines to give a uniform look and feel to the work that is being produced. Uniformity will help reduce the ramp-up time for users of the platform and ideally minimize the ceremony of getting up to speed on it.

- Who has the ability to add code? Your development model can dramatically affect the controls that you need to have in place around the platform. Do you have centralized development, where a single group owns and manages the code? Or do you have a federated development model, where multiple groups can contribute to the code base? In either case, you need to understand who is providing the active oversight of the changes being committed to ensure that they are in line with the vision and quality of the platform.

- Are there design patterns that can help the adoption and operation of the platform? As the platform matures, try to identify and name the patterns and idioms that emerge. These can help raise the level of conversation that needs to occur during the development of new features.

- What about internationalization? The global nature of what most companies are dealing with today makes internationalization of a platform something that needs to be in place from the very initial development efforts.

Platform Involvement with Mergers and Acquisitions

Mergers and acquisitions can be a great way for companies to increase their revenue growth or to acquire new capabilities that are missing from their product portfolio. However, trying to bring in a new acquisition and "merge" its capabilities into the overall platform development model you are trying to hone and refine can be very challenging without requiring a significant development effort. To help minimize this:

- Have someone familiar with the platform involved with the acquisitions team to help evaluate the overall fit of the assets that are being purchased with respect to the platform.
- Have an understanding of how you would incorporate the new acquisition into the platform. Try to look for how closely the architectural styles will interact with each other. For example, the purchase may be for installed desktop software, but you have a cloud-based software as a service (SAAS) solution.
- Look for open-source issues, regulatory issues, and legal issues that may exist and reduce the overall value of the purchase.
- Get a clear understanding of any identity or entitlement issues.
- Understand the overall goals of the acquisition and merger. They may be more about revenue growth than platform expansion. If this is the case, those who are making the purchase need to be aware of the overall capability sprawl and customer confusion that may result from the purchase.
- Make sure the costs of the changes to mainstream these capabilities into the platform are accounted for in the overall cost structure of the purchase to enable the development work that will need to occur after the acquisition is completed.

One of the problems that can occur when the platform team is not involved in mergers and acquisitions is that duplicative capabilities may be bought by business units that are not fully aware of platform capabilities. This can lead to future issues when the business wants to centralize these capabilities and the redundancies need to be removed.

Platform Involvement with Consolidating Company Assets

As the development of key platform capabilities occurs within a company, working to consolidate related company assets into the platform can be challenging. Those who need to begin leveraging the platform may have little or no interest in giving up the control of the duplicative capabilities they currently manage. Others will gladly move to the platform to help reduce their overall expenses and to access new capabilities. The platform will enable them to focus on their area of specialization within the business. Having the right level of high-level executive directives and oversight to drive the right behavior within the business is needed to make the platform successful.

Platform Involvement with Divestitures

As the company expands, grows, and changes, it may choose to divest certain assets within its overall portfolio. This may be done for a variety of reasons. As you consider what is being divested, take the time to closely consider all of the integration points the divested area may have within the business. These include business systems, technology systems, services, hardware, networking, and staffing. A significant amount of effort may be required to untangle the divested asset and get it rehosted outside of your environment. There are usually a lot of hidden costs that are amortized across different business functions.

Be Cautious about Expanding Where the Platform Extends and Grows

As you consider the direction for the platform, you need to be aware of the willingness of the business to invest in a particular area. If the support is not there, be cautious about expanding into that area.

As a platform architect, be willing to consider taking the occasional "weird" app that doesn't match your core capabilities to help expand your horizons.

The decisions you make will likely last at least a decade; choose carefully.

Platform Development

Normally the development challenges around creating a platform are more complex and need a more strategic-thinking set of developers than for other projects. Taking the time to groom the right team is critical to enable high-quality code that is leverageable.

- Do you use contractors? The challenge is that they cost a lot and may allow you to deliver quickly, but the risk is a loss of quality. Hire right.
- Are there ways for you to show off your new technologies within the organization and attract the top talent? You need to understand what areas are of interest and what areas cause concern within the development community in your company and region. This will help you craft your hiring message.

- How do you manage demand for the development of features? Heavy demand may cause adoption of the platform to slow down due to lack of access to development resources. You may have been very successful in selling the platform to others but not have all of the features to cover their "core" capabilities. These gaps need to be identified and placed on an overall architectural roadmap. This will give your partners a sense of when they can join the platform and the costs that may be involved in doing so.

- Does the development staff have a clear understanding of the quality of service you are seeking to deliver? Are they developing or acquiring tools to ensure this level of quality? Platform development requires high-quality code. Make sure that the developers have this in their mindset; that when features are being added they follow the standards your team has established; and that the operational tools for monitoring, configuring, and deploying are all fully accounted for.

- How are you managing operating systems, JVM configurations, and other tools or services? The level of documentation around a platform tends to be higher than for typical application software development. Appropriately documenting the runtime and other operational requirements can make transitioning new capabilities into production a simpler process.

- Are you transforming from application to platform? If so, try to minimally impact your current customers. You need their support, especially in the early days.

- When to tech refresh? You want to stay current with technologies as they advance to keep your platform relevant and avoid atrophy. The challenge is to do this in a manner that minimizes disruption and does not cause you to abandon current customers.

- What is the cost of any licensing or support with respect to certain technologies? You need to be careful about being too expensive. Your goal needs to be to maintain cost-effectiveness. The business needs both speed to market and low cost to help maximize profit and maintain market leadership.

- Where is the appropriate and cost-effective place to deploy? Should this platform be deployed on physical servers? Cloud servers? Virtualized servers? Or should it be some mix based on environment and demand? The right combination of deployment options can help you manage your overall costs. Using virtual or cloud deployments can help with your ability to move quickly into lower development and testing environments by avoiding some of the long provisioning processes that are likely to exist for physical servers. Do you need to perform large-scale testing efforts? If so, do you have the hardware infrastructure to account for them, or can you access one of the production sites to help? Routing live traffic to one of the other production sites can help get real-scale testing in and help minimize the cost of maintaining a separate scale environment.

- Are there requirements to be able to deploy the platform on customer sites? If so, who owns the deployment and upgrade schedule? Make sure these items are covered in any contractual talks with the customer. What kind of access do you need or will you have to the systems? What kind of support is required? How will this affect your documentation? How will this affect your ease of deployment? Are there service personnel involved? Can this be managed externally? Doing on-site deployments may address the security and regulatory concerns of the customer, but they dramatically increase the complexity and cost structure of managing the platform. These issues need to be weighed carefully within the business to ensure that this is an area that you are willing to commit to. Exploring secure cloud deployments that are in the regional or national boundaries of the customer may be an acceptable alternative. Ensure that whatever path you are selling to the customer is one that you have both the technical and operational depth to manage.

- How often and when do you do deployments? What impacts are there to the applications on the platform? How do you manage through API changes? How do you ensure minimal impacts to customers? Deployments have the ability to dramatically impact live customers. Regression testing can play a critical role in assuring that the new software will behave properly for all of the partners that you have on your platform during deployments. You need to ensure that your API changes are versioned and that your changes are backward compatible. You need to ensure that as you do your deployments you have drained the site or instances in a manner that does not impact live customers. You need to message your changes to partners far enough in advance that they can react and plan for any changes that may impact them. The challenge with most platforms today is that there is an expectation of their being up 24×7. Having the ability to do rolling deployments, to roll back changes, to turn features on and off at runtime through operational controls, and to be able to target the release of features to a limited set of users or partners are all areas of concern for large-scale platform development.

- How do you manage your intellectual property? Have you applied for any patents? Do you regularly meet with an intellectual property lawyer to determine if there are any ideas worth pursuing for a patent? Taking the time to ensure that all of the work you have done to build the platform is protected is important from a business perspective. It helps the business to manage the platform as a financial asset for the company.

Acknowledging the Costs Associated with the Platform

Developing platforms is a fun and exciting endeavor. However, the development, maintenance, and operational costs are higher than for other projects. Unless the ability to significantly leverage the platform exists, it may not be worth the investment required to support the associated costs (see Figure 6.4).

There is also added risk to the set of applications using the platform due to the common dependencies of the platform if something goes wrong. If the applications are not properly managed, they also have the ability to impact one another.

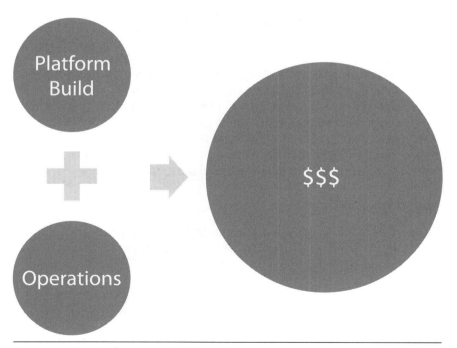

Figure 6.4 Platform costs: building platforms is an expensive proposition but with many benefits.

Platforms raise the promise that they can create an environment where the time and effort to develop applications is significantly reduced and the costs associated with managing the operations can be shared. This can enable the businesses that use the platform to invest in other areas. Determining the actual costs, cost savings, reduced risks, improved product velocity, and other measurable positive benefits including attributable revenue can be challenging for platforms due to their multidimensional nature.

Managing Platform Quality

The quality of a platform is directly related to

- **Focusing on loose coupling between capabilities.**
- **Aiming for a high percentage of code coverage.** Focus on the error paths through the system; the happy paths will take care of themselves.
- **Encouraging a high level of mocking.** This helps focus tests on the class being tested, not its dependencies, including other classes and time-consuming resources such as accessing databases.
- **Managing tech debt.** If there are areas of the code that everyone is afraid of, get rid of them; they will cause entropy to occur in those areas of the system and cause everyone to naturally want to steer clear of them.
- **Performing a variety of different kinds of tests** (functional, scale, ad hoc, automated, end-to-end, and user).
- **Determining the time frame of backward compatibility.** If you extend backward compatibility for a long time, it adds to the complexity of the code base; if you don't, you may be forcing changes on your customers who are not in a good position to deal with change.
- **Being cautious about database and data model changes.**

Platform Integration

Understanding how others desire to integrate with your platform can help determine how you structure features and access points. You need to consider the following:

- At what points within the architecture stack will you allow access? Having well-defined access points within the architecture stack will help aid your partners in understanding how they need to approach platform integration.

- Are your customers looking to provide their own user interface and simply want to access a services layer? Or are they simply looking for providing a new skin on an existing platform application with simple and quick configuration to deal with branding and look-and-feel-related items? Having different levels of leverage will make your platform more appealing to a broader set of potential customers. It may also cause customer confusion about what they should leverage.
- Are there ways for you to leverage other internal or external platforms and avoid the ownership expenses (establish core capabilities versus adjacent capabilities)? The ability to leverage other platforms may create synergies and cost reductions that might not otherwise be achievable.
- Are there ways to leverage common assets to enable cleaner integrations? Is there a notion of modules or componentization that can make smaller units of the platform usable without having to consume the entire platform? The more that each of the capabilities has loose coupling with the other capabilities of the platform, the more orthogonal development and growth can occur. Otherwise, platform atrophy will be encroaching.
- Once decisions have been made to consolidate to a platform, how do you work toward consolidating applications? Consolidating hardware? Consolidating business models (which may not need to be done)? Consolidating capabilities? Developing a roadmap of how the consolidation will occur can help ease everyone's concerns about the timing and help to identify issues that may be lurking.
- Is the type of integration more synchronous and transactional, or is it more batch and bulk oriented? How others intend to integrate with the system can have a dramatic impact on how the system scales. Make sure you understand this early on to ensure that the access you are providing into the platform will work well for them and for you.
- Does your system need to support mobile? If so, is it simply mobile web or does it require a native application? If it is native, what platforms does it need to support? Does it need to support offline mobile? Mobile concerns are higher up in the overall architectural stack and as a result can deal with more variability and changes as market needs change. The key is to clearly identify the location of key capabilities within the architectural stack and to understand the impacts of offline access to those capabilities.

I have seen instances where a platform started out with capabilities tightly integrated with specific business systems. This tight coupling of the business system and the platform enabled the users to get up and running quickly. Unfortunately, this tight coupling also caused the platform to be a major source of pain and delay for new applications that wanted to utilize the platform because they used different business systems.

In the end, be flexible and allow for flexibility in the different kinds of integrations that various businesses may want with the platform. The easier it is for them to leverage the platform, the faster the platform will become a success.

Scalability

For detailed information on scalability, please see Chapter 7, "Architectural Perspective."

Security

For detailed information on security, please see Chapter 8, "Governance."

GUIDING PRINCIPLES

Adhering to guiding principles can help establish a solid platform and extend its overall life.

Seek Exceptional Quality

The nature of leverage and reuse embodied within a platform drives the need for much higher levels of quality than would be necessary in a typical application. The wide variety of uses of the platform tends to stress it in many different dimensions, which results in the need for high-quality code and high-quality automated testing to ensure that not only are the new features solid, but no unintentional changes within the platform are introduced to those who depend on its stability. In general, this makes development efforts for platform code a more expensive proposition and also highlights the need to focus on adding only those features that will be heavily leveraged.

Seek Operational Excellence

The operational needs of a platform are usually much more complex for a multitenant platform environment. Your ability to ensure that security, regulatory, and privacy concerns are addressed is table stakes in a platform environment. Take the time to purchase and develop the appropriate operational tools to

- Ensure that the platform operates with the insights necessary to help with growth planning
- Diagnose specific customer issues
- Detect security breaches
- Detect failures
- Alert when resources are approaching critical levels (such as storage full)
- Enable dynamic feature access and controls

Having the appropriate operational tools for the platform can help make dramatic growth both feasible and sustainable.

Seek Configurability over Hard Coding

In the development of platform code, it is easy to simply add in branching logic within the platform to choose which code to execute. Although this may be the "quick fix" to get something working, it adds brittleness to the overall code base. Take the time to learn how to enable the same behavior through external configuration, inversion of control, or dynamic operational controls.

If you do introduce technical debt, keep track of it and create stories to deal with it quickly. Technical debt can weigh down your future development velocity dramatically if you don't stay on top of it.

Seek Leverageability

Platforms need to be developed in a manner that supports the broadest set of use cases and the greatest number of partners. Adding partner-specific code to a platform dilutes its overall value. One way to address this is to partner with customers for new feature requests and generalize what they are requesting. This will allow for the features to be more broadly applicable and enable the leverage opportunities that you are seeking for the platform.

Seek Redundant Architecture

Platforms should have multiple levels of redundancy built into them to enable scale, availability, and reliability. This includes having multiple physical locations, using clustering techniques, using caches with nearby persistence, making backups, and using other approaches that enable critical components to fail but allow the overall system to continue to function with minimal disruption. Redundancy generally favors a scaling-out approach versus a scaling-up approach.

Seek Linear Scalability

Platforms need to be able to scale linearly to ensure that the cost of adding new users does not become prohibitively expensive as the popularity of the platform grows. One of the best ways of ensuring this is to do regular scale testing with monitoring of key metrics within the system over time and ensure that scale is not degrading as new features are added to the system.

Avoid Platform Entanglement

Each change that is made to the platform can cause tighter coupling to occur within the platform. As changes are introduced, take the time to refactor the code base and the architecture to reflect the new directions of the business. A platform needs to change to grow and stay vital.

Avoid Platform Sprawl

It is easy during the midlife of a platform to want to say yes to all new development that shows up. Being willing to say no to adding things that don't clearly align with the platform will help extend the overall life span and usefulness of the platform without diluting its central purpose.

Keep Upgrading to Current Technologies

One of the best ways to kill a platform is to minimize the investment in keeping the platform current with technology. Platforms are like any other system. You need to upgrade them every one and a half to five years as technologies go out of favor and are replaced with newer and better approaches and techniques. This should be done on a rolling basis, not as a big bang.

SUMMARY

The road to platform development begins with

- Managing platform capabilities
  - Defining the set of platform objectives
  - Defining the set of platform capabilities

- ▪ Focusing on leverageable capabilities
- ▪ Developing a strong conceptual model
- ▪ Embracing APIs, configuration, and eventing as the keys to the platform
- ▪ Focusing on the platform ecosystem
  - ▪ Knowing the platform users
  - ▪ Understanding platform ownership
  - ▪ Understanding platform management
  - ▪ Driving platform development
  - ▪ Acknowledging platform costs
  - ▪ Managing platform quality
  - ▪ Understanding platform integration
- ▪ Guiding the platform growth through principles

My experience has been that working on platforms from an architecture perspective is challenging and fun. The set of customer interactions and learning is a constant, which makes it exciting to go to work.

REFERENCES

Benioff, Marc, and Carlye Adler. 2009. *Behind the Cloud: The Untold Story of How Salesforce.com Went from Idea to Billion-Dollar Company and Revolutionized an Industry*. Jossey-Bass.

Gharajedaghi, Jamshid. 2011. *Systems Thinking: Managing Chaos and Complexity: A Platform for Designing Business Architecture, Third Edition*. Morgan Kaufmann.

Godinez, Mario, Eberhard Hechler, Klaus Koenig, Steve Lockwood, Martin Oberhofer, and Michael Schroeck. 2010. *The Art of Enterprise Information Architecture: A Systems-Based Approach for Unlocking Business Insight*. IBM Press.

Leffingwell, Dean. 2011. *Agile Software Requirements: Lean Requirements Practices for Teams, Programs, and the Enterprise*. Addison-Wesley.

Levy, Steven. 2011. *In the Plex: How Google Thinks, Works, and Shapes Our Lives*. Simon & Schuster.

Meadows, Donella H. 2008. *Thinking in Systems: A Primer*. Chelsea Green Publishing.

Reynolds, Chris. 2009. *Introduction to Business Architecture*. Cengage Learning.

Ross, Jeanne W., and Peter Weill. 2006. *Enterprise Architecture as Strategy: Creating a Foundation for Business Execution.* Harvard Business Review Press.

Simon, Phil, and Mitch Joel. 2011. *The Age of the Platform: How Amazon, Apple, Facebook, and Google Have Redefined Business.* Motion Publishing.

Chapter 7

ARCHITECTURAL PERSPECTIVE

"To design something really well, you have to get it. You have to really grok what it's all about. It takes a passionate commitment to really thoroughly understand something, chew it up, not just quickly swallow it."

—Steve Jobs

"A little perspective, like a little humor, goes a long way."

—Allen Klein

"A lot of people in our industry haven't had very diverse experiences. So they don't have enough dots to connect, and they end up with very linear solutions without a broad perspective on the problem. The broader one's understanding of the human experience, the better design we will have."

—Steve Jobs

"Perspective gives us the ability to accurately contrast the large with the small, and the important with the less important. Without it we are lost in a world where all ideas, news, and information look the same. We cannot differentiate, we cannot prioritize, and we cannot make good choices."

—John Sununu

"So when these people sell out, even though they get fabulously rich, they're gypping themselves out of one of the potentially most rewarding experiences of their unfolding lives. Without it, they may never know their values or how to keep their newfound wealth in perspective."

—Steve Jobs

Architects are usually the first technology people to get involved with the business on a new idea. Depending on the timing and the level of engagement of the business, this can be as early as ideation or as late as when the product is already wireframed and an estimate is needed. If all goes well, the architect will be included earlier rather than later.

The spanning type of role for architects gives them a unique view into the world of building products. Architects therefore need to understand not only what the business wants to accomplish, but also what is logical, feasible, cost-effective, scalable, and intuitive to multiple levels of the technology organization.

This chapter unveils one of the essential skills needed by a software architect: the ability to provide architectural perspectives for a project.

ARCHITECTURAL PERSPECTIVE DEFINED

Perspective is the ability to step back and view architecture from many different vantage points. Each perspective is not necessarily fully accurate, but being able to see, analyze, and conceptualize from multiple views gives a holistic view of the landscape.

Knowledge of common principles, adages, and rules of thumb can help you measure the nature of the perspective:

- Does it look right?
- Does it meet the expectations of the customer?
- How does it compare to other architectures?
- What are the differences/variances in what is being perceived?

Viewing architecture from multiple perspectives can give valuable insights into the solution (see Figure 7.1).

ARCHITECTURAL PRINCIPLES

As you develop the architecture for a system, a core set of architectural principles can be used to evaluate decisions that are being made. The principles don't always have to be followed, but you should have some solid rationale for why you are going in a particular direction.

The Principle of Least Surprise

The *Principle of Least Surprise* is the concept that the idea or approach being taken would not surprise a reasonably knowledgeable person in the subject area being developed when first encountering this element of the system.

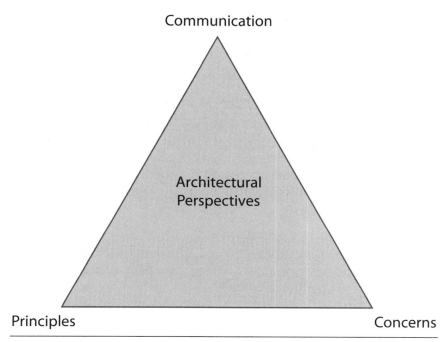

Figure 7.1 Architectural perspectives

This principle can apply to nearly every aspect of the architecture. It can apply to the domain model, where the nouns that are being used represent entities, and the verbs describe the actions that are being performed. Would the words being used surprise an end user?

It can apply to the visualization of the user interface. For example, does the sequence of actions flow easily and naturally? From a hardware perspective, does the configuration of the hardware represent a pattern that the data center personnel are familiar with? If so, is the pattern named or in common use? Naming patterns can go a long way toward establishing context in architectural conversations.

In some very real sense, this principle could be renamed the Principle of Natural Intuition. When this principle is applied, the users of a system should be able to quickly and intuitively understand what to do and what to do next.

When you are reviewing the architecture and you encounter nonintuitive elements, this is the time to closely evaluate the cause. Sometimes the solution is as simple as renaming items. Other times, it requires a major overhaul. Either way, getting the architecture to have the right fit can make the overall system easier to work on, create fewer issues, and give the users a quality experience that will make them want to come back again and again.

The Principle of Least Knowledge (aka the Law of Demeter)

The *Principle of Least Knowledge* is a concept about minimizing dependencies. As you are architecting the system, the goal is to strive for proper coupling and cohesion. That is, you want loose coupling for capabilities that are more independent of one another, and you want high cohesion for capabilities that are highly correlated to one another (they should do one thing well).

Establishing these boundaries from the outset makes it significantly easier for the development teams to stand up new capabilities; they will have a clear, well-defined purpose. In a similar fashion, the ability to scale new capabilities will be straightforward. Ideally, the capabilities are self-contained. That is, they have no or very few dependencies on other capabilities within the system.

What you want to avoid is a giant mud ball, one in which everything is dependent on everything else within the system. It is very hard to test, to deploy, to refactor, to scale, or to reuse systems that are tightly bound, such that if you touch one part of the system, another seemingly unrelated part of the system changes.

If you are not extremely diligent, there is a natural entropying of the careful boundaries that were laid between various capabilities of a system as the system progresses through time. When you are first architecting the system, take the time to cluster capabilities that form a cohesive group and likewise isolate capabilities that are not related to one another. As the system ages, guard these boundaries diligently, and you can extend the life of a system for years and years.

The Principle of Least Effort (aka Zipf's Law)

"In simple terms, the Principle of Least Effort means, for example, that a person in solving his immediate problems will view these against the background of his future problems, as estimated by himself. Moreover, he will strive to solve his problems in such a way as to minimize the total work that he must expend in solving both his

immediate problems and his probable future problems. That in turn means that the person will strive to minimize the probable average rate of his work-expenditure (over time). And in so doing he will be minimizing his effort. . . . Least effort, therefore, is a variant of least work."

—George Kingsley Zipf

The *Principle of Least Effort* has applicability to almost every aspect of software architecture, software development, and software usage. At every stage, we tend to follow the path that is the easiest (requires the least effort). This principle generally points to the idea that the start determines the end, so start well; others will perceive that the path of least resistance is simplicity combined with excellence. It sets the initial system expectations high and enables people to do great things, because that is the way things are done for the project.

When considering changes to the design of a user interface, remember that users will find a certain way to accomplish a task, and they will repeat that pattern endlessly to get the task complete unless there is a significantly easier way to perform it, in which case they will change.

The same is true for architecture: if you find a path to architecting systems that works, you are unlikely to change unless you find a significantly better way. Take the time to find a path to architecting that exhibits the qualities you are seeking and the rest will naturally follow. If you take this approach, the next system and the next system will also likely exhibit those same qualities. The previous architectures will act as templates for all of the work you do.

If you are unable to produce an architecture that you like, look to other architects around you for whom you have a high level of respect and emulate the work that they do. Their work can act as a template for you, and eventually the architectures that you produce will feel natural, and you can innovate with your own brand of architecture. You can look for architects inside or outside your organization. There are many architecture resources available.

The Principle of Opportunity Cost

The *Principle of Opportunity Cost* is based on the notion that resources are scarce and that every choice that is made has a direct impact both on the choices that were excluded (missed opportunity) and on the value that is not being realized by the choice that was made.

Architecture is fundamentally about weighing choices against one another and pragmatically trying to maximize the overall value of the project for the business. The choice is not only what should be, but what should not be.

By making a more tactical decision now, you may enable the business to save money and make additional investments in other promising areas. Alternatively, the exact same situation may enable the creation of critical infrastructure—a more strategic solution—which in turn will lower the cost of future projects that can leverage the new infrastructure.

As you compare the opportunity costs between multiple options for a project, consider the following:

- What is the right answer? The answer may be that all options are valid.
- Who needs to weigh in on the decision? There are likely many opinions on the matter, but who are the critical stakeholders, and how do you explain the alternatives to them in a manner that is understandable and not unduly biased?
- Have all the critical options been considered? If not, it may be opportunity lost.
- How much time do you have to evaluate the options available? My experience has been that the time frame for producing an architectural approach is very limited, and the limited time in which to come up with a single viable option, let alone multiple options, is challenging.
- Do you have a significant enough view into the product pipeline to know not only what is being requested today, but what is being considered for the next year or two? If you don't have this kind of insight into product development, your ability to evaluate some of the options for the current project will be very limited.
- Are you willing to put your reputation on the line for architectural infrastructure that may or may not reap a return on investment? What is your gut feeling? Can you sell this?
- Are you willing to say no to the business because of the technical debt that will be incurred because of the tactical approach that would need to be taken to get the project done for the price the business wants to pay?

- How will you answer when your boss's boss wants you to explain why he's heard from his peer in the NPD organization that the project costs too much? Make sure you have taken the time to vet the solutions and their costs (not just financial) informally before they are published publicly; corrections made in private don't get noticed as much.

Saving your development dollars as long as possible, avoiding speculative feature development, and keeping a low burn rate will enable the business to have more resources later once the stakeholders better understand what they want.

Within agile, there is a concept of making decisions at the last responsible moment (see the section on that principle later in this chapter). This idea applies to building what you know while looking to the future to determine what and how you can build the system in a cost-effective manner. The key is to be open to change and let the business know what the impacts of the change are.

The Principle of Single Responsibility

The *Principle of Single Responsibility* is the concept that a module or capability of the system should have only one responsibility. Keeping a service narrowly defined enables everyone who is using it (including testers) and everyone who is developing it to be well aware of what its intended purpose is.

This narrow definition also helps you name the capability correctly. If you are having a problem naming it, take the time to figure out what is wrong with the name or wrong with the definition of what it is doing. Names matter; each name should clearly state what the item does and should be intuitive. If you have to do a lot of explaining to get people onto the same page about what something does, you need to clarify it.

The Principle of Parsimony (aka Occam's Razor or KISS)

The *Principle of Parsimony* means eliminating what is unnecessary; it means defining the minimal assumptions necessary to complete something. The goal of Occam's Razor and KISS (Keep It Simple Stupid) is to reduce complexity.

The areas of relevance to software architecture are everywhere. The principle applies to the interfaces that expose our software to users, the services that reveal the capabilities of the system, the data structures that represent the information our system manages and maintains, and the workflows that orchestrate a series of complex tasks.

As we add features and capabilities to our architecture, we want to do it in a manner that promotes essential elegance, ease of understanding, and the usability and maintainability of the system being produced. The keyword here is *essential*; it doesn't mean eliminating the hard problem or a key differentiator of a capability, it simply means removing the clutter.

A good indication of the level of complexity is whether or not you can explain the item of interest in just a few minutes. If you can't, take the time to look at what can be removed or what doesn't belong without removing the value of what is being developed.

From a product development point of view, the minimum viable product serves as another variant of Occam's Razor. The goal here is to focus on the minimal set of essential features that are necessary to complete the system. Taking this approach will speed development, minimize development costs, reduce time to market, and enable quicker feedback from users.

The Lean Startup has refined the process around the minimum viable product. It utilizes quick iterations with customer feedback to help learn what is essential and to steer the evolution of the minimum viable product.

The Principle of Last Responsible Moment (aka Cost of Delay)

The *Principle of Last Responsible Moment* means waiting to make a decision until you need to. In general, early and potentially uninformed decisions have the potential to hurt you far worse than waiting to make a decision later. By waiting, you have the ability to allow the problem to more fully reveal itself and have a better sense of all the dependencies and risks involved.

The goal is not to wait indefinitely and cause delays in the project implementation and missed shipped dates, but rather to wait to narrow the options until you are better informed. The key is to weigh the cost of delaying the decision. That is, if you wait, what are the impacts, costs, and risks involved?

One of the most effective ways to mitigate these risks and to help weigh alternatives is to engage in prototyping and proofs of concept. Taking the time to jump in and prototype or POC key areas of risk associated with the various alternatives can help give you the insights needed to ensure that when the last (sometimes referred to as the most) responsible moment arrives, you are able to make an informed decision.

The Principle of Last Responsible Moment can be used throughout the life cycle of a project to help manage micro-level decisions, to enable the business to have better visibility into what the real options are, and to help stakeholders visualize what they are really asking for.

The Principle of Feedback

The *Principle of Feedback* means making decisions about what to do next using feedback loops to help provide the navigation structure for the decisions. The Principle of Feedback is demonstrated in many different areas:

- **Agile and Lean development** (the evolutionary development of software through small incremental development with direct user feedback to guide the overall solution)
- **Lehman's Sixth Law** (guiding continuous change or system evolution through feedback systems)
- **Quality-of-service monitoring** (measuring key metrics to ensure SLAs and system performance)
- **System optimization** (measuring and visualizing the key performance aspects of the system to ensure that the right areas are being optimized; using conjecture in this area usually leads to solutions that are not effective)
- **User interface design** (directing the attention of the users through visual elements such as contrast and proximity)
- **Usability testing** (observing and measuring how users navigate and react to your system)

The key to developing systems that are able to evolve to meet the ever-changing needs of customers is to employ the Principle of Feedback.

ARCHITECTURAL CONCERNS

Architectural principles give us a means of evaluating decisions to validate that they are in line with our overall goals for the project and for the technology organization. Architectural concerns are different perspectives of the system often referred to as the "-ilities." These concerns enable us to consider very narrow dimensions that are typically nonfunctional elements of the system but are critical for the system to behave properly.

Availability

Availability is the notion of how available your system needs to be or conversely how much downtime your business is willing to accept. The answer is often directly related to how much revenue or expense impact there will be if the system is down for some period of time or to what the reputational impact of the system not being available is.

It is not uncommon for the business to initially say it wants 100% uptime; more uptime sounds like a good idea, so why not have a lot of it? This is usually the case until the stakeholders begin to understand the costs associated with having a truly 100% uptime requirement. There are always situations that will force some level of downtime, whether due to maintenance or some form of system failure. The key questions are:

- What amount of time is the business willing to accept for the services to be unavailable?
- How much is the business willing to spend to meet its service availability requirements?
- Do you have or does your hosting provider have the operational staff to support the service availability requirements you are seeking?
- Do you have or does your hosting provider have the operational tools and monitoring in place to detect service unavailability?
- When the service is determined to be unavailable:
  - What are the processes and procedures to begin a recovery process?
  - Are these processes automated, manual, or a mix of the two?
  - How much time does the person responsible for a manual recovery process have to get the job done?
  - What are the validation steps that are required once the service has been restored?
  - What are the notification and auditing requirements for when an availability issue arises?
  - Is root-cause analysis required for determining what the root issue was?
  - Are you required to have a mitigation plan to avoid the issue in the future?
- How quickly can you recover from downtimes?
- What mechanisms can you put in place to mitigate a lack of service availability?
- What types of problems are you trying to protect yourself from?
  - **Storage full.** On the surface this one seems silly, but I have seen systems become unavailable due to storage becoming full. The

question here is what processes need to be in place to prevent this from occurring. It could be something as simple as monitoring storage full percentages in conjunction with knowing the answers to these questions:

- How fast does the storage fill up?
- Who needs to receive an alert in order to resolve the situation?
- How long does it take to expand or replace the storage (does it need to be ordered, is there additional storage on standby that simply needs to be allocated and made available)?
- Does the data on storage lose value with age? Are these log files that are okay to purge within a specified period of time?

- **Storage failures.** These could potentially be handled by something as simple as ensuring that this storage is replicated to a separate storage device.
- **Server failures.** These may be able to be mitigated by clustering servers or by load balancing servers. In either case, you basically have a redundant server or servers that can do the equivalent job if the other server is not available.
- **Maintenance windows.** These could be handled by simply having a scheduled system outage or a failure over to other hardware.
- **Power outages.** These can be dealt with by having backup power whether through battery or power generation. The big question is how long you can make this last in a real emergency.
- **Site outages.** If the site where your servers are hosted goes out of commission, what do you do? Do you have a second or third site that is significantly far away that can act as a backup site? How does this backup site stay in sync? How much data loss are you willing to tolerate if not all of the data was synchronized in time?
- **Site loss.** Is having a complete site loss acceptable? It might be extremely rare, but what is the impact to the business? Do you have another site that can be quickly or dynamically switched to?
- **Software compatibility issues.** Do you have lower environments that can be used to test and verify software compatibility?

- Are you contractually obligated to provide a certain level of availability? Be cautious about what you allow the business to specify as an availability requirement and imposing any financial penalties for missed SLAs until you have had an opportunity to fully understand what it will take to meet those obligations. It may cost the business significantly more than it is willing to invest.

Scalability

Scalability enables a system to gracefully respond to the demands that are placed upon it. These can range from storage I/O, to database access, to CPU utilization, to memory utilization, to app server farms, to network utilization. The nature of the application determines what will get stressed out. It is not uncommon to fix one scalability issue only to have another hiding behind it.

The challenge is to understand the nature of the demand that will be placed on the system. It has been my experience that most people incorrectly predict what areas of the system to optimize without testing and detailed monitoring in place to validate the system behaviors that are observed.

When you are first designing the system, you need to determine if you are planning to scale up (buy bigger hardware) or scale out (have multiple sets of hardware that can respond to the same requests). Generally speaking, a scale-out approach is more cost-effective. It will allow you to start out small and add system resources as the demand for the system's capabilities increase over time.

There are a variety of areas to take into consideration when you are working toward building a system that is capable of scaling to your product's needs:

- How many users (online and batch) will concurrently access the system?
- How much data will the system be able to manage?
- How many read/write operations per second does the data store need to handle?
- What is the peak concurrent access to the system?
- How much data can be cached to minimize the depth within the system that the requests need to travel before being responded to? Can data be cached outside the system in a content distribution network (CDN) to help keep traffic away from the site? Consider if the content has a significant hit rate (is it worth caching)?
- Is data replication required for the system? How long is it acceptable for the data synchronization to take place?
- How much logging and eventing are required for the system to support the operational needs of the system for immediate as well as future system performance analysis?
- Are there areas of data contention?
- Are there CPU-intensive operations?

- Are there long-running operations?
- How do you plan to measure usage of the system?
- Do you plan to meter services to throttle excessive usage?
- Do you have the ability to auto-provision additional servers to meet demand?
- Can you schedule batch operations to occur at nonpeak times?

Anytime a system resource exceeds 80% utilization, you need to consider some kind of operational warning to give the operations team a chance to find ways to remedy the situation. If it goes beyond 90% utilization, a more urgent notification needs to be sent to the operations team. Ideally, key system resources and error rates are monitored over time and presented in a graphical manner to both the operations team as well as key stakeholders. This gives everyone a chance to keep track of system health and to respond accordingly.

The key to scalability is to test and validate that your assumptions about the system's behavior are correct. When you are testing, you want to drive the system past its limits to find out where the breaking points are and to find out how the system fails under load. If it does not fail gracefully, look for ways to protect the system.

Extensibility

Extensibility enables a system to be easily added to or changed. From a business perspective, the ability to add to, modify, or change certain aspects of a system quickly and easily can be a critical factor in the ability to scale revenue associated with the system.

Extensibility can include items such as

- Handling deployments to diverse geographic locations
- Enabling alternative styling and branding of the user interface
- Enabling the user interface to be adjusted according to client needs
- Modifying or customizing system capabilities/functionality

The key to handling extensibility is to listen closely to the business early on during the ideation phases and actively listen for areas where the business may want to be able to alter the behavior of the application to address customer needs. Typically, a variety of design patterns can be employed to enable the changes in system behavior or presentation without significantly affecting the architecture or incurring heavy development costs when the requests for change come from the business.

Repeatability

Repeatability is the ability of a system to behave in a consistent manner. This consistency of interaction between the user and the system is what builds trust. It is not uncommon for "new and improved" systems to fail to gain adoption in the user community because this trust factor is broken.

Features that on the surface appear to be less than ideal and consequently appear to be great candidates for change to the system designers may in fact have gained widespread adoption in the user community, and even though they are not perfect, their flawed state is highly useful and "loved" by the users, who are not seeking change.

The notion of repeatability within a system is paramount for setting user expectations.

Compatibility

Compatibility is the ability to introduce nonbreaking changes into the system or, minimally, a grace period when old functionality is still available while the new or changed capability is rolled out and being adopted.

Compatibility can often be achieved by supporting versioned APIs or historical versions of a system. Eventually these older versions can be deprecated or dropped from support. Providing compatibility with the past allows your user base to find a convenient time to make the required changes within their systems to upgrade to the new versions.

From an architecture perspective, laying changes out in a roadmap can inform your user community of coming changes and allow them to prepare and plan for the changes in their upcoming releases.

This level of transparency with your user base can go a long way toward establishing trust and cultivating long-term relationships. Users will know that their investments will not be quickly thrown out the window if they choose to partner with you and have guarantees of long-term support.

Sustainability

Sustainability is the ability to keep the architecture relevant through change without causing unintended entropy within the system. It goes beyond maintainability in that the intent is to enable continued growth and evolution, not just prevent a degradation of current capabilities.

Sustainability is best achieved by maintaining a proper separation of concerns and not allowing a slow entanglement of capabilities that eventually lead to a large mud ball. Enabling these changes through configuration, inversion of control, and independent deployment of new capabilities leads toward a sustainable system.

Sustainability is essential to the long-term health of the business and helps maximize the return on investment made in technology.

Security, Disaster Recovery, Business Continuity, and Open-Source Licensing

For more information on these topics, see Chapter 8, "Governance."

Third-Party Integration

As you consider integrating with third-party solutions, you need to look closely at their solutions with respect to the architectural concerns discussed previously. Your customers will expect the same level of service from third parties as they do from the rest of your offerings.

Your business partners may be extremely excited by the possibility of adding a new capability to their portfolio and are likely not to be focused on the architectural concerns; they just expect everything to work out. Make sure you have an opportunity to see the contracts with the third-party providers before they are signed to ensure that the appropriate language is in place to enable everyone's success.

ARCHITECTURAL COMMUNICATION

The architectural principles and architectural concerns help guide architects in the development and evolution of an architecture, but it is through active communication that the architecture comes to life.

This communication often takes place as whiteboarding sessions, where the architecture is diagrammed and key aspects of the architecture are discussed. Developing a set of common architectural artifacts can serve as a long-term communication tool for the organization.

Generally speaking, the most effective way to communicate architecture is through pictures and diagrams. There are a variety of different vantage points from which to view the architecture. Typically, these vantage points are from the perspective of key consumers of the architecture.

Domain Model

The *domain model* is usually developed first in the ideation and discovery phases of a project when it is critical to discover the language of the end users, that is, the nouns they use to describe things and the verbs they use to describe the actions related to the nouns. The model can form the basis of a common language with which to talk to customers, new product development, marketing, sales, and technology. Using the "native" language of the domain can help form natural relationships and cardinality; various parts of the system will naturally work together even if the design teams of the different parts of the system don't work that closely together.

Process Diagram

A *process diagram* is used to show the flow of work. It can represent many different aspects of the system that is being developed. A process diagram typically shows the key steps that users take to do their work and their interactions with the system. It gives a sense of where key decision points are within the flow as well as what parts of the work will be automated (controlled by the system) and what parts of the work will be performed outside the system, whether manually or by another system.

Process diagrams can also be used to lay out

- How builds and deployments will work
- How migrations from legacy systems to new systems will occur
- How batch workflows will work and how error conditions will be handled

Key considerations for process flows include the following:

- Where does the process begin?
- What are the prerequisites for the process to begin? For each step to occur? For the process to be considered complete?
- What are the postconditions that need to be considered?
- What are the critical decisions within the flow that will require different actions based on the outcome of each decision?

- How will error conditions and exceptions be handled?
- What are the transitions of work between various actors and roles?
- What subprocess flows need to be created for a deeper level of understanding?

The type of diagram shown in Figure 7.2 may not be produced by the architect, but it is essential to understanding what the user is attempting to accomplish when using the system. If a business analyst is not available to create one, taking the time to produce some basic process flow diagrams can significantly improve your and the project team's understanding of what needs to be built.

From an architecture perspective, showing the basic flows of processes can help you understand the sequencing that needs to occur within the solution. Showing decision points and alternative flows can also help inform key aspects of the workflow.

Context Diagram

A *context diagram* is used to help define the boundaries of the system. It can help with scope discussions to give a visualization of what areas the system will or will not be responsible for managing. Establishing these boundaries early on can help avoid misunderstandings and help clarify the intent of what you are trying to accomplish.

During the life span of the context diagram, the boundaries that define what is in and out of scope may change, but the key outcome is to get everyone on the same page. The diagram may change from release to release as the capabilities of the system expand.

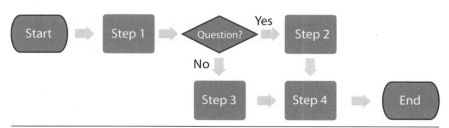

Figure 7.2 Basic process diagram

User Interface Mock-ups

User interface mock-ups, even if they are wrong, are extremely important for understanding what the business is looking for. Requirements documents, epic-level user stories, and all other textual forms of specifications for what the business desires to be built typically fail to adequately convey the nuances of what is being requested.

The form of the mock-up doesn't matter so much; it could be wireframes, it could be sample HTML pages, it could be diagrams on a napkin. The key is to begin expressing visually what is desired. The visualizations will spark significantly deeper conversations and reveal nonverbalized dependencies between capabilities and potentially with other systems that were not stated in the textual descriptions.

Early on, before the project is formed, not all of the details are going to be known or fully understood, and they shouldn't be. The goal is to find out the direction in which the business wants to go and approximately the types of capabilities that are desired. By the time the project completes, the set of capabilities desired is likely to have changed as the business learns more about what it actually wants—as the business people go out and interact with customers and get feedback on the potential direction things are heading.

The business will want to modify its course to align better with customer expectations. This is a great thing, except that it may feel as if you are following a rabbit trail. Changes earlier in the project are easier to accommodate, whereas after a significant portion of the system has been built, changing directions can become expensive.

Logical Architecture Diagram

The *logical architecture diagram* describes the key components of the system. A typical diagram takes a separation-of-concerns approach where there is a section relating to the user interface, a section for the core system capabilities (this is where most of the business rules exist), a section for the persistence layer (your data storage mechanism), and a section for any crosscutting concerns such as security, logging, reporting, and so on.

This diagram typically has a very functional bent to it (see Figure 7.3).

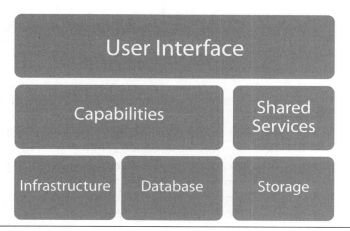

Figure 7.3 Logical architecture diagram

A logical architecture diagram can take many forms. The intent is to show key logical groupings of the architecture and show some of the separation of concerns. The logical architecture can also guide the planned implementation, including the various design patterns that may be considered.

Executive Overview Diagram

An *executive overview diagram*, a high-level conceptual diagram for executive stakeholders, should basically have five boxes or fewer. You need to significantly raise the level of abstraction for the system under consideration. You should include basic descriptions of the boxes and answers to a few questions that you expect to be asked, such as what other alternatives were considered. The executives need to be able to understand the diagram in less than two minutes; it needs to be intuitive, and they will naturally dive into whatever areas of detail they sense are not solid or have issues.

Be prepared for them to dive in two to four layers deeper than what is shown at the highest level. Be prepared for them to find the area of vagueness where all the details have not been figured out; they have a natural instinct for finding these areas.

Hardware Environments Diagram

The *hardware environments diagram* is essential for interacting with the data center folks. These diagrams will help answer the following questions:

- What environments will the project support?
  - Sandbox (aka development lab)
  - Development (aka continuous integration)
  - Quality assurance
  - Demo
  - User acceptance testing (QED), typically sized near production
  - Production
- Who has ownership of each environment—development group, data center operations, networking, database admins?
- How much of each type of hardware is needed? Will this be physical hardware, virtual hardware, or cloud-based hardware?
- What is the configuration of each type of hardware? Are the servers clustered? If so, how? What servers need access to which storage? How much internal storage is required? How much network-attached storage (NAS) is required? What operating system is required? What type of licensing is required?
- What purpose does each type of hardware serve? Are the servers app servers? Database servers? Network switches? NAS filers?
- What are the delivery time frames of each type of environment?
- For each type of hardware and environment, what groups are to be notified when issues arise or maintenance is required?
- What naming conventions will be specified for the hardware?
- What networks do the servers need to be connected to?

Sometimes to aid in the understanding of the hardware environments you are trying to stand up, taking the time to name the pattern of the hardware configuration can make the capital purchasing much simpler. People who are reviewing the purchase will recognize the pattern name and quickly understand the approximate cost and operational needs of the request. This can make reviews of the purchase go much more quickly and require less documentation and explanation to get the purchase approved.

Risks, Assumptions, Issues, and Dependencies (RAID)

One of the key areas of documentation for an architect to produce is the risks, assumptions, issues, and dependencies (RAID) associated with a project (see Figure 7.4).

RAID is an effective tool for ensuring coverage of key executive concerns and those of a wider audience.

Later on, when the project is midway through execution and something goes horribly wrong, the architect is usually one of the first people called

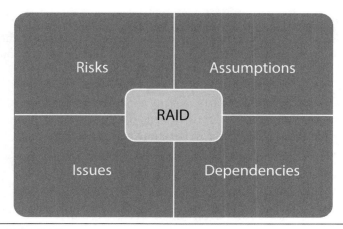

Figure 7.4 RAID

in to help determine why this occurred and why the problem wasn't recognized earlier. This usually invites executives to get involved. The best time to prepare for this is when the project is getting started. This is the time to clearly call out the risks, assumptions, issues, and dependencies.

Risks

Risks are the events that have a reasonable likelihood of occurring and may have a significant impact on the architecture or success of the project. When considering the architectural risks, consider the following:

- What risks may cause the project to be delayed or not delivered?
- Are there software development skills that are not currently employed in your areas?
- Are new technologies required for the project that your company or area is not familiar with?
- Are there specific contracting needs for the project?
- Are there scaling needs that the business is not willing to pay for?
- Are there lower environment needs that will not be fulfilled?
- Are there testing efforts that will not be funded?
- Are significant business risks being introduced?

Documenting risks lets stakeholders know the key areas of uncertainty that may derail a project. It allows them to develop risk mitigation plans in the event that a risk becomes a reality. It also serves as a mechanism of full disclosure and transparency that help build trust.

Assumptions

Assumptions are the prerequisites for your architecture. They are the things you believe to be completed or true. As you build and document your set of architectural assumptions, consider the following:

- What assumptions are you making about the project?
- Are you assuming that
  - You can successfully develop some new capability?
  - Certain groups will do particular parts of the work?
  - Certain refactoring will occur within an existing system?
  - Certain integrations will be required or will explicitly not be supported?
  - Some research and development needs to occur?

Your documented assumptions will help level-set people's thinking about the architecture and will serve as an issue-resolution mechanism later on when problems arise.

Issues

Issues are the outstanding questions that have not been resolved. These include the following:

- What areas of the architecture have not been finalized?
- Are there areas of technology that have not been spiked, contain areas of concern, or have known problems?
- Are there contractual issues in play?
- Has a key resource recently moved to another part of the company?
- Is the deadline for delivery overly aggressive?

It is critical to identify issues in your architectural documentation. Doing so will give those who are working on a project a sense of what areas of the architecture have not been resolved and may still need to be dealt with.

Dependencies

Dependencies are the items, tasks, or projects that your architecture is dependent upon or that are dependent on your architecture. As you identify your architectural dependencies, consider the following:

- What projects are you dependent on for your project to complete? If you call out a dependency like this, you may want to consider adding the cost of the portion of the project you are dependent on to your estimate. It is not uncommon for dependent projects to be late, to not complete the feature that you need, or to change the feature that you need in a manner that renders it useless. The alternative solution that you provide may be a tactical solution, but it will be financed and you will have the opportunity to complete on time instead of waiting or being stuck with nowhere to go.

- What licensing agreements are you dependent on to provide needed functionality?
- What purchases or other procurements are needed?
- What business arrangements are needed?
- What hardware needs to be purchased or operationalized?
- What infrastructural software needs to be operationalized?
- Is software integration with specific tools or services required?

Basically, dependencies are anything that you need that will block you from delivering the project if you don't have them.

Dependencies need to be very clearly stated and made visible to the executive staff. This will help them manage the dependencies for you on the outside chance that the dependencies get off track. They may be able to apply the necessary influence to enable your dependencies to deliver. After all, it will be in your management's best interest to make sure your dependencies deliver and your project delivers as promised.

BRINGING IT ALL TOGETHER

Following the architectural principles, dealing with architectural concerns, and developing effective architectural artifacts can help you deliver solid architectures for the business.

Remember
Abstractions live longer than details.

Don't let one vantage point drive you to an extreme. These are not laws; they are for guidance. For every rule there are conditions that justify breaking it.

SUMMARY

The road to architectural perspective begins with

- Knowing and understanding architectural principles
- Knowing and understanding key areas of architectural concern
- Creating architectural artifacts to bring clarity to what is being created

Having an architectural perspective on a project can result in a broad understanding of it. It can help raise and clarify key risks, assumptions, issues, and dependencies to help enable a smoothly running project where both the business and technology have a common understanding of what is being produced.

REFERENCES

Bass, Len, Paul Clements, and Rick Kazman. 2012. *Software Architecture in Practice, Third Edition*. Addison-Wesley.

Clements, Paul, Felix Bachmann, Len Bass, David Garlan, James Ivers, Reed Little, Paulo Merson, Robert Nord, and Judith Stafford. 2011. *Documenting Software Architectures: Views and Beyond, Second Edition*. Addison-Wesley.

Janert, Philipp K. 2013. *Feedback Control for Computer Systems: Introducing Control Theory to Enterprise Programmers*. O'Reilly Media.

Poppendieck, Mary, and Tom Poppendieck. 2003. *Lean Software Development: An Agile Toolkit*. Addison-Wesley.

Reinertsen, Donald. 2012. *The Principles of Product Development Flow: Second Generation Lean Product Development*. Celeritas Publishing.

Rozanski, Nick, and Eóin Woods. 2011. *Software Systems Architecture: Working with Stakeholders Using Viewpoints and Perspectives, Second Edition*. Addison-Wesley.

Chapter 8

GOVERNANCE

"Architecture is the reaching out for the truth."

—Louis Kahn

"In any architecture, there is an equity between the pragmatic function and the symbolic function."

—Michael Graves

"As a designer, the mission with which we have been charged is simple: providing space at the right cost."

—Harry von Zell

Have you ever looked across the business and observed duplicate implementations of the same software, and thought to yourself, "How in the world could this happen? Why aren't they sharing the implementation?"

On further investigation, you realize that not only did both groups believe they acted in the best interests of the company, but neither group knew of the other's implementation.

Another variation of this situation is when the business has bought multiple companies that actually do the same thing. You think you are Alice in Wonderland and the world has turned upside down.

In the world of architecture, the architect serves as a conduit to the business to help make sound business decisions with respect to business processes, technology, and integration. The ability of architects to recognize challenging situations, to provide alternative low-cost solutions, and to recognize leverage opportunities makes them highly valued from a business perspective.

This chapter unveils one of the essential skills needed by a software architect: the ability to provide governance for software projects and acquisitions.

GOVERNANCE DEFINED

Governance is the oversight of projects and platforms that provides the boundaries for design and development. These boundaries are not absolute but are reasonable guidelines to help mitigate risks, reduce costs, and promote leverage for the business.

Governance is best chartered with the senior leadership within your organization. This will help build the support that is needed from them to successfully implement a governance program. As the program progresses, standards that are crafted toward your organization will arise from good governance.

GOVERNANCE PRINCIPLES

Governance principles are principles to help enable proper oversight of your projects and platforms. They should be adhered to and carefully considered when projects are about to begin and when they are approaching major releases.

Avoid Vendor Lock-in

Vendor lock-in occurs when you consistently choose a single vendor for a particular solution. On the surface, this seems like a good idea:

- You can gain broad standardization.
- You can initially obtain great pricing discounts.
- You can gain broad operational knowledge.
- You can quickly integrate due to broad technical knowledge and know-how.

The list goes on and on, especially if you listen to the sales representatives of some vendors.

However, once vendors are tightly integrated into your business and operations, they have you over a barrel, especially if the cost to swap them out is high. This is the point where vendors begin increasing the price for their products dramatically. You have the sense that if you were a fish, the hook would be set deep and it's going to be painful to get away.

As you look across the set of projects, ensure that there is an awareness of alternative options for products and services when they are available; standardization is great, but vendor lock-in can be disruptive to your cost structure (see Figure 8.1).

Figure 8.1 Avoid vendor lock-in—it's expensive to exit.

Effective vendor management is critical because vendor lock-in can destroy a business case. Have a plan for how to deal with potential vendor lock-in, execute the plan, and have an exit strategy. This requires some discretion. Sometimes leveraging one vendor can provide significant cost savings. In these circumstances, you always need to remain agile. Mature procurement practices can help monitor and control this if you have a technology procurement area whose charter is to support vendor management.

Encourage Open-Source Usage

Open-source tools offer excellent software at great prices—typically free. The key challenges for open-source software typically include

- **Ensuring that the open-source licensing model does not impact your intellectual property or your ability to charge customers for the products that you create.** Apache licensing is usually a very safe option. Other licenses should be evaluated by your lawyers; they can vet the impacts related to licensing and any potential issues with using multiple open-source software tools that have different licensing models. Ideally, if you can create and maintain a list of "approved" licensing models, you can keep the usage approval process to a minimum.

- **Ensuring that the open-source community support is active.** If the open-source tool is not actively supported by its community, it will atrophy in usage and bugs will likely not get fixed. You still have the option of contributing work to fix defects that impact you. You need to ensure that you are not legally liable for negative impacts related to the coding changes made by employees at your firm. This is a good area for your legal counsel to validate.
- **Ensuring that your usage of the open-source software complies with the license associated with the tool.**
- **Ensuring that you actively keep track of the open-source tools that you are leveraging.** If there turn out to be critical issues or litigation related to the open-source software, you want to know the areas of your business that are likely to be impacted or may need immediate attention. There are tools that you can leverage that will scan your software and report on which open-source tools are in use and flag the ones that may be problematic.
- **Ensuring that you actively keep track of the open-source issues and bug lists.** For instance, if there is a significant security hole related to some open-source software, you want to be aware of it quickly so you can react appropriately.

Be aware of the support costs related to open source and understand your ability to influence the priority of development or a bug fix by the development community. This potential lack of an SLA could put you in a bad position with your customers if you are not able to deal with an issue in a timely manner.

Your open-source usage should be incorporated into your acquisition, procurement, and third-party integration processes. The use of open source can be an effective tool in negotiating with vendors whose pricing is higher than desired.

In general, open-source tools are a great way to reduce the cost structure of your products and often are better supported and more open about issues than commercially available tools.

Minimize the Cost of Disruption (aka Enable Business Continuity Planning and Disaster Recovery)

Minimizing the cost of disruption means focusing on the ability to recover from a disaster or unplanned event and resume normal business operations in a relatively short amount of time. Disasters are rare, but they do happen, and if you are not prepared they can be devastating to your products and potentially lethal to your business. Consider what would happen if

- The data center where your servers are located floods, and all the servers are destroyed
- Your primary database server that houses your business-critical data has a complete disk subsystem failure
- The building where all of your employees work is destroyed by an earthquake during nonworking hours

These are all relatively unlikely events, but they can happen. What preparations have you made to ensure that your business will continue to operate with minimal disruptions after an event such as these has occurred?

When a business or product is small and first starting out, disaster recovery may not be on the top of the list of areas to focus on. However, by the time the business has grown and the product is successful, implementing disaster recovery mechanisms can be an expensive proposition.

If your business operates with servers in a data center, have you considered

- Storing copies of your data off-site?
- Having warm site/hot site redundancy?
- Having a passive secondary or alternative active set of servers that is geographically separate from the primary site?
- Having data replication plans in place to support the secondary site?
- Having the operational plans and support in place to handle switching the secondary site to become the primary site?
- Having other geographic locations for your business?
- Creating a disaster recovery plan and having it aligned with the business's larger continuity plan? The two need to be in sync.
- Rehearsing the disaster recovery plan? You do not want to find a hole in the plan when it needs to be used; it is much better to find the hole during a drill.

There should also be written business continuity plans (BCPs) in place so everyone knows his or her responsibility if and when a disaster occurs. This plan should include not only the services you are directly responsible for, but also integrations with your third-party providers. Holding tabletop exercises and talking and working through simulated disasters with the crisis management group can be a great way to practice, prepare, and bring life to your business continuity plans.

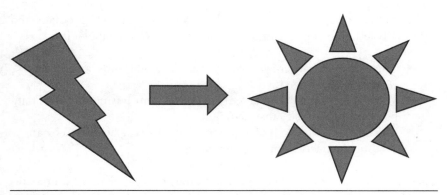

Figure 8.2   Proper disaster recovery can transform a disaster into simply an inconvenience.

These types of plans will help ensure that your business is alive and well even when disaster strikes (see Figure 8.2).

Enable Loose Coupling between Business Units

Enabling loose coupling between business units is essential for the continued successful operation of both units.

The common areas of concern when two business units integrate systems include

- **Managing to two different operational models.** Are the operational models of both business units known and documented? Is everyone aware of the differences and potential impacts of these differences? For instance, when is it okay to take a system outage or have the system perform some maintenance activity?
- **Managing to two different customer usage cycles.** Different business units often have different important times of the year, which typically leads to decisions that are based on assumptions that are relevant to the party that is making the decision. For instance, is everyone aware of when
  - A critical system demo is occurring for a major contract?
  - A major conference for the business unit is occurring?
  - The busiest day, week, or month for the business unit's systems is?
- **Managing issue escalation procedures across two business units in a timely fashion.**
- **Managing to two possibly different disaster recovery approaches and business continuity plans.**

The coupling that occurs between two business units needs to be well documented and well communicated to both organizations. The coupling needs to be extremely loose to enable both parties to flex as needed without dramatically impacting the other organization. Think of the 80/20 rule: too many exceptions will dilute the operational model and create complexity.

A tight integration between the two could end up spelling disaster for both organizations instead of just being an issue for one organization. For example, instead of creating a multitenant architecture with many operational exceptions for each tenant, consider creating separate services using shared library components.

Leverage Common Capabilities

Leveraging common capabilities, especially in the form of a platform, is a dramatic way for multiple applications and potentially multiple business units to compound the value of the investment in building the application or platform.

Typically, the infrastructure necessary to set up an application is one of the more expensive portions of building it. Your ability to leverage and reuse the work that was done can dramatically improve the ROI of future applications, assuming there are in fact leverage opportunities.

The areas of challenge for leveraging common capabilities are

- **Adjusting the requirements of the application to meet the capabilities of the leveraged system.** The two rarely line up exactly. The key questions are the following:
  - Is it acceptable from a product perspective to make the compromises necessary to leverage the capability?
  - Is it worth the investment necessary to change the leveraged code and to do it in a fashion that is acceptable to all other parties that are leveraging the same capability?
  - Is it possible to place feature access controls around the change that is needed by the requesting business unit to prevent changes to the other partners?
  - Is it possible to dynamically load code that the requesting business unit needs and maintain independent operations of the leveraged system?
- **Aligning the operational aspects of both business units to enable smooth, uninterrupted customer experiences.**

- **Ensuring that the security, confidentiality, regulatory, and privacy concerns of both systems are maintained when the systems are integrated.**

Leveraging common capabilities between systems is a huge strategic advantage for a company when the systems are built correctly and the requirements of the two systems line up.

For example, service-based organizations may be able to leverage a common private cloud and create communities to consolidate capabilities and reduce costs based on their requirements, including regulatory.

Alternatively, leveraging capabilities between systems for the sake of leverage when the two systems' requirements do not line up is a recipe for disaster. It will likely negatively impact both organizations and result in a negative user experience with both systems.

As always, architecture is about making pragmatic decisions. Principles and rules are guidelines for behavior, not commandments that have no exceptions. You are being paid to think, not blindly follow previous decisions or the hottest trend flowing through the industry.

Common capabilities should always be evaluated in the context of the business. Based on the outcome of the evaluation, an informed business decision can be made.

Ensure Regulatory Compliance

Regulatory compliance is essential for certain lines of business. Areas such as health care, insurance, aviation, financial services, and many others are closely regulated by governments. The challenge for many of these industries is that there are regulations at the federal level, state level, and potentially the local level. Be aware of the basics behind

- PCI DSS (credit card compliance)
- SOX (corporate responsibility compliance)
- FISMA (federal agency security controls compliance)
- NERC (compliance related to power generation and distribution)
- FedRAMP (federal security related to cloud compliance)
- HIPAA (health-care-related compliance)
- DIACAP (Department of Defense–related compliance)

Having someone within the business who can track the appropriate regulatory requirements for your system and the jurisdictions with which it needs to be compliant is critical. The challenge for many of these is that the person tracking the laws and regulations may not be technically oriented, which can make tracking and interpretation challenging.

From an architectural governance perspective, the key is to know who the person or department responsible for compliance is and work with that person closely to establish a common vocabulary that can be used to communicate.

Before attempting compliance, make sure you understand the requirements to be in compliance; it may be a longer, more complicated, and more expensive road than you first think. Consider developing a risk matrix, and ensure that you understand the frequency of assessment for compliance; it may have to be done annually.

The key to most regulatory compliance efforts is to demonstrate due diligence. Being out of compliance may not be bad if it is documented and there is a roadmap to achieving compliance.

Staying on top of regulatory changes and doing so in a timely fashion is critical for the business and for the customers who use your software.

Ensure Security

Security is a multidimensional problem. It is complex and if implemented incorrectly has the ability to render your software nearly worthless if your user community doesn't trust your system.

Security has many elements to it. These include

- Secure authentication and authorization (see the section on identity and access management later in the chapter)
- Data classification and security
- Sequestration
- Secure Synchronous Data Link Control (SDLC)
- Privacy
- Physical and programmatic access
- Provisioning and timely deprovisioning (this is often a huge gap in most organizations)
- Geographic location of servers and data

From a governance perspective, each of these areas has its own set of concerns. Ensuring that the threats associated with these areas are properly addressed is critical for the business, especially in the context of how the system is being used.

Increasingly customers' IT groups are auditing applications for adherence to security requirements. These can be costly to implement, especially for legacy systems. For this reason, make security a priority in new development and consider how to cost-effectively achieve compliance with older systems. This is becoming a larger part of the architecture process.

The Principle of Least Privilege (aka the Principle of Least Authority)

The *Principle of Least Privilege* means giving out the absolute minimum security rights to accomplish a task or a set of tasks. By limiting what users have access to, you limit the chances that they will have access to something they are not supposed to have access to, and you may prevent a "dangerous" operation from accidentally occurring.

Creating a flexible and effective security system is tricky, especially if the users can have multiple roles and individual security rights can be added and revoked. If you get complex security requirements from the business, work to simplify the model.

The more complex it is, the more likely it is that there are holes in the system and the more difficult it will be to test the software to ensure that it is working correctly.

Keep it simple, limit users' access to what is necessary, and protect operations that have broad impacts.

Seek Unified Identity and Access Management

Identity and access management (IAM) is the ability to manage the identity of users and their associated access to systems. Ideally, you would create/leverage a single unified identity and access management system to help ensure that access to your systems is managed well and to provide a simpler user experience for those who are accessing your systems. This can be a challenging problem to solve if you are dealing with a variety of legacy systems that have approached the problem differently.

There are several key elements to unified identity and access management:

- **Single sign-on (SSO).** This is the ability to sign on once and access multiple systems based on this action.
- **Multifactor/-level authentication.** This is the ability to have more than one authentication mechanism to validate the identity of the user.
- **Identity interchange.** This is the ability to exchange identity information between two identity providers with standards such as SAML.
- **User provisioning and deprovisioning.** This is the ability to create, manage, and deactivate user accounts and their associated entitlements.
- **User activity compliance.** This is the ability to log, audit, and report on a user's activities to validate them and perform root-cause analysis for compliance purposes.
- **Web access management.** This is the ability to provide IAM for web applications.

Seek Data Portability (aka Avoid Data Lock-in)

As you leverage systems in which you do not control the persistence of the data, you need to be aware of potential data lock. That means that the raw information that resides within the system is not accessible or is not easily accessible. Either ensure that the data is available to you contractually, or ensure that there are APIs or services that allow you to easily export your data so that if you choose to move it to another system, it is a relatively straightforward process.

Seek Integration and Automation

As you develop systems, you want your governance to be integrated into the normal development process. Ideally, the governance will be adopted and maintained by the development team. To the degree possible, you want to automate the governance checking.

AREAS OF GOVERNANCE

For an architect, a variety of areas require some level of governance or oversight (see Figure 8.3).

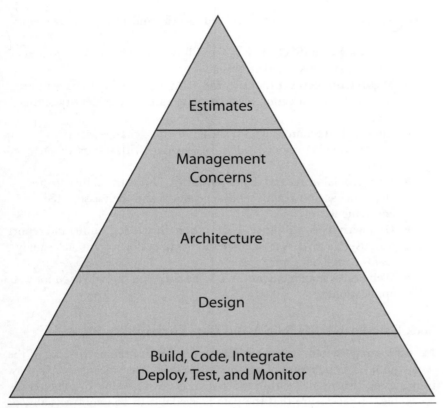

Figure 8.3 Governance areas

Estimates

Estimates produced by the technology teams and operational teams, whether for informational purposes or to produce a business case, need to be validated against the architectural approach that was prepared prior to handing over the estimates to the business.

Key considerations when reviewing an estimate include the following:

- Have all areas of the estimate been accounted for?
- Does the estimate align with your thoughts about what the estimate should be? If not, take the time to meet with the specific teams to

understand where there is a difference of opinion. If it is unclear, go
with the higher estimate.

- Do all optional elements of the estimate have their dependencies
  properly accounted for? If an optional element is selected, are the
  costs associated with the dependencies included?
- Are your risks, assumptions, issues, and dependencies in alignment
  with the estimating team's?
- Has the business indicated what the desired cost of the project
  would be? If the estimate is higher than the amount the business
  wants to spend, are there any alternative approaches that should
  be considered?
- Has your management had a chance to see the estimate? *Management hates surprises*—let them see the numbers before they are
  formally published.

Having a good requirements-gathering and RFI (request for information)/
RFP (request for proposal) development process will help facilitate solid
estimates.

Management Concerns

Management concerns can take many forms, such as the following:

- **Procurement governance.** This is usually overseen by a group
  within finance. The goal of procurement governance is to help
  ensure the best possible costs of a product or service, to enable
  leverage of the product or service across multiple business units, to
  prepare for potential future uses and growth, and to ensure that the
  licensing models of the product or service do not conflict with current or future business needs.
- **Portfolio management.** This is usually overseen by a project
  management office (PMO). The goal of the PMO is to manage the
  overall portfolio of projects that are being executed by an organization. They tend to oversee and manage dissemination of information around schedules, resources, financials, and certifications. The
  goal for an architect is to partner with the PMO on the management
  of projects and to ensure that the projects they are responsible for
  are successfully released.
- **Product lines.** These are usually overseen by new product development and marketing. They will determine the overall suite of projects and how they are presented to the different market segments.
  From an architecture perspective, the goal is to be supportive and

suggest ways that you might approach the products when appropriate. In the end, the business owns the products and you need to respect their wishes.

- **Finance.** Finance controls the purse strings and normally has rules around the allocation of funds and any variances to the allocated amounts. As an architect, the more you can help keep costs inside the parameters set by finance, the less executive oversight you will incur.

- **Regulatory compliance.** Regulatory compliance means ensuring that you are compliant with the regulations for the products that you produce and the environment in which they are produced. Normally, this is overseen by a compliance group, a security group, or a legal group. Your job is to make sure you know the rules or, better yet, know who knows the rules to help ensure that you are in compliance.

- **Legal compliance.** Legal compliance normally deals with areas such as patents, intellectual property, lawsuits, legal holds, and other related areas. As an architect, the best option here is to know who your legal counsel is and work with him or her on a regular basis to deal with any questions you may have. Ideally, getting a brief overview of how legal can help you will give you a sense of when you should engage an attorney.

- **IT compliance.** This is usually managed by the data center for an actual implementation and deployment of hardware. It is usually the responsibility of the architect and the business unit partner to articulate the compliance needs for a project to the data center.

Architecture

Architecture reviews can take many forms, such as the following:

- **Approach review.** This is typically done by the estimating team, including the business owners. The purpose of this review is to understand the architecture in order to create an estimate, but also to validate the business objectives against the architecture as well as the risks, assumptions, issues, and dependencies.

- **Executive review.** This is typically done by technology VPs or the CTO of the local business unit. The purpose of this review is to validate the architecture for purposes of alignment with business goals and strategy; to validate the cost of the architecture approach, including what alternatives were considered and either approved or rejected; and to validate the assumptions, risks, issues, and dependencies.

- **Enterprise review.** This is typically done by a member of the enterprise architecture team for larger projects or by local architects or VPs for smaller projects. The purpose of this review is to validate the architecture against the standing enterprise architecture policies that are in force.
- **Peer review.** This is typically done by members of the architecture staff from the local business unit. The purpose of this review is to validate the architecture against the business objectives of the project; to validate the approach against the standing strategic architecture goals of the local business unit; and to validate the assumptions, risks, issues, and dependencies associated with the approach being taken.
- **Development review.** This is typically done by the development team that will develop the solution for the project. The purpose of this review is to familiarize the project team with the desired architectural direction of the project.
- **Hardware review.** This is typically performed by technology staff related to the data center operations. The purpose of the review is to validate the capital request against the goals and strategy of the data center operations and to validate the amount and type of hardware being requested against the approach being taken and the expected performance characteristics of the system as a whole.

For any given project, all of these reviews are not likely to occur. The only exception is when the project is extremely large and likely has multiple architects assigned to it. The goals of the reviews are communicating to all of the key stakeholders and ensuring that there are no large gaps in the approach being taken.

Different reviewers will have different criteria of importance; learn what they are interested in and address their concerns. You will need to convince them that you have considered everything, including all reasonable alternatives.

The key is to ensure that multiple reviews occur and that they are project based. Each review acts as a filter and helps improve the overall quality of the architecture.

Design

Design reviews are intended to validate that the design approaches being taken by the development team are in alignment with the architectural approach for the system and that they align with the current thinking of the business owners. It is not uncommon that the business will adjust its requirements to better align with its current understanding of what the marketplace is looking for.

Design reviews can occur at any point in the project. Having one big design and associated design review up front really doesn't make sense. Designs should be reviewed closest to the moment the coding associated with the design will occur. The formality around the design review can vary based on the communication needs of the organization. It could be as simple as a whiteboarding session with the relevant team members, subject matter experts, and the business partner.

The intent is to be relevant and not clutter the thinking with gold plating or things that may be needed sometime in the future. The review needs to be focused on what is known today and what needs to be implemented within the next few iterations.

The design review will likely include some form of interface design (API), class structure, and related sequence or state machine diagrams. It will likely show how the architectural concerns such as authentication, authorization, disaster recovery, and other key areas will be handled.

The exact principles, guidelines, and standards will vary by organization to match the particular business needs of each. There are many sources of great material for this online and in other books (see the references at the end of the chapter).

Building, Coding, Integrating, Deploying, Testing, and Monitoring

Oversight of the build systems, coding, integration, deployment systems, testing, and monitoring systems for a project is really one of the chief responsibilities of an architect.

Creating and laying out guidance, principles, and rules of thumb for the development teams can help enable them to be more independent and align them more naturally to your style of thinking. For example, "Prefer configuration over coding" gives the development team an indication of the direction you want to take to handle common system changes.

I believe this is the best way to drive governance; hard, fixed rules generally do not serve you well, and most rules were meant to be broken.

For more detailed information, see Chapter 5, "Management."

GOVERNANCE AND A HEALTHY TENSION WITH AGILE

The purpose of governance is to help identify and mitigate risks, help reduce costs, and help promote leverage for the business. It is not about managing the functionality of the system; this is the responsibility of the business, and the business should be able to ask for whatever it is willing to pay for.

Governance and agile development on the surface seem to be at odds with one another. When you look at agile in more detail, you notice that it is also about mitigating risks, reducing costs, and promoting value for the business. Agile often has a reputation for being footloose and fancy-free when in reality it is trying to elicit the real requirements from the business just in time and to meet the real business demands that exist.

The key challenges for governance are to provide relevance to those who are involved, to minimize the amount of documentation required for effective communication, and to create living standards that match the current business needs. If the work being done is not relevant to those involved, the amount of sincere effort put into governance will be shoddy at best and promote an environment where open communication is not encouraged.

The key for governance is to strike the right balance between innovation and the need to ensure that quality systems are being produced (see Figure 8.4). The goal should be to enable the sustainability of the business. Note: properly implemented governance does not inhibit innovation.

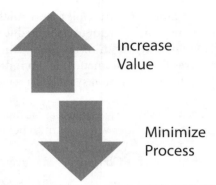

Increase
Value

Minimize
Process

Figure 8.4   The goal of governance is to increase the value of solutions for the business without introducing undue process.

Summary

The road to governance begins with

- Getting management support and sponsorship to do governance activities
- Understanding and embracing the governance and the underlying principles
- Using governance as a mechanism to help guide both the architecture and its associated systems
- Focusing on creating value for the business, not undue process

Governance in and of itself doesn't necessarily excite me, but seeing the outcomes of projects that had good governance and the positive outcomes for the business shows that it is an endeavor that can pay great dividends. I have also seen governance be more passive and not be relevant to the projects at hand. When this occurs, governance wastes valuable time.

The key is to find the right balance of governance and help mitigate risks, help reduce costs, and help promote leverage for the business.

References

Ambler, Scott W., and Mark Lines. 2012. *Disciplined Agile Delivery: A Practitioner's Guide to Agile Software Delivery in the Enterprise.* IBM Press.

Hiles, Andrew. 2010. *The Definitive Handbook of Business Continuity Management, Third Edition.* Wiley.

Humble, Jez. 2010. *Continuous Delivery: Reliable Software Releases through Build, Test, and Deployment Automation.* Addison-Wesley.

McGraw, Gary. 2006. *Software Security: Building Security In.* Addison-Wesley.

Nygard, Michael T. 2007. *Release It!: Design and Deploy Production-Ready Software.* Pragmatic Bookshelf.

Pfleeger, Charles P., and Shari Lawrence Pfleeger. 2006. *Security in Computing, Fourth Edition.* Prentice Hall.

Ries, Eric. 2011. *The Lean Startup: How Today's Entrepreneurs Use Continuous Innovation to Create Radically Successful Businesses.* Crown Business.

Taylor, Laura P. 2013. *FISMA Compliance Handbook, Second Edition.* Syngress.

Todorov, Dobromir. 2007. *Mechanics of User Identification and Authentication: Fundamentals of Identity Management.* Auerbach Publications.

Whitman, Michael E., Herbert J. Mattord, and Andrew Green. 2013. *Principles of Incident Response and Disaster Recovery.* Cengage Learning.

Chapter 9

KNOW-HOW

"The future belongs to the curious."

—Unknown

"Develop a passion for learning. If you do, you will never cease to grow."

—Anthony J. D'Angelo

"You don't learn to walk by following rules. You learn by doing, and by falling over."

—Richard Branson

"I am always doing that which I cannot do, in order that I may learn how to do it."

—Pablo Picasso

"Technical skill is mastery of complexity, while creativity is mastery of simplicity."

—Erik Christopher Zeeman

Have you ever seen a demo, read a blog, been at a conference and thought, "Wow—that looks and sounds amazing. We need that!"?

This is usually one of the first glimpses into the evolutionary needs of an architecture. Seeing what others are doing can serve as an inspiration to architects and other development staff about what the possibilities for the business may be. One of the best ways to figure out if this new area will apply to what you are doing is to work on incorporating it into your body of know-how.

This chapter unveils one of the essential skills needed by a software architect: developing and maintaining your body of know-how.

KNOW-HOW DEFINED

The concept of *know-how* is literally having the practical understanding of how to do things and the nuanced knowledge of when and where that knowledge should be applied. For the purposes of software architecture, there is a strong focus on technology and the business domain.

For architects, there is a career-long need to stay current and relevant within the technologies and the domains in which they work. This need drives a tension among the following (shown in Figure 9.1):

- **Relevance** (the direct applicability of what you know compared to what is needed)
- **Currency** (the minimal distance between your knowledge and the current wave of knowledge in your industry)
- **Excellence** (the level of craftsmanship, mastery, and nuanced knowledge of an area)

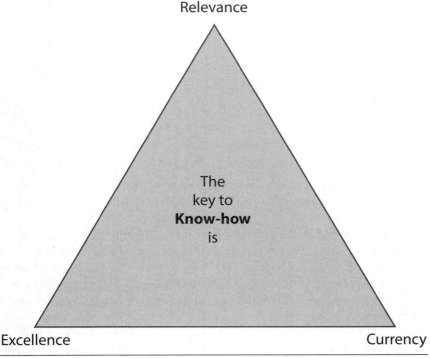

Figure 9.1   The key to know-how is balancing the competing forces of relevance, currency, and excellence.

DEVELOPING KNOW-HOW

As an architect, staying current and relevant on the latest technologies can help you to guide software projects, maintain your technical expertise, and give the business opportunities to stay competitive.

There are a variety of ways to increase your architectural know-how, some of which are shown in Figure 9.2.

Developing Know-how Relevance

As you consider how to develop and maintain your know-how, one of the best ways to help determine where to focus your time is to consider how

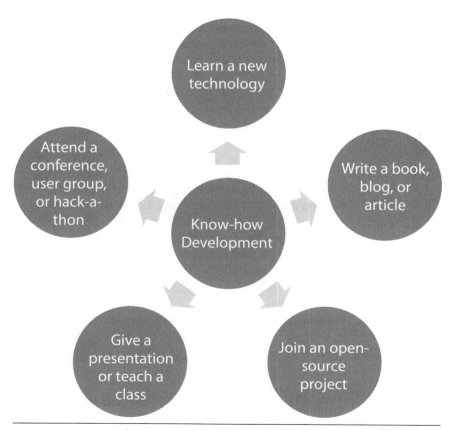

Figure 9.2 Know-how development—it's critical to your staying relevant as an architect.

relevant the area that you are interested in is to the work you are currently doing or hope to be doing soon.

Applying Know-how to Your Domain

For architects, knowing what the currently available technologies are and what they are capable of doing is critical for making decisions on directions to head for projects.

Here are some key questions to ask about a technology:

- What types of applications is the technology being used for? Are other areas within your industry using it?
- What problems does it solve? Does the technology align with your product development needs? What percentage of the capabilities will you use? If it is a relatively low percentage, you need to question if the extra overhead is worth it, especially if you are paying any significant amount for the technology.
- What problems does it introduce? You need to understand the operational impacts this technology will have on your organization.
- Where are people struggling when they implement it?
- Is there good online support? Does it have an active community? Can you find information about it in Stack Overflow? You need to have a strong support community when real issues arise and you absolutely, positively need to resolve them fast.
- Is there active development around the technology? Is it a fad that has passed, or is there a growing level of interest in it?
- What are the alternatives? Which option best fits the problem that needs to be solved?
- Does it have a roadmap? Where is it going and does that align with where you anticipate your business going?
- Are there books written about it?
- What revision is it? Has is gone beyond a 1.0 release? Using a technology before a 1.0 release can be very tricky when things go wrong.
- What are the costs associated with it? Is it a one-time charge? Is it a charge per user, per some computation unit (server, CPU, etc.), per some usage unit? You need to know the costs associated with a technology before you begin "selling" it to your business. The costs could eat up all of your profit.
- What are the licensing implications? Do they affect your intellectual property, the ability to charge for your product, the ability for others to resell your product? You need to understand the licensing impacts

on your business. If they impact your ability to generate revenue, you need to understand how this technology limits you.

The challenge is to balance your passion and enthusiasm for a new technology with the environment that already exists. For instance, are you trying to apply a big data solution to something that a single server can handle? This is not a great use of the limited time you have to investigate and bring in new technologies. The technology needs to be appropriate for the problem at hand.

Developing a Model

Can you model the new business challenge with a view toward how you would use it in your product portfolio? This could be a domain model, a physical hardware diagram, a logical architecture diagram—basically some visual representation. Ideally, each of these diagrams will fit on a single printed page.

The key is to give enough information to allow for an understanding of the domain without all of the detail.

Dealing with a Certain Level of Ambiguity When Determining Relevance

It is simply not possible for architects to dive into every last detail of every problem that is on their plate. This is primarily due to time constraints, which force assumptions to be made, and risks and issues to be identified but not necessarily resolved. In this environment, key decisions about relevance need to be made, ones that will have significant project impact. Learning how to deal with ambiguity is a necessity for architects to get their work done on a daily basis.

For me, getting to the point where I know of at least one way that a problem can be reasonably solved goes a long way toward easing my anxiety about the problem. I don't have to know the exact solution now; I just need to know that the problem can be solved. This drives toward the need for determining a solution's relevance to my product portfolio and specific problems at hand.

Vetting and Selling Know-how

Architects are constantly involved with selling many different aspects related to technology. They need to be able to sell management and development staff on the direction that a particular solution should take and what directions should be avoided. They need to be able to present an authentic view of where technology and the business are going and have confidence that what they are saying is achievable. Selling a solution means making it relevant by being able to

- Weave a coherent story about the solution (all of the things you are saying need to hold together—minimize any inconsistencies)
- Clearly express the advantages of the direction being chosen
- Clearly express areas of concern
- Tell the same story repeatedly, but adjusting the details to the audience being addressed
- Anticipate different areas' interests (what will engage them about the technology)
- Anticipate counterpoints
- Make management feel confident in your work by showing your passion, your management of risk, and your ability to pick great solutions that are appropriate to the problem at hand

Developing Know-how Currency

In the fast and ever-changing world of technology, architects need to ensure that their know-how is current within the industry and domain in which they operate. If as an architect you don't maintain currency, you may quickly become irrelevant to the business.

Having a Broad Knowledge of Technology

For architects, having a broad-based knowlege of technology is essential for making decisions on where to guide projects. There are a variety of ways to accomplish this:

- Attending a conference can give you a sense of what other companies are doing, what vendors are promoting, and what is trending within the industry. You won't necessarily find out all of the details, but you will get a good sense of areas to focus on. You will also get a sense of what technologies may be starting to transition from bleeding edge to leading edge.
- Attend a local user group; local user groups can give you access to real experience within the industry. These are the technologists who are truly passionate about the technology. They are willing to share the details of what they are working on, where they are struggling with the technology, and where they are having successes.
- Read blogs and magazines, or watch online training videos (through sites like Pluralsight) that are in the general areas of interest that

you have. They can give you a small snippet of code to enable you to do some quick prototyping and allow you to kick the tires of the technology. They can also make you aware of some of the pitfalls of the technology.

- Network with other technologists in your area and your community. Technologists naturally love to talk about technology. Establishing a broad network of individuals who are passionate about technology will give you access to an amazing wealth of information. Contractors are also a great source of information about what is currently happening in your area. They are hired to work on areas where other companies are having challenges staffing. The fact that they move around and see what other companies are doing gives them a tremendous level of knowledge about what works and does not work (at least not currently). Follow topical experts on Twitter.

Learning Technologies Quickly

Architects usually have very limited amounts of time to jump into a particular area in depth. The challenge is that it takes time to formulate a sense of where a technology is best applied (what purpose it serves best and where it doesn't fit).

Doing small prototypes or having someone on one of your teams do some prototyping with respect to a particular technology can help you begin to establish the validity of the tool for the set of problems you are attempting to solve.

The challenge is that new tools, no matter how seasoned they may be, are likely to have operational issues that you are unaware of when first introducing them into a new area.

These types of challenges are easier to manage earlier on in the life of a project. Later, once the cadence of a project is established and the expectations about delivery time frames are real, introducing new technologies into the project is usually a risky proposition. The amount of time you have to recover from a misstep is very limited.

Look for ways to learn the new technologies by leveraging the teams you work with. You cannot be an expert in everything. Knowing how much to learn is critical so you can manage your overall time commitments, and allowing the teams to work on fun new technologies will raise their engagement level. Take the time to pair program with developers.

Learning New Programming Languages, Frameworks, and Methodologies

One of the best ways to keep up on the ever-changing world of technology is to spike solutions with new technologies and do proofs of concept (POCs). These may never be used in active development projects, but the spikes and POCs will give you a sense of

- The features and direction where the current version of a technology is heading
- The problems that technologies are attempting to address and how they are attempting to address them
- The rough edges related to a technology, giving you a sense of whether the technology is ready for prime time or is more experimental in nature
- Any new technical language surrounding a new technology (this will allow you to be aware of subtle references related to the technology when talking to others or when reading online or a hard copy)
- The operational nature of a technology

Attending a Conference

Attending a conference related to your primary area of work can be an excellent way to get a sense of

- Where the industry is heading
- What trends are emerging
- What other companies are doing, what technologies they are adopting or have recently adopted, and what kinds of experiences (positive or negative) they have had in trying to bring the technology in-house
- What is coming into favor, what is falling out of favor, what is capturing the attention of other developers, and where the money is

If travel budgets are tight, you can often find local conferences to attend. There has also been a trend toward smaller free conferences hosted by interest groups with a set of local sponsors where you can see local talent give presentations on interesting topics. This may take the form of a meet-up or an un-conference. Another option is to consider a virtual conference. Some conferences put selected session videos online.

Attending conferences will give you a chance to network, learn about new technologies, discover interesting projects that are in development in your geographic area, and add to your current know-how.

Attending/Hosting a Hack-a-thon

If your business has a particular problem to solve, one great way to generate ideas and potential solutions is to host a hack-a-thon. This can give the business a great sense of what some of the technical challenges of a particular problem are. It can also provide some new insights into what the real problem is and a variety of ways to consider for solving it. This type of hack-a-thon is usually more internally than externally facing.

If you are looking for an exciting way to demonstrate or hone your technical skills, attending a hack-a-thon can give you a chance to look at a problem you may not have considered before and force you to think differently from the way you have in the past. It may also lead to new employment opportunities that you were previously unaware of.

One area that needs to be addressed with a hack-a-thon is who owns the intellectual property of the solutions that are generated. This needs to be clear before the event occurs.

A similar idea to a hack-a-thon is an innovation contest under the broader umbrella of open innovation.

Leveraging Online Resources

In today's world, there are many different ways to learn new technologies. There are often tutorials, free online courses, and endless sample code just waiting for you to dive in and train yourself.

Taking the time to train yourself through online research is an excellent way to learn what is available on the web and to find the top sites for the areas you are interested in. One way to make this more efficient is to use tools like Google Alerts that will bring relevant information to you instead of you needing to search for it.

Developing Know-how Excellence

Architects need to gain a deep level of knowledge with respect to the technologies that they are using or about to use. They need an understanding of the many nuances related to the technology and what the impacts of those nuances are on the solutions they are developing.

Technical know-how also adds to your credibility as an architect. You want to avoid being a PowerPoint architect.

Developing a Proof of Concept

One of the best ways for architects to maintain their software development skills is to do POCs when technology decisions need to be made. POCs have many benefits:

- Architects can maintain and enhance their coding skills. This enables them to remember just how long some "easy" tasks can take to develop.
- They can experience firsthand some of the challenges and some of the benefits of a new technology or development approach.
- They enable better communication with the business when the architect has firsthand knowledge and is able to personally demo the work.
- They relieve the primary development staff from balancing forward-looking research with the immediacy of the hot fix that needs to get to production or the looming deadline that is quickly approaching.

To help maintain my development skills and keep current with the latest technologies, I try to focus on a single area each month with the goal of producing a prototype in that area. This lets me investigate 12 things per year. I try to spend on average an hour a day focusing on this, perhaps more or less depending on my other commitments.

My focus varies depending on what I am interested in or if I am trying to prepare for an upcoming project where I may not be familiar with some aspect of the technology stack that we would like to adopt. It gives me a chance to do coding without creating dependencies within a project on which the team is waiting for me to get code completed. I will focus on areas such as big data, mobile, semantic search, user interface, analytics, or whatever area seems important to get up to speed on.

Creating or Joining a Local User Group

If you are extremely passionate about a particular area, find a local user group that meets on regular basis where a wide range of topics with respect to your area of interest are discussed.

If a local user group doesn't exist, you may be able to create one if you can attract a set of similarly interested parties. This may be an offshoot of another user group or something that was kicked off from a local conference.

The key to a successful user group is to have passionate members and enough time to support and manage the organization to keep it fresh, interesting, and in depth for those involved. Make sure that everyone who attends feels welcome. The local user group can be a great way for local enthusiasts to get together and share ideas about how solve their current problems. It is usually surprising just how many others are facing similar problems or have solutions to the problems you are encountering.

Giving a Presentation at a Local Conference

One great way to learn a topic in more detail is to give a presentation at a local conference. There is nothing like the fear of public speaking to drive you to know the subject matter in extreme detail.

Ideally, you can pick a topic or area that aligns with the work you are already doing and is in an area that you want to learn more about.

Public speaking will help you become more effective at work, allow you to be more confident in dealing with crowds, and help you to think on your feet.

For technology-related presentations, live demos will help keep the audience's interest. The key is to pick small representative examples that can be shown in a relatively short amount of time. If you show multiple alternatives for how to use a technology, giving recommendations (the pros and cons) for which alternative is the best in certain situations can help the audience walk away with valuable information to use in case they run into a similar problem.

On the odd chance that everything goes south for the demos, have slides prepared that show the same set of live experiences you wanted to demo and the results of the demo. This will give you a fallback in case everything else goes up in flames.

For most people in technology, seeing is believing; and if something is easy enough to use in a live demo, it may actually be possible to use it in a real project. If nothing else, live demos nearly always keep the audience's attention and help draw out questions and observations for the presentation, making it more fun for everyone involved.

If possible, make the coding examples available after the presentation. They will give the attendees a great starting point from which to learn the technology in more detail after the conference.

Speaking at conferences is an invaluable experience. It will help build your résumé and help you make new professional connections.

Teaching a Class

"To teach is to learn twice."

—Joseph Joubert

Teaching a class is one of the best ways to learn a subject even when you think you are an expert in an area. The questions you get from class attendees will give you a perspective on what is obvious and what is not easily comprehended. It is a great way to learn the nuances of a particular technology and brand it on your mind.

The class could be something that is internal to your organization, it could be taught through a local community college, or it could be offered through some other technical organization.

A class that includes lots of examples and where attendees actively participate will keep the discussions lively. PowerPoints are great for guiding a conversation, but doing is the best way for students to learn. Developing hands-on exercises will invariably cause you to discover new tricks, bugs, and gotchas.

If the topic is challenging enough or the class is large enough, you may need to have helpers to field the questions and to help students overcome any technical issues they have with implementing the solution or variants of the solution they are attempting to create.

Sometimes meeting together physically in a room for teaching is not possible or practical. A class taught virtually through a webinar or other online format can potentially reach a broader audience. The challenges of virtual teaching are to make sure you have thought through how you will present to the class and handle questions from students, whether you will have a camera aimed at you (in a context that is easy to watch), how you will administer polling, and how you will give tests or quizzes (if needed).

Teaching a class is a good way to help build your résumé and also is an opportunity to provide community service. It can often give you a chance to mentor some of the students in an ongoing manner.

Writing a Book

If you are feeling really motivated, try writing a book. Writing a book is a great way to get your name out in the industry and establish your expertise in a certain area.

One way to test out an idea for a book is to give a presentation at a conference. It will help formulate the ideas in your head more clearly. The feedback from attendees at the conference can indicate the interest level in the topic and enable you to make any adjustments that may be needed to improve the concept. The fact that a conference was willing to accept your proposal can help you persuade a publisher that there is a market for your book.

One challenge in writing a book is to pick a topic with a long enough shelf life that by the time you have completed the book and gone through a few revisions, the topic will still be relevant. Another challenge is making a significant time commitment to complete the project, and to complete it on time.

Writing a Blog

If writing a book seems a bit overwhelming, a good alternative is writing a blog, even if it's just internal to the company you work for. This allows you to publish your ideas in smaller segments and to stay current with topics that may have a relatively short shelf life. It also lets you focus on areas that you are passionate about and get live feedback from those who read your blog.

Becoming an Active Participant in an Open-Source Project or Online Community

Participating in open-source software is another great way to expose yourself to new technology. Find an area that you are passionate about and see if there is an active open-source project that is focused on a particular problem in that space. If none exists, consider starting an open-source project to solve the problem you are interested in. At a minimum, have an account and follow projects.

Participating in open source is also a great way to get involved in a community and be recognized for the work you do. Open-source software can have a higher level of quality than what a normal business may be interested in investing in. As issues arise and get resolved, there is a sense of accomplishment and a sense of fulfillment for helping out the community.

Open-source projects can also be hosted internally within a business as a means of promoting code and knowledge sharing.

One advantage to contributing software to the open-source community is that there is broader support for the software, including new and innovative ideas. Another advantage is that open source usually allows you to more consistently take a strategic approach to solving problems.

Become an active member of an online community by asking and answering questions on sites like Stack Overflow.

Knowing How to Instrument

The only real way to know what is going on within a system is to have it provide the information you need. This usually requires some form of system instrumentation.

One of the best ways to display information from instrumentation is to create a dashboard (see Figure 9.3). The dashboard can give both a real-time and a historical perspective on how things are working. It also allows anomalies to be displayed visually.

The challenge is that if you instrument everything, your system will spend all of its time logging information and never really get around to servicing the requests for which it was built.

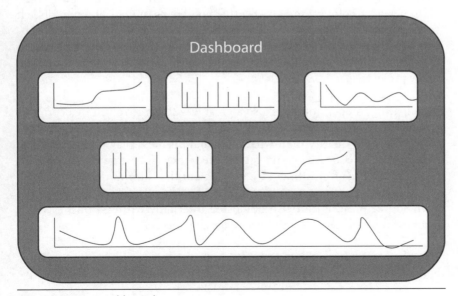

Figure 9.3 Dashboard

One way to minimize this problem is to focus on the edges of the system, what is going in and what is going out. If you have the basic inputs and outputs, your ability to reproduce problems is significantly higher.

Focus on counting activities that the system is performing; this will give you a sense of where the system is being heavily used and what the normal daily trends in activity are. This data can help inform when system maintenance is best performed. It can also give you a sense of when abnormal things are occurring by logging error rates and other activities that may require someone's attention.

Acting on the basis of knowledge is critical to making good decisions.

Knowing How to Scale and Performance Tune

Before a system ever has a single line of code written, having a sense of how you might approach scaling is important. Are you going to scale out? Are you going to scale up? Once you have a basic idea of how you are going to approach scaling, you are in a position to start thinking about how you might provision the hardware and middleware that are needed for your system and begin the process of defining capital solutions.

Once the system is being built and you have the appropriate instrumentation to measure what is happening within it, you can begin dealing with the areas that are blocking you from getting the performance you are looking for. This may be solved by

- Providing more hardware in a scale-out solution
- Providing a caching solution for common requests to be serviced at the edge of the system
- Providing intelligent locking mechanisms to prevent blocking
- Isolating certain functions or users from one another to prevent overconsuming resources
- Rewriting algorithms to be more efficient
- Ensuring that all of the proper indexing is available for data retrieval
- Minimizing the amount of data transfer through the system
- Moving the code to where the data is, instead of the other way around
- Being more event driven than request driven
- Parallelizing portions of a request

There are usually many alternative routes to improving scale and performance; the challenge is to be cost effective and still meet the business needs and timelines. If possible, you want to identify and deal with these architectural issues early in a project so their impact on cost can be managed effectively. Another key element of this is to defer any irreversible or costly decisions until the last (or most) responsible moment.

Knowing Where Money Can Be Saved without Compromising the System

Every project seems to run short of money at some point, and the inevitable question is asked: "Can we do some things differently to save money?" The project that has been a poster child for strategic development suddenly turns tactical.

There are an endless number of ways that a system can be hacked to achieve the desired goal. For example, you can

- Skimp on testing
- Just add in the code without refactoring (the begging of a god object)
- Just shove some data into the database in a field that is not being used
- Create yet another tie to a legacy system that is scheduled to go out of commission

All these things are achievable and will deliver the functionality that is desired, but you are adding technical debt to the solution.

Software is like a garden; you need to keep the weeds out. If you don't do the right things most of the time, your system will begin to develop entropy and eventually will need to be replaced.

If you have to hack the system, have a clear plan to fix it and implement it in an isolated manner. This will enable a refactoring of that area to occur without impacting other areas of the system. Document it for what it is—a hack.

Having a deep sense of the nuances related to a technology can help inform what the best solution will be.

Having a Basic Knowledge of Project Management

Project management is something that most architects are more than happy to let someone else on the project take care of. For most large projects, the architect has the best view of the project dependencies and the approximate amount of time needed to complete tasks. The architect is also one of the first technology people involved with a project, often before the project ever comes into existence.

It is important for an architect to be able to

- Lay out a high-level schedule (release plan) for a project (at least at the very beginning of a project when others are first being added to the project)
- Lay out dependencies between tasks and other development areas
- Identify risks and areas of concern
- Help to start populating an initial backlog of stories

Partnering with project managers can help make the job of architecture run more smoothly. Having open conversations about where the project is and what the current challenges are and having a game plan for how to address current issues will help the project manager stay abreast of areas that need attention and areas that need to be communicated to key stakeholders. All of this works toward establishing trust and transparency.

> **Note**
> Establishing a common front with architecture and project management is a key to success when interacting with executives. Executives who sense any division will instinctively dive into the area of division and focus on it for months to come.

Knowing the Software Construction Process

Architects need to be well versed in the software construction process.

Your ability to know and understand the software construction process is critical to having the appropriate oversight of a development team, including developers, configuration management, and testing.

KNOW-HOW SYNTHESIS

Know-how synthesis is about putting all of your know-how together into a coherent whole. Working through individual areas independently can be helpful, but until you take the time to figure out how the areas interact with one another and determine what works well and what doesn't work, you haven't really added value to your business.

Know-how means jumping into the details and learning how things work, what dependencies exist, and where things are best used. Synthesizing it will lead to success and longevity in the role of an architect (see Figure 9.4).

KNOW-HOW-DRIVEN ARCHITECTURE

Know-how-driven architecture is driving architectural solutions based on active knowledge about the space you work in and providing influence on a daily basis.

You can't possibly know everything, but you need to be broadly familiar with nearly all of it.

Architecture that is based on know-how has one of the best chances of being successful (see Figure 9.5).

Know-how-driven architecture is about balancing the relevance, currency, and excellence related to your know-how. In the end, it is a lifelong process

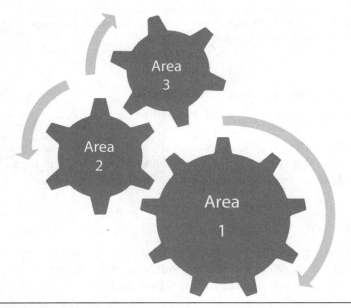

Figure 9.4 Know-how synthesis

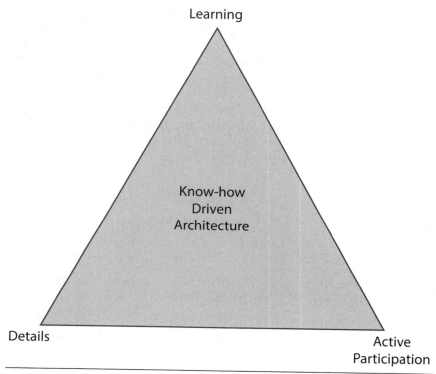

Figure 9.5 Know-how-driven architecture

of learning, curiosity, and incorporating new details into your knowledge base through active participation with the industry you work in, the company you work in, and the teams you engage with regularly.

Even if you don't know everything you would like to, you should be capable of jumping in, learning, and driving the business toward great solutions.

SUMMARY

The road to know-how begins with

- Engaging in activities that increase your know-how
- Expanding the basis of your knowledge
- Staying current with the directions of the industry
- Filling in any gaps that are critical to your area of responsibility
- Staying passionate about software

Software architecture is a great job and requires broad, active know-how to be successful in decision making. The great challenge is to balance the incessant demands on your time with the need to stay relevant. There will always be far more things to do than you can possibly get done. The keys are to

- Focus on what will provide high value to the business
- Avoid major misses that will make executives unhappy
- Follow the areas you are naturally passionate about
- Surround yourself with experts and maintain a strong professional network

REFERENCES

Lafley, A. G., and Ram Charan. 2008. *The Game-Changer: How You Can Drive Revenue and Profit Growth with Innovation.* Crown Business.

McGonigal, Jane. 2011. *Reality Is Broken: Why Games Make Us Better and How They Can Change the World.* Penguin Books.

McGrath, Rita Gunther. 2013. *The End of Competitive Advantage: How to Keep Your Strategy Moving as Fast as Your Business.* Harvard Business Review Press.

Pink, Daniel H. 2006. *A Whole New Mind: Why Right-Brainers Will Rule the Future.* Riverhead Books.

Robinson, Ken. 2010. *Sir Ken Robinson: Bring On the Learning Revolution!* www.ted.com/talks/sir_ken_robinson_bring_on_the_revolution.html.

PART III

VISIONARY SKILLS

"There are three classes of people: Those who see. Those who see when they are shown. Those who do not see."

—Leonardo da Vinci

"'Think simple' as my old master used to say—meaning reduce the whole of its parts into the simplest terms, getting back to first principles."

—Frank Lloyd Wright

"I don't know why people hire architects and then tell them what to do."

—Frank Gehry

"Design is not making beauty, beauty emerges from selection, affinities, integration, love."

—Louis Kahn

"I feel coming on a strange disease: humility."

—Frank Lloyd Wright

Part III focuses on the three essential visionary skills for an architect. These chapters focus on exploration, planning, and execution of an architectural vision. The chapters are organized as follows:

- Chapter 10, "Technology Innovation," will enable you to
  - Develop relevant trend awareness
  - Align technology innovation with the business
  - Enable strategic research
  - Apply innovation principles to technology
  - Take a pragmatic approach to technology innovation

- Chapter 11, "Strategic Roadmapping," will enable you to
  - Develop roadmaps using strategies and principles
  - Know the role of an architect in building roadmaps
  - Be aware of some of the key risks related to roadmaps
  - Know where and when to use roadmaps
- Chapter 12, "Entrepreneurial Execution," will enable you to
  - Architect with an entrepreneurial spirit
  - Take calculated risks
  - Deliver results
  - Use entrepreneurial principles as an architect

Visionary skills are the third layer of technical skills needed to be an architect (see Figure PIII.1).

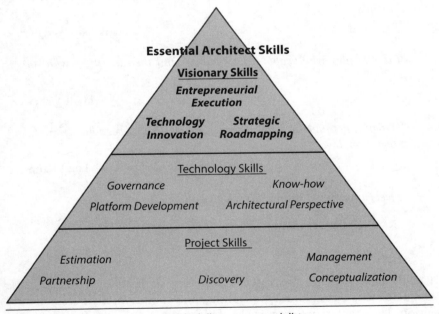

Figure PIII.1   Essential architect skills (visionary skills)

The visionary skills will enable you to explore innovation, strategically plan, and entrepreneurially execute architectures that align with the strategic goals and vision of the business (see Figure PIII.2).

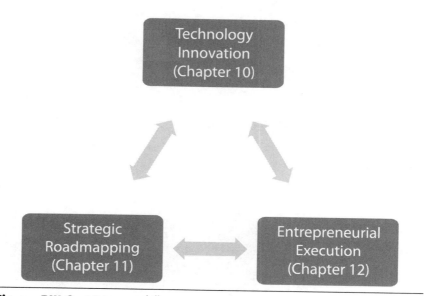

Figure PIII.2 Visionary skills

Chapter 10

TECHNOLOGY INNOVATION

"Innovation is the central issue in economic prosperity."

—Michael Porter

"Innovation has nothing to do with how many R & D dollars you have. When Apple came up with the Mac, IBM was spending at least 100 times more on R & D. It's not about money. It's about the people you have, how you're led, and how much you get it."

—Steve Jobs

"Because, you know, resilience—if you think of it in terms of the Gold Rush, then you'd be pretty depressed right now because the last nugget of gold would be gone. But the good thing is, with innovation, there isn't a last nugget. Every new thing creates two new questions and two new opportunities."

—Jeff Bezos

"I believe in innovation and that the way you get innovation is you fund research and you learn the basic facts."

—Bill Gates

"Learning and innovation go hand in hand. The arrogance of success is to think that what you did yesterday will be sufficient for tomorrow."

—William Pollard

Have you ever been at a conference and attended a really cool presentation? It focused your attention on a new area you were not familiar with, and it captured your interest. Later in the week, you noticed more sessions that were focused on different perspectives of the same technology or approach.

This kind of clustering of conference presentations—or magazine articles or blog posts—is usually a signal that a new trend is emerging. It may not have wide appeal yet, and it may not emerge into anything concrete, but it sounds fascinating and seems to address a real issue you are dealing with. Your ability to recognize these types of new trends can open up opportunities for your business and enable you to be a leader in the implementation of a new technology within your organization. On the other hand, the new opportunity could lead you down a rabbit hole with technology that has little support or interest from the wider development community internally or externally.

This chapter unveils one of the essential skills needed by a software architect: the ability to identify, assess, and infuse new and potentially disruptive technologies in a business-centric fashion.

TECHNOLOGY INNOVATION DEFINED

Technology innovation is the ability to

- Look where research, technology, and your industry are heading
- Identify trends and opportunities that are aligned with your business's strategic goals and objectives
- Partner with the business and customers to discover solutions
- Make recommendations about the adoption of new technologies into the organization and their timing

Technology innovation is linked to the theory of Moore's Law, which predicts the doubling of computing hardware capacity every two years. Many digital devices are impacted by Moore's Law as processing power, memory, and other technical capabilities improve over time, speeding exponential growth and technology innovation.

Technology innovation is best done in partnership with the business to align with the company's strategies and goals. It also helps ensure that technologies are not selected simply for their "cool" factor (see Figure 10.1).

TREND AWARENESS

Trend awareness is your window into where interesting technologies are heading. It provides you with a glimpse of the possible new disruptive technologies, business models, processes, and so on that can either give you a leg up on the competition or put you at a disadvantage.

The trend diagram in Figure 10.2 shows the typical peaks and valleys in popularity that new technologies tend to follow over time. Observing the

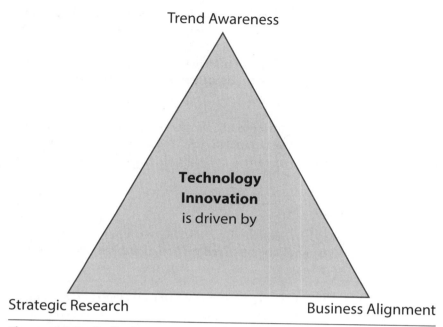

Figure 10.1   Technology innovation

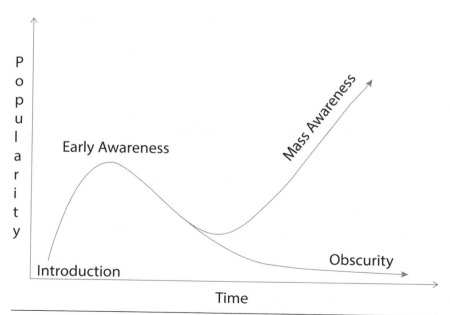

Figure 10.2   Trend diagram

popularity of technologies, business models, processes, and related areas can give you a good sense of what is happening in the industry at the macro scale. Companies such as Gartner, GigaOM, and Forrester Research typically gather and publish this kind of information on technology topics such as big data, mobile, gamification, and others as they start to gain critical mass and awareness.

Your ability to quickly identify promising new technology trends and predict their eventual success or failure will help you avoid spending time and resources on those technologies that end up toiling in obscurity and eventual failure.

Areas of Trend Awareness

A wide variety of trends are potentially applicable to your architectural areas of responsibility and should be observed on a regular basis. These include the following:

- **Industry.** What are the economic conditions that affect your industry? Is it in a cycle of growth, stability, or decline? The economics that are pervasive in your industry can and will affect the degree to which you will be able to attract technology investment from the business.
- **University research.** What areas are universities researching that may be of interest to your business and lead to potential partnerships? Knowing what schools are doing in research areas that are of interest to your business partners can be a great source of new information and talent in the form of interns and new hires as well as an area for potential joint research projects.
- **Open-source tools.** What tools and technologies are gaining or declining in popularity and community support, especially those that have more business-friendly licensing arrangements? These are potential candidates for adoption if they are growing in popularity and community support or candidates for elimination or replacement if the community interest is declining.
- **Conferences.** Conferences can be a great way to get a quick glimpse of what the new and emerging "hot" technologies are. The presentations at these conferences can give you a jump start into background information about new technologies and some of the early experiments and results. This will help you become aware of which areas are working well and which areas are still rough around the edges and need more time and testing.

- **Regulatory compliance.** Being aware of the types of changes that regulatory bodies are considering can help prepare you to plan the aspects of the architecture that may need to remain flexible to account for new regulatory requirements.
- **Hardware capabilities.** Hardware is constantly changing. Taking the time to keep up with key vendors and their roadmaps can help you prepare for hardware that may enable better performance or less expensive solutions in the near future.
- **Cloud capabilities.** The area of cloud computing is evolving quickly. Understanding the capabilities provided by cloud vendors can enable elastic growth with little or no effort. The key challenges are to understand the costs and data lock-in that may be associated with the varying solutions.
- **Customers' competitive knowledge.** One of the best ways to keep up with your competitors is to closely partner with your customers. They can be an excellent source of information about what your competitors are up to and what they are promoting as strategic advantages and differentiators.
- **Vendor capabilities.** A large number of vendors make capabilities available for a price. Some vendors are leaders in their areas of expertise. They often have a solid understanding of what others are doing and what is working well and what is not. Working with these types of vendors can be a great partnership. The key is to ensure that the value being added by the vendor is greater than the cost of using their products.
- **Intellectual property.** Working with your intellectual property counsel or in-house general counsel can help you keep up to speed on areas where the business may want to go after the development of patents or other intellectual property.
- **E-mail alerts.** Many online sources allow you to set alerts based on keywords. When you hear of a new technology or development, you can put an alert on it using the keywords associated with the technology. Then when there are new updates or recent news, you'll be one of the first to know, which will help you consistently monitor the space.

Applying Trend Awareness

Trending information can be used as a source of guidance when you are trying to determine if a particular area is worth diving into in more detail. It can serve as an early warning that there is a technology-related change in direction that could impact the business, it can serve as an alert that there is a new opportunity for your business, or it may just serve as a confirmation that there is no cause for concern in this area, at least for now.

Remember that the rate of change may be exponential, and you should expect that things will change quickly in a given technology focus area. Your ability to check in on a regular and frequent basis will help you stay on top of the trends that signal technological changes that could impact your industry and disrupt your business.

BUSINESS ALIGNMENT

Business alignment is a critical success factor to technology innovation.

Paying Attention to Trends on Customer Inquiries

If you are receiving a fair number of inquiries from customers about a particular new trend, it may well be worth your time to consider investing in this area. It is quite possible that they are using this new capability as a differentiator and a means of comparing and contrasting different solutions.

Although the capability may be not be a primary use case for what they want to use the product for and it may not even be used that often, it is something they can put on a checklist and use to make a decision.

Such items can help them gain support and excitement within their organization about why using the product they are considering is a good choice. It can help them justify the cost for the change or the purchase to begin with.

Getting Customer Feedback

Your customers are one of your best sources of information. There are different kinds of customers:

- **Fans.** They always have great things to say. Listen for patterns. The key is to find out what is behind the patterns. What is driving their adoption, and what maintains their enthusiasm for your products?
- **Utilitarians.** They are using your product because it is convenient, it is easy, it is practical, and it makes financial sense. The key here is to understand the key value proposition that keeps them coming back.
- **Captives.** They are using your product because they have to. Either they are not the decision makers about buying your product or there are no competing products in the marketplace. The key here is to

understand who drives the purchasing decisions and what influences them.

- **Followers.** They are using your product because others said it was a great product. The recommendation can come from many different sources; it could be from a friend, or it could come from online comments. The key here is to find out what people are recommending and why. This is your real value; it's an endorsement. In a similar fashion, hearing the negative things others are saying about your product can give you insights into what you need to improve.

No matter who your customers are, you want to make it easy for them to provide feedback. If you use a survey, keep it short, provide some multiple-choice questions, and provide a place for them to type in their comments in their own words. They may praise your product or roast your product, but getting a wide variety of feedback from your customers can give you insights into where you need to go and what improvements you should pursue. It may be as simple as adding link on the product's website to solicit ways to improve the product.

Analyzing Customer Feedback

Once you get the customer feedback, ensure that internally everyone has access to the information, whether it is good or bad. The more access everyone has to this information, the more it can help influence their daily decisions about the work they do (see Figure 10.3).

Look for common patterns in what is being said. You are looking to tell a story that can be used to help understand how your product is doing in the marketplace and help drive where investments should be made.

When to Be Cautious about Trends

There are a variety of situations when following or looking to follow new trends is simply not a good idea. For example:

- There is a great new technology and you want to reimplement a system that already works and that customers love.
- You are coming to the close of a major release and the team is working to stabilize the system.
- Your current system is already experiencing significant operational challenges, and the root cause is not known.
- Switching costs outweigh any perceived or realized gains.

Figure 10.3   Customer trend analysis: customer feedback can give you
investment insights.

One of your major goals as a technology architect is to manage risk, not
introduce it. You need to ensure that you have adequate time to recover
from destabilizing the system after the new technologies, approaches, or
patterns have been introduced. As the idiom goes, "Discretion is the better
part of valor."

The last thing you want to do is harm your reputation unnecessarily or be
viewed as reckless by the executives who are overseeing the work that you
do. To mitigate this risk, always go in with your eyes wide open and be willing to listen to other people's perspectives, whether positive or negative.
Seek to understand their concerns and make sure you're considering feedback from all levels.

Any change is difficult, and you don't want to make it harder by pushing something your company and its people or customers aren't ready for.

Patience and persistence are valuable skills at this time. If you are right, as mass awareness grows eventually people will come around to seeing the value of your approach and recommendations. Remember that being too early can be just as bad as being too late. Timing is everything.

When to Embrace a Trend

There are a variety of situations that naturally lend themselves to exploring trends and bringing new and innovative approaches to the problems that need to be solved. These include the following:

- The business wants to do a technology refresh and modernize the technology stack for an important application or system.
- The business wants to establish a presence in a new market with a new set of applications or systems.
- The current set of technologies, approaches, and processes has been determined to be inadequate for solving the problems at hand, and a new approach is not only warranted but welcomed by everyone involved.

If you seek to introduce new ideas at the appropriate times, you will gain the trust of the business that you can take a pragmatic approach to moving the business forward. This form of partnership will serve you well.

STRATEGIC RESEARCH

"Research is formalized curiosity. It is poking and prying with a purpose."

—Zora Neale Hurston

At any given time there are only a limited number of research projects or areas that can be undertaken. Several factors should be considered when determining what areas are the ones that should be explored. These include

- **Alignment with strategic business goals.** Research should be focused on an area that both the business and technology need to learn about in order to be able to move forward with a particular set of projects or areas that the business wants to pursue or invest in.
- **Agreed-upon prioritization.** Both technology and the business should agree that this area of research is needed, that the limited funding available for this type of research would be well spent, and that this is a high priority for both areas.

- **Agreed-upon purpose.** Both technology and the business should be in agreement about the purpose and desired outcomes of the research. Is it to determine the feasibility of pursuing a particular area? Is it to reduce the risk? Is it to help appropriately size the investment request? Is it to better understand the threat that this technology poses to the business? Is it to better understand the opportunities a particular area may offer? Are there legal and regulatory issues that need to be fleshed out?
- **Agreed-upon time and resource allocation.** Both technology and the business should agree upon a time box that this research will fit into. Ideally, this is measured in days. The goal should be to do the research in a cost-effective manner, and to the greatest degree possible limit the amount of time, money, and resources being used to pursue it. Are there other areas in the business with which you can share the cost of this research if it turns out to be a larger endeavor?
- **Agreed-upon report-out mechanism.** As the research is pursued, how will the progress and lessons learned be reported out to the business? Are there natural points at which these report-outs can help determine if this area of research is worth continuing to pursue? Are there other areas of the business that would be interested in the outcomes of the research? Can you post these findings in an internally accessible collaboration area to let others know how the research is progressing? If necessary, can you control who has access to the research findings, depending on the nature of the research?

The key is to partner with the business to determine the parameters that surround strategic research.

Research Approaches

Several different approaches to pursuing research can be taken, such as the following:

- **Business unit driven.** This research is done internally within a business unit. The resources working on it typically are not devoted 100% to research.
- **R & D.** This research is done by a dedicated research and development team. It is often staffed with resources who have Ph.D.s in specific areas of interest to the business. They also are typically actively involved in the broader academic research community.
- **University partnership.** This research is done in partnership with a university. It allows the university to get exposure to challenging

business problems and information that is generally not publicly available, and the business gets access to professors and students who specialize in a particular area of interest.

- **Open innovation challenges.** This is a research challenge that typically is constructed in partnership with a company such as InnoCentive. Working with you and your team, they will help frame the research problem or question into a challenge. They will also handle any intellectual property treatments and any awards for the winners of the challenge. The challenge itself can be open to the public or open only to those within your business. A successful challenge typically results in a crowdsourced solution to a specific business problem.
- **Corporate innovation labs.** These are effectively start-up groups that are formed within the overall business. They focus on rapid experimentation and validated learning through interacting with real customers. They often employ A/B testing to help drive decisions about which alternative solution is working better.

The goal is to pick the approach or mix of approaches that makes the most sense for your business situation. The key is to find ways to inject new ideas and approaches into the business that will enable it to grow.

TECHNOLOGY INNOVATION PRINCIPLES

Technology innovation has the ability to bring disruptive technologies to the business. The challenge is to bring these technologies forward at the right time and in partnership with the business to enable the best possible chances for success.

Seek Approved but Minimal Time and Funding to Explore

Ideally, you should be able to get a limited amount of business-approved work time to explore new technologies and trends. This may take the form of

- Small research projects
- Exploratory prototypes
- Reading research papers
- Attending conferences that are focused on the area of business interest
- Reading blogs, magazines, or books that may enable new capabilities

Citing successful and innovative companies such as Google, 3M, and HP that allow employees "innovation time" to focus on and research new areas may also help in your efforts to obtain approval.

Ideally, your research request would be done in conjunction with your business partners in an area that

- They are looking to move into
- Is currently extremely hard for them to solve
- Requires a significant amount of manual effort to deal with

Make Small Bets

The goal is to survive to live another day. You don't want the entire business riding on a single investment if you are unsure of its long-term future. Being prudent with these kinds of decisions allows you to fail quickly, with the least amount of disruption to the business, and learn how to improve.

Use Technology Scouting to Scan and Track the Trends Regularly

The goal with scouting technology trends is to learn about new things on a regular basis (see Figure 10.4) and find out

- What is applicable to the business
- What things need to wait on the back burner while they mature
- What things warrant further investigation

Keep an eye on new and emerging trends using the scouting method of scanning the landscape to identify what's new and interesting, then track those trends that look promising and apply them to your business. Scanning and tracking technology trends is of less value if the information obtained is not shared, so try to find a venue to share your findings and continue to make updates so your research is up-to-date and relevant.

Note

Maximize the quality of your trend analysis and limit the amount of time you spend by staying hyper-focused and hyper-aware using a technique called "scanning and tracking."

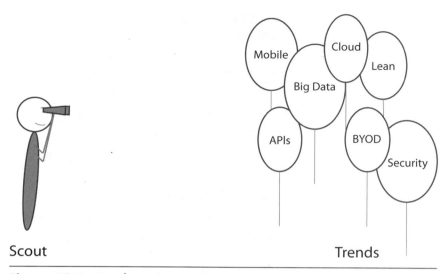

Figure 10.4   Trend scouting

Unless you are in some special circumstance, trends and trend investigation should not consume a large portion of your time. Major trends change less frequently—you may see the direction change every 6 to 12 months—while minor trends change more rapidly.

By quickly *scanning* an area of research interest and *tracking* any major changes, you'll build up a knowledge base that will make your efforts more efficient the next time you *scout* the area. Catching these changes, whether the trends are gaining momentum or fading, gives you an indication of whether or not it is worth spending additional time and resources to learn more about a particular area and report out your findings.

Have a Lab Area

Having a lab environment can allow you play around with new technologies without a lot of visibility from other areas. For the areas in which you find success, you can bring them forward and have them progress toward a production environment.

Setting up a small lab typically doesn't cost too much and allows you to do things that would scare the data center folks to no end.

Use Rapid Experimentation with User Feedback Loops

Experiments allow you to get firsthand knowledge of what is working or not working and a sense of what the real problems are. When experiments are combined with user feedback, you gain the ability to navigate toward customer needs. In many respects, this is similar to driving a car. You use the information that surrounds you to navigate toward your desired goal.

Show the Business and Customers Prototypes

As you have success with new technologies, show the business what is possible. A working example is worth an amazing amount to the business:

- It demonstrates initiative on your part.
- It reduces risk on the part of the business if it chooses to pursue the opportunity.
- It engages your mind in thinking of new ways and approaches to solving problems.
- Small innovations can grow into large enterprises and help sustain the business for the long haul.
- It engages the development team and shows them that working in your company will give them the opportunity to work on cool things and stay current with the industry.

Introduce New Technologies at the Edge

As you look to introduce new technologies into existing systems or even new systems, try to find areas near the edge of the systems that will have minimal impacts on the core (see Figure 10.5). This enables you to operationalize the new technology in a quiet manner.

If it fails, the impact will be relatively small and the executives will be less likely to take notice.

On the other hand, if you take out the core revenue-generating software for any period of time, you are likely to get a direct call from senior executives and have some very unpleasant meetings in which your judgment is questioned.

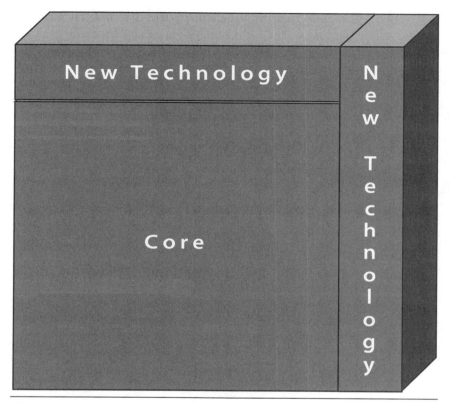

Figure 10.5   Keeping trendy areas near the edge of your activities will minimize the overall risk of trying out new things and the visibility of failures.

If this does occur:

- Be the first to approach the executives.
- Let them know what the situation is.
- Let them know what the possible resolutions are.
- Let them know what path you recommend.

You are much better off being proactive in this situation than reactive. It gives you an opportunity to be in control and to some degree manage the message that is delivered.

PRAGMATIC TECHNOLOGY INNOVATION

The key to pragmatic technology innovation is not so much what is here today; the key is to see what is emerging and anticipating the future needs of your business partners and their customers. Watching Gartner's Hype Cycles, attending leading conferences, and following blogs can help give you a sense of where the industry investments are being made.

Take the time to play around with these technologies; if possible, find a low-profile project to test them on. The important point is to understand what problems are being solved or what business needs will be met.

How does this apply to your business? Think about these questions:

- Where is your business going?
- Where are your chief competitors going?
- Where are your competitors investing?
- Is the business landscape changing?
- Are there new emerging competitors?
- Is your customer base changing? Is it expanding? Shrinking? Aging?
- What is happening to your customers' business model?
- Do you know why your customers' business model is changing?
- What affects your market adoption?
- Do you need to be more aligned with trendy marketing and product appearance?

Taking the answers to these questions into account can help you navigate the tricky waters of what trends to be aware of, what trends to act upon, and what trends you should ignore.

Today, large sweeping trends are influencing technology. These include the following:

- **Big data.** The big data movement is transforming people's thoughts about data analytics, data visualization, and content processing. Hadoop and MapReduce are becoming widely used technologies across all industries. An ever-growing set of technologies is integrating with the Hadoop Distributed File System (HDFS) and making access to big data ubiquitous. Your ability to understand customers and craft user-centric experiences has never been more important. Incorporating information life-cycle semantics into your architecture can enable significantly improved user experiences as your understanding of the users increases.

- **Mobile.** Expectations of mobile as a primary application access point are becoming commonplace. Understanding the user experience within your application as being lean forward (highly interactive) versus lean back (consuming content) is critical to ensuring that the user has a great experience. This understanding along with anticipating users' tendencies to multitask can drive your architectural approaches for the best ways to deliver content.
- **Networked platforms.** With the rise of cloud computing and the proliferation of devices and sensors, platforms are slowly becoming more and more interconnected. Understanding the need to interact with users as well as systems can help drive the architectural layering and the secure API development that are needed to enable networked platforms.

The trends are constantly changing. The key is to be aware of them and to understand their ability to impact your areas of technology innovation. The trends tend to move relatively slowly, but your awareness of them and your ability to apply them appropriately to your business at the right time are critical to keeping your architecture current and relevant to the business.

SUMMARY

The road to technology innovation begins with

- Being aware of the trends
- Aligning with the business
- Engaging in strategic research
- Using innovation principles
- Being a pragmatic technology innovator

Watching and following trends can be fun and exciting. They can easily distract you from the job at hand. However, they are also the eyes into the future that may provide opportunity or peril. Architects need to be familiar with the trends that are swirling around them and approach them with caution.

Technology innovation is a critical aspect of software architecture. Learning when and where to introduce new and potentially disruptive technologies into the business is essential for business growth and operational stability.

REFERENCES

Blank, Steve. 2013. "Spotlight on Entrepreneurship: Why the Lean Start-Up Changes Everything." *Harvard Business Review*, May.

Chesbrough, Henry William. 2005. *Open Innovation: The New Imperative for Creating and Profiting from Technology*. Harvard Business Review Press.

Davenport, Thomas H., and Jeanne G. Harris. 2007. *Competing on Analytics: The New Science of Winning*. Harvard Business Review Press.

Howe, Jeff. 2009. *Crowdsourcing: Why the Power of the Crowd Is Driving the Future of Business*. Crown Business.

Ries, Eric. 2011. *The Lean Startup: How Today's Entrepreneurs Use Continuous Innovation to Create Radically Successful Businesses*. Crown Press.

Chapter 11

STRATEGIC ROADMAPPING

"Map out your future—but do it in pencil. The road ahead is as long as you make it. Make it worth the trip."

—Jon Bon Jovi

"All you need is the plan, the roadmap, and the courage to press on to your destination."

—Earl Nightingale

"A good plan is like a roadmap: it shows the final destination and usually the best way to get there."

—H. Stanley Judd

"I can't change the direction of the wind, but I can adjust my sails to always reach my destination."

—Jimmy Dean

"Follow what you are genuinely passionate about and let that guide you to your destination."

—Diane Sawyer

"The essence of strategy is choosing what not to do."

—Michael Porter

Have you ever been working with the business and started to realize that a new vision was emerging, one that is radically different from where you are today? A vision that would be a real game changer and, if realized, would have a significant impact on your business, possibly your industry, and maybe even the world?

Your mind begins to swirl with all of the things that would need to happen to make this vision come to life. There are what appear to be endless dependencies that would need to align for this to become a reality. Over the course of weeks and months, you begin sorting this out with the business, and you begin to realize that there is a glimmer of hope that if things aligned reasonably well, the vision has a real shot (albeit a long shot) at becoming a reality.

This chapter unveils one of the essential skills needed by a software architect: the ability to lay out a roadmap for how a potential destination can be reached.

STRATEGIC ROADMAPPING DEFINED

Strategic roadmapping is the process of laying out major milestones that are likely to be required for a particular vision to be realized. The exact sequence of the milestones may not be well defined, but their general order is roughly correct.

Roadmaps make strategies actionable.

Representing roadmaps visually can give a sense of the steps, dependencies, and their approximate ordering to achieve a particular vision (see Figure 11.1).

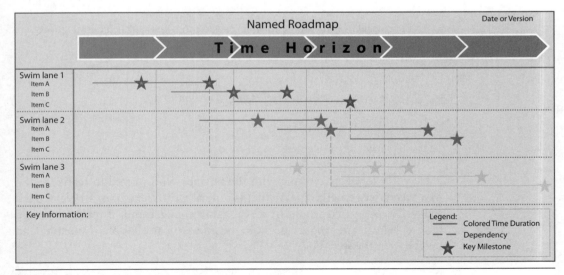

Figure 11.1   Roadmap visualization

ELEMENTS OF A STRATEGIC ROADMAP

Strategic roadmaps tend to incorporate the core elements described in the following sections.

Strategically Focused

The roadmap should be aligned with the strategies, mission, and goals of the organization. There should be an end state toward which the roadmap is driving. Some level of fuzziness in the end state is normal and can be clarified along the way.

Time Sequenced

The roadmap itself should target a specific time horizon. Typically, it can range from 6 months to 36 months depending on the nature of what is being pursued and how urgent the end result is to the organization.

Organized by Swim Lanes

The swim lanes on the roadmap typically represent groups that will do or oversee the work, strategies being pursued, or some other logical grouping that is highly relevant to the group to which the roadmap is targeted. Within each swim lane, you should include key items that need to be addressed, their approximate start and end dates, and key milestones that need to be achieved to demonstrate that progress is being made.

One useful organization of swim lanes is

- A product swim lane (key capabilities, features, or releases)
- A technology swim lane (key technology deliverables that are dependencies for the product or products)
- An infrastructure swim lane (key third-party and operational dependencies)

Dependency Aware

There are typically many dependencies among the items that are represented on the roadmap. These dependencies need to be clearly called out to help the audience that is consuming the roadmap understand their relative order. The items should be sequenced according to their relative start and end dates in relation to the other activities and dependencies that exist.

Visually Represented

The roadmap is best represented in a visual manner. The use of time spans, sequencing, colors, shapes, symbols, and icons can help make the dense amount of information being presented more consumable and relevant to the audience.

Collaborative in Nature

The development of the roadmap is collaborative in nature. It typically requires input from a wide group of individuals with expertise in varying areas. This collaboration enables dependencies to be identified and key milestones to be established that will need to occur to reach the end goal.

Code Named

The effort that is represented by the roadmap often has a code name associated with it. This naming allows a context for discussions to be established among those involved with the effort. A code name also minimizes information to those who are not familiar with the effort if confidentiality is a concern.

Context Dependent (Personalized)

There is no right way, process, or format for developing a roadmap. The roadmap itself needs to be highly relevant to the organization that is developing it. It needs to use domain-specific names, categories, symbology, colors, goals, and strategies that are common and familiar to your business and industry. You need the roadmap to be easily consumable by a broad audience. The more foreign language and unfamiliar concepts that are introduced into the process, the more challenging it will be for people to understand what is to be accomplished.

Multidisciplinary and Specialized

Most roadmaps go beyond the knowledge and expertise of a single person and often of an organization. Gathering the right set of people who can speak to the nuances of the plan to be pursued is critical to developing a roadmap. If you don't have all of the expertise that is required within your organization, you may have to bring in external experts or consultants to help speak to the areas that are new or unknown to the organization.

Prioritized

Roadmaps are as much about what you want to exclude as what you want to accomplish. They are about making tough decisions and prioritizing what to include and when it needs to be accomplished. A roadmap is not just a wish list.

Iterative in Nature

Roadmaps are inherently iterative in nature. As the roadmap is socialized to a broader audience, new details, new dependencies, and new risks emerge and some fade away. This updated information needs to be fed back into the roadmap, which leads to its evolutionary and organic nature.

Updated

Roadmaps need to be living documents. The group that owns and develops the roadmap needs to keep it relevant by updating it on a monthly, quarterly, or yearly basis to reflect progress, changes, new dependencies, or changes in sequence. Over time, it can be interesting to see the progression of a roadmap as it evolves. When new versions of the roadmap are created, a date or version identifier should be placed on the roadmap to let those who are consuming the information understand whether it is current or historical in nature.

Published

Roadmaps should be published to a location that allows for them to be consumed and commented on by a sufficiently broad set of people. Access to the roadmap may be limited to those who are directly involved with the effort or those who are relatively close to it due to confidentiality or strategic concerns. The goal is to engage the broadest possible set of individuals who can provide appropriate feedback. Because of their strategic nature, most roadmaps are not publicly available.

Measurable

Progress on execution of the roadmap should be clearly measurable. The steps that are identified in the progression toward the end state need to be small enough that a regular heartbeat of progress is visible to all who are involved with the effort.

The elements of a strategic roadmap can be used to give you a sense of how to approach roadmapping.

ROADMAPPING STRATEGIES

Whiteboarding the Roadmap Using Sticky Notes

When you start to develop a roadmap, keeping it simple and minimizing the ceremony around its creation can help get things jump-started and moving quickly. One of the best ways to approach this is to simply use a large whiteboard and place sticky notes on it where you've written things that need to happen to achieve the goal. Sticky notes can easily be moved and sequenced relative to one another.

As this roadmap develops, natural sequences and groupings will begin to form. This helps inform what the swim lanes for the effort should be. As dependencies are discovered, note them on sticky notes or use tape and string to connect them. As you make progress, take pictures of the roadmap. Later, this can help trigger ideas from others as they see the roadmap developing.

Starting with the End (aka Work Backward)

Sometimes just getting started with a roadmap can be a bit daunting. One way to alleviate this is to start at the end. Ask what is needed to accomplish the end state. Once those items have been identified, repeat the process with these new items as goals and determine what needs to be in place to be able to accomplish them. Keep repeating this process until you are back to your current state. This process will help identify key dependencies and potential gaps that need to be considered.

Holding Workshops

Given the collaborative nature of roadmapping, holding workshops where all the relevant participants can meet in person is a great way to get a strategic roadmap kicked off and align participants. It allows for the participants who may not have worked together in the past to get to know one another. In the future, this will help reduce the barriers for people to share ideas if they have a sense of trust and an established relationship with the other participants.

Before the workshop, give the participants information about what the agenda will be and access to any preparatory materials so that the time together can be less about discovery and more about the actual roadmap development and conflict resolution.

As the workshop progresses, capture any actions that evolve out of the discussions. When the workshop is nearing the end, review the action items that are outstanding and relevant, and capture information about what went well and what could be improved about the workshop.

Thinking of Roadmapping as a Project

One way to help with the sustainability of the roadmap is to consider the roadmapping exercise as a project itself. The roadmap is the product and the work that happens surrounding the roadmap can be thought of in terms of stories, iterations, release planning, and other development steps.

Capturing Underlying Guiding Principles

As the development of the roadmap progresses, often guiding principles are established to help the participants make decisions. Capturing these guiding principles can help others later on to understand why one decision or path was chosen over another. They help describe the overall rationale behind the roadmap.

The strategies for strategic roadmapping are only suggestions. As stated previously, there is no right or wrong way to develop a roadmap. The key is to discover the information that is needed to pursue the goals that the organization finds most desirable and to do it in a manner that fits with the organization's culture.

ROADMAPPING PRINCIPLES

The goal of roadmapping is to establish a path to reach a specific set of goals. The following principles can be used to help guide the creation and maintenance of the roadmap.

Keep It Simple

Roadmapping should be done with as little ceremony as possible. Find quick and relevant ways to express your ideas to those who will consume the roadmap, use low-tech mechanisms to gather the roadmap information, and minimize any title or role recognition within the roadmap-building workshops. The goal is to get to the task at hand and keep those participating in the roadmapping effort as engaged as possible so they can make significant contributions.

Partner with the Business

Partnering with the business is essential for any roadmapping exercise. You may be able to lay out architecturally what needs to happen, but without input from the business, you will likely not be aligned with its direction and vision. In practice, this is the only way you will achieve the funding levels that are needed to deliver the vision. (For more information, refer to Chapter 1, "Partnership.")

Get Moving

Sometimes looking at a roadmap can seem a bit overwhelming because of everything that needs to be accomplished. One of the best ways to alleviate this is to just get started.

Usually, once you start moving, your anxiety tends to go away and the job at hand keeps you focused. Once you start making progress, there is a tremendous amount of satisfaction that you are moving toward a better state, and it will add energy to what you are doing.

Have Fun

Have some fun along the way. Life is short. If you don't enjoy what you are doing, look for ways to make it more interesting. Maybe look for ways to partner with others. Usually, traveling along with others tends to make the work seem less like work, and the fun can begin.

If you can't find any ways to make it interesting, look for something else to do and come back to it later. Sometimes the work can't be made interesting, and you just need to put your nose to the grindstone and get it done.

Strategies without Goals Are Pointless

Sometimes roadmapping exercises start with strategies in mind, but without a clear goal of what the destination is. Be cautious when this occurs. You need to have a vision and a clear set of goals in place to begin mapping out how to get there. If these are not well understood, take time to back up and get this information clarified or raise your concerns about the endeavor. There needs to be a "why" and a "where" before there can be a "what" and a "how."

Identify Areas That Require Research and Innovation

If you encounter a great chasm during roadmapping development and there is no logical path to the next step, the goal being pursued may be more research or innovation oriented. If this is the case, a focused research or innovation effort may be needed. (For more information, refer to Chapter 10, "Technology Innovation.")

Identify Skill and Knowledge Gaps

During the course of roadmapping, as dependencies are identified, it usually becomes clear what skills and knowledge the organization lacks. This information can be used to help determine training needs, hiring needs, or consultant opportunities. The key is to identify these areas early enough that you can remedy them before they block the progress of the roadmap.

Be Flexible on the Timing of Getting to the Destination

Sometimes the deadlines that we drive toward are simply self-imposed.

If you and the business can be flexible about when something must be done, you have the opportunity to do things at the right time versus forcing something that is really not ready to be addressed. Sometimes if you wait, other solutions will appear or new approaches may come to light that make achieving what you want much simpler.

Be Willing to Take a New Route

A roadmap is an approximate plan for how to accomplish a particular goal or set of goals. The challenge is that with most roadmaps a significant number of unknowns and challenges lie between where you are and where you want to go.

Occasionally, when you are traveling down the road toward your goal, roadblocks appear. There are several choices at this point:

- Do you barge forward in the direction you are traveling? You may already have a significant amount invested, and you feel you are close to a solution.
- Are you able to time-box how much time you are willing to invest in continuing on the current path? This will allow you to limit the collateral damage and get moving toward a different solution.

- What other choices are "in the vicinity"? There are often adjacent solutions that may not be exactly what you had originally planned but are close enough that you can move forward without significant cost or delay.
- Do you need to back up and take a fresh look at what you are attempting to do? Do you really need to do it? Are there other avenues that still get you to your end goal but allow you to go around versus through the current roadblock? Stepping back and taking a broader view of a roadblock can often give you ideas about how to approach the goal.

Taking the time to step back and clearly consider what your best alternatives to moving forward are can help keep you moving toward your ultimate goals in an effective manner.

It's Not about the Details; Focus on the Destination and Key Milestones

For nearly any end-state vision, there are many, many different paths to achieving the goal. The details involved in getting there are often not as important as simply getting there. There may be major milestones that are essential to hitting the end-state target.

The key is to focus on the destination and be willing to vary how you are going to achieve the goal. Sometimes simply changing the approach can have a dramatic impact on the overall cost and effort required to achieve what you want.

Some of the best ways to do this are to

- **Talk to other architects.** They may be able to tell you how they have approached similar problems.
- **Talk to other areas of the business.** This will help you get a sense of the different perspectives on the problem you are attempting to address.
- **Talk to some of the executives.** They usually have a remarkably good sense of what is essential and what is nonessential.
- **Talk to some customers.** Customers who work in the area you are focusing on can normally tell you if what you are concerned about has any relevance to what they do.

In nearly all situations, talking to others (collaborating) can help

- Clarify what you are concerned about
- Provide alternative approaches or solutions
- Simplify or eliminate problems altogether
- Confirm that you do indeed have a tough issue

Regardless of the feedback, you will have confirmation that you are on the right path or need to make some adjustments.

Follow What Energizes You

If the roadmap that you have developed doesn't energize you, you are likely on the wrong path or have a vision that doesn't fit the current business (or strategic) environment. Even if you are on the right path, if you don't have passion about the goals and vision you are attempting to move toward, you are unlikely to inspire anyone else to want to take the trip.

The key to finding what energizes you is to follow what you are passionate about. Look at what you are trying to accomplish and try to determine the answers to these questions:

- What is of interest to you? These areas of interest will be easy to go after even when you are tired and have been on the journey for a while.
- What is not of interest to you? These are the energy drains. If you do not have interest in doing these things, consider alternatives.
- Are there ways to repackage the item to make it interesting?
- Can you change the approach?
- Can you delegate this area?
- Are there ways to simply eliminate the item altogether?

At the end of the day, you need to believe in what you are doing. If you don't, you are not likely to succeed, which is bad for you and for the delivery of the roadmap goals.

WHAT IS AN ARCHITECT'S ROLE IN ROADMAPPING?

Given the collaborative and multidisciplinary nature of roadmaps, architects are rarely the only ones at the table. Architects normally excel at roadmapping due to their detailed product, technology, and infrastructure knowledge. This detailed knowledge lends itself to knowing and understanding key dependencies that exist, which in turn leads to helping sequence the major milestones. It is common for architects to help draft the first copies of the roadmap.

WHERE CAN YOU USE ROADMAPS?

Roadmaps can be used to describe many different things. It really depends on what you want to communicate about future plans.

Roadmaps can be used for

- Capital planning
- Product or platform capabilities
- Project or product integrations
- Compliance milestones
- Major release milestones

Use roadmaps as a communication vehicle to help others understand the direction where things are going and the general timing of when the goal will be delivered. This will help others plan when they can leverage the solutions identified in the roadmap.

ROADMAP CONSIDERATIONS

"You'll learn more about a road by traveling it than by consulting all the maps in the world."

—Anonymous

"Experience, travel—these are as education in themselves."

—Euripides

As you go through the process of developing a roadmap, there are a large number of considerations that should be taken into account, such as the following:

- Does the roadmap show a replatformization? Key migrations? Major technology changes? These are all large cost drivers that you will need to have accounted for.

- Does the roadmap align with your technology innovation efforts? If it does, it may allow for some natural synergies.

- Does the roadmap drive you toward the revenue model you want to achieve? Does it give you the premium or value brand you are shooting for? Understanding the revenue and value impacts is critical when seeking approval and funding for implementing the roadmap.

- What are your competitors doing? Can you create a likely roadmap for them? Trying to get a sense of what your competitors are doing and are likely to do will give you a sense of how you will need to compete and what issues you may need to address in your roadmap.

- Have others published their roadmaps at conferences? Any external information that you can gather will help you understand how others are approaching similar problems or give you insights into your competition.

- Have others in your company released a roadmap? If they are integrating with you or you with them, do you show up on their roadmap? If not, why not? Creating synergies and following successful patterns can help simplify your justification for implementing the items on your roadmap.

- Does your roadmap vary per platform (mobile versus desktop versus cloud based)? Understanding how platforms impact the work you do can help you structure the architecture in a manner that is platform friendly or agnostic depending on the nature of what you are doing.

- Are there regulatory concerns that need to be addressed? Regulatory needs and requirements can add significant cost to the work of implementing a roadmap. You need to understand these early on and clearly articulate how you are addressing them.

- Are there certifications that are being pursued? Are there dependencies between the certifications? Are there pre-evaluations that need to be performed? Certification dependencies for a roadmap are very important to know up front so that you can include the requirements and costs of pursuing certifications clearly in your roadmap.

Roadmaps are rarely derailed by the known items. It is the unknowns that creep up and derail the effort. Keep a vigilant eye on the roadmap and its adjacencies. This knowledge may give you insights into risks of which you were previously unaware, and it can help give you the maximum amount of time possible to mitigate these risks.

ROADMAP SOCIALIZATION

Roadmapping is an essential communication tool for an architect. It allows for a malleable future, one that is not set in stone but instead gives a sense of priorities and a sense of key dependencies to help inform current decisions.

It can also be used as a tool for others to understand when to engage with a new platform or to understand when their dependencies may need to change.

Once the roadmap has been established, it needs to be socialized within the organization (see Figure 11.2); this will help establish buy-in for the chosen direction.

The roadmap can act as a form of sales tool to show that you are aware of certain deficiencies today, to show alternative ways to address them in the future, and to show approximately the time frame in which they may be addressed.

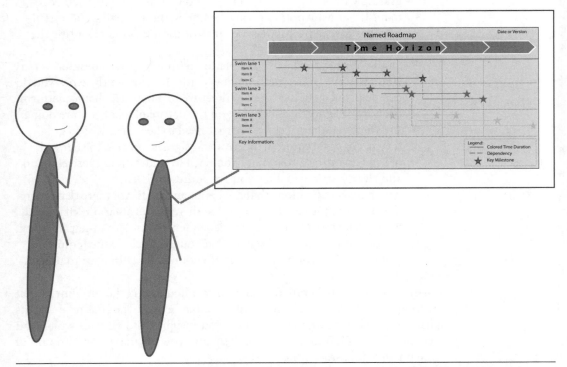

Figure 11.2   Socializing your roadmap can help align the expectations of all the groups with which you interact, allow for clarifications, and allow for adjustments to be made.

The key is that a roadmap invites conversation and a way to gather other people's insights (positive or negative).

It is likely that some of the roadmap may not be definitive. Socializing it invites the kind of feedback you are looking for:

- Are we directionally correct? There is a natural tension between directionally correct and the need for course correction based on different perspectives.
- Does it invite excitement and passion? If it does, you are probably on the right track.
- Does it invite skepticism? This may be okay, although you may have a challenge on your hands to work through it.

Managing group dynamics during roadmap development is critical to keeping the flow of information and critical thinking open and respectful. When a respectful environment exists, people are more naturally willing to express their true thoughts.

A roadmap really is a communication tool. It's a plan. It's okay for it to change as new things are learned. It also gives you a sense of history when you look back and see what you were thinking and where you actually ended up.

CELEBRATING MILESTONES ACHIEVED

Once the roadmap has been established and the project or projects that support it are well under way, take the time to celebrate the milestones as they are achieved.

Recognizing that you are making progress on the road to success can keep the teams engaged and provide valuable feedback about where you have been, what lessons you have learned, and what you need to continue doing to ensure that you will complete the journey.

SUMMARY

The path to roadmapping begins with

- Understanding the elements of roadmapping
- Leveraging the roadmapping strategies
- Understanding the roadmapping principles
- Knowing where roadmaps are best used

- Being observant of new risks
- Socializing the roadmap
- Knowing your role in roadmap development
- Celebrating milestone successes

For architects, roadmaps are an essential communication tool for helping to establish a vision of what needs to be accomplished and its approximate sequencing. When the business and architecture are on the same page regarding where a product or platform is going, this partnership can help propel the success of the business.

REFERENCES

Highsmith, Jim. 2009. *Agile Project Management: Creating Innovative Products, Second Edition.* Addison-Wesley.

Lafley, A. G., and Roger L. Martin. 1999. *Playing to Win: How Strategy Really Works.* Harvard Business Review Press.

Lawley, Brian. 2007. *Expert Product Management: Advanced Techniques, Tips and Strategies for Product Management and Product Marketing.* Happy About.

Mckeown, Max. 2012. *The Strategy Book: How to Think and Act Strategically to Deliver Outstanding Results.* FT Press.

Nimmo, Geoffrey, Rich Scheer, Jack Eisenhower, Michael Radnor, Julie Glasgow, Louise Vickery, Catherine Farrell, and Deborah Howard. 2001. *Technology Planning for Business Competitiveness: A Guide to Developing Technology Roadmaps.* Australian Emerging Industries Section Department of Industry, Science and Resources.

Osterwalder, Alexander, and Yves Pigneur. 2010. *Business Model Generation: A Handbook for Visionaries, Game Changers, and Challengers.* Wiley.

Phaal, Robert, Clare Farrukh, and David Probert. 2001. "Technology Roadmapping: Linking Technology Resources to Business Objectives." Centre for Technology Management, University of Cambridge.

Whalen, P. J. 2007. "Strategic and Technology Planning on a Roadmapping Foundation." *Research-Technology Management*, May–June, pp. 40–51.

Chapter 12

ENTREPRENEURIAL EXECUTION

"The five essential entrepreneurial skills for success are concentration, discrimination, organization, innovation, and communication."

—Michael Faraday

"Your time is limited, so don't waste it living someone else's life. Don't be trapped by dogma—which is living with the results of other people's thinking. Don't let the noise of others' opinions drown out your own inner voice. And most important, have the courage to follow your heart and intuition. They somehow already know what you truly want to become. Everything else is secondary."

—Steve Jobs

"It takes 20 years to build a reputation and 5 minutes to ruin it. If you think about that, you'll do things differently."

—Warren Buffett

"Choose a job you love and you will never have to work a day in your life."

—Confucius

"Vision without execution is hallucination."

—Thomas A. Edison

Have you ever noticed that the most challenging problems require you to step back, throw away your assumptions, and look at the problem carefully from a different perspective? This process requires you to dive deeper into the problem and contemplate whether your approach is right, if your models hold up correctly, if there are similar solutions to the problem, how solving this problem really helps the customer, and whether there are other ways to solve the problem. You talk to others and slowly the solution begins to reveal itself as you immerse yourself in the details.

Entrepreneurial execution is about finding new and innovative ways to solve problems and, as Richard Branson suggests, to "make other people's lives better." It is this quest that makes the life of an architect an exciting journey.

This chapter unveils one of the essential skills needed by a software architect: the ability to apply entrepreneurial execution to software architecture.

ENTREPRENEURIAL EXECUTION DEFINED

"Entrepreneurship is the pursuit of opportunity without regard to resources currently controlled."

—Howard Stevenson

"Entrepreneurship is at the intersection of an idea that solves a problem and the actions taken to implement the idea."

—Randy Blass

Entrepreneurial execution is the vitality that breathes life into architecture. It is the spirit of adventure and of solving epic problems that inspires you day by day. It is knowing that what you do will make a difference in the world and will enable others to do great things.

The elements of entrepreneurial execution include vision, innovation, solving problems, throwing out the past, persistence (relentless drive), identifying the small change that changes the world, recognizing patterns from other domains that apply to yours, perceiving a problem that others don't yet see, recognizing a solved problem, taking calculated risks, and delivering results.

Entrepreneurial execution is where an idea meets action (see Figure 12.1).

It is the spirit of exploration—the "Go west, young man" of Horace Greeley—that drives entrepreneurial execution.

ELEMENTS OF ENTREPRENEURIAL EXECUTION

Entrepreneurial execution is about bringing an entrepreneurial spirit to the work that you do, taking calculated risks, and delivering results (see Figure 12.2).

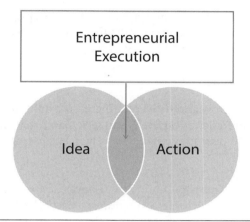

Figure 12.1 Entrepreneurial execution

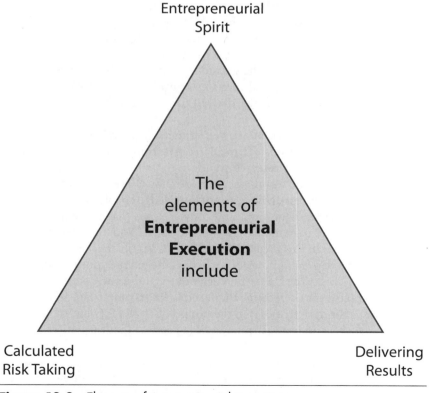

Figure 12.2 Elements of entrepreneurial execution

Entrepreneurial execution, sometimes known as intrapreneurship within a corporation, can help you deliver results that bring innovation and add significant value to the company.

Entrepreneurial Spirit

Businesses need to grow and deliver an increasing amount of value to their customers. This need drives businesses to seek teams that embody an entrepreneurial spirit to help maximize that value. The essence of an entrepreneurial spirit is

- **Innovation.** This is the ability to discover new and creative ways to deliver value to customers. It requires a natural level of curiosity and constant observation of the things that surround you. (See Chapter 10, "Technology Innovation.")
- **Passion.** This is the enthusiasm that you radiate when you love what you do. Passion can supply the fuel necessary to keep you motivated and continuing to drive toward a solution.
- **Thriving in adversity.** As the old saying goes, "Necessity is the mother of invention." Adversity can help drive you to new solutions by enabling you to better deliver value to your customers through refining and adapting the solutions you are trying to create.
- **Optimism.** This is the almost unstoppable belief that you can get where you want to go regardless of the storms that are swirling around you.
- **Depth of knowledge.** When you immerse yourself in a problem space for long periods of time, look at it from nearly every possible vantage point, and research solutions to issues in this problem space extensively, you naturally begin to develop a level of expertise that few others possess. This depth of knowledge enables you to quickly navigate around questions and conversations that are centered in this area and to demonstrate your expertise. You know what is easy and known in this area and what the hard problems and unknowns are. This depth of knowledge will become part of your brand.
- **Focus.** This is the ability to block out the noise and concentrate on the top two or three items that need to be accomplished and delivered. This directly ties into the notion of an MVP (what is essential to deliver) and product/market fit (a product that can satisfy the needs of the market).
- **Trusting your gut feeling.** This is about learning to listen to your gut feeling and having the confidence to follow it. It will help guide your decisions when all the facts are not readily available.

- **Credibility.** This is about establishing trust with those who will invest financial capital or allocate resources to your ideas. You need to be authentic and have integrity in what you say and do to gain credibility. You need to deliver on what you commit to.

Calculated Risk Taking

There are always risks to projects. The challenge is to minimize the impact of the risks in a manner that allows you to change, grow, and improve while not putting your core assets at risk.

There are a variety of ways to accomplish this:

- **Learn from others.** Take the time to gather the experiences of others who have traveled or tried to travel down this path. Experience is a great teacher, and learning from others' experiences can shorten your path to success.
- **Utilize POCs (proofs of concept).** POCs are great tools to help determine the viability of solutions or to help navigate the decision-making process about which path to follow. Using them allows you to fail, learn, and adjust your direction early and quietly without a major impact to the project. The key is to do them quickly and minimize the effort required.
- **Enable and use A/B testing.** In areas where you are trying to measure customer interest, A/B testing can help you compare two or more variances of a solution and determine which ones attract the most interest. The key is to make sure you vary only one element of the solution at a time. Gathering and comparing the results of the users' behavior can give you great insights into which approach or approaches work best.
- **Minimize the required investment.** If you can minimize the required investment to the point where a loss is affordable (see the section on principles that follows), you can take the risk and not endanger your ability to survive to another day. This is one of the key ideas behind an MVP. The challenge is to ensure that there is still enough value to engage your customers with the solution.

You may notice a pattern here. The key is to do, measure, learn, and repeat. You always need to keep your end goal in mind to ensure that you are heading in the right direction. Otherwise, a series of small decisions can leave you pointing in the wrong direction.

From an architecture perspective, the key is to enable the ability to measure key performance indicators and enable low-cost system changes without impacting the overall design or quality of the system. You want to be data driven.

Delivering Results

One of the most import things a business needs from an architect is the ability to deliver results. Working closely with the business to navigate the creation of a product or platform and making the pragmatic daily decisions necessary to deliver customer value through techniques such as MVP are essential to delivering results consistently.

ENTREPRENEURIAL EXECUTION PRINCIPLES

The goal of architecture is to enable the business to achieve its goals. One of the chief goals of most businesses is to grow. The following principles embody the spirit of entrepreneurship and can help align architectural decisions to lean toward successfully growing the business.

Affordable Loss Principle

The *Affordable Loss Principle* is looking at what the potential loss would be if this decision is made or not made and making a determination of whether or not you can afford that loss, whether it be financial, reputation, time to market, scalability, or some other type of loss. From an architecture perspective, this is what drives many of the nonfunctional requirement decisions such as disaster recovery, security, and identity management. It is important to note that what is determined to be an affordable loss may change over time as the business or product grows.

Lemonade Principle

The *Lemonade Principle* means taking a different perspective on the problems at hand. Maybe instead of being problems, they are really opportunities that are waiting to be recognized (making lemonade out of lemons); for instance, when you are trying to build a roadmap and you reach a point where there appears to be no known solution for how to get from point A to point B. This may be a problem that many different organizations and companies are encountering, and solving it may be the real product or solution that you should research and build. It may be an opportunity to pivot. It is important to note that the business is about delivering results, not necessarily the results that were originally intended.

Patchwork Quilt Principle

The *Patchwork Quilt Principle* means solving the problems of your current set of investors (those who are footing the bills). The advantage of taking this type of approach is that you have one of the critical issues solved—having someone who cares enough about what you are doing to give you money. They are already committed, and the advice they give you may be self-serving, but it will be real, and not just opinions. Generally speaking, if you can make at least one person truly happy with your solution, you are off to the races.

During platform development, your current investors are often those who are willing to fund new features in the platform. They aren't just making suggestions ("It would be really nice if . . ."); they are making a real commitment to spend limited investment dollars and use your platform. Let these committed partners guide and help craft your vision.

Bird-in-the-Hand Principle

The *Bird-in-the-Hand Principle* means using the things you have to drive and create solutions. There is always that great new shiny object that if you only had it (better known as "shiny object syndrome"), you would be able to easily produce the system that is being sought. From an architecture perspective, can you use an existing technology (sometimes the new technologies don't operationalize very well), or can the current development staff learn the needed skills (sometimes existing domain knowledge is critical to solving the new problems)? The key is to leverage what you have to the greatest extent possible; it usually has more value than you think.

Pilot-in-the-Plane Principle

The *Pilot-in-the-Plane Principle* means that the future is not the outcome of some inevitable trend, but rather is the outcome of human choices and actions. It is the pilot in the plane who will have the most direct effect on the success of the flight based on the pilot's actions or inactions. The great news is that you have the ability to determine your future. As an architect, your actions or inactions will directly impact the success or failure of a project; you get the opportunity to help craft that future.

Seize the Moment

For entrepreneurs, there is no time like the present. In reality, this is the only time you are guaranteed to have. Action is something that can help you engage in innovating and developing new solutions for customers.

There is often a tendency to want to wait for just a few more details to arrive and then start, but in reality you need to start doing, and that can enable the learning process to begin. It will also give you time to fail and restart a few times.

For architects, beginning to explore an area by beginning to model problems, "playing" with technology, visually beginning to represent knowledge that is acquired, and getting feedback on the thoughts surrounding a particular solution can enable the moment to be seized and a jump on the competition to be afoot.

Follow Your Passion

Following your passion (the areas that fundamentally interest you) is your internal compass. It is naturally focused on areas that can maintain your interest for the long haul. It will make the journey you are on seem like an adventure with some days being very exciting, some days being a bit scary, but overall the path presents the opportunity to fulfill your destiny.

If you are not sure what your passions are, consider the following:

- What areas do you naturally like to talk about?
- In what areas do you lose track of time when you are engaged with them?
- To what areas does your mind naturally drift off when you are daydreaming?
- What areas give you a sense of fulfillment when you are pursuing them?

These are your areas of passion. Think about what you need to do to find ways to pursue these areas. Your daily grind will become a much more enjoyable experience when you pursue the areas you are passionate about.

Most people who interact with you can probably easily tell you what you are passionate about. You are likely overflowing with information about that area. You know the pros. You know the cons. You know what works and what doesn't work. You truly have a wealth of information.

People can tell your passion without you having to state it because it's who you are.

Learn to Pivot

Pivoting is the ability to recognize that the current path is not working and change is required. Having the confidence and ability to make course corrections is an essential element of entrepreneurship. It is unlikely that the exact course you have planned for going from point A to point B will work. Learning to pivot when roadblocks are encountered is a necessity (see Figure 12.3).

When you need to pivot, take the time to see where the big opportunity lies (your end state, your vision), adjust your course based on all of the

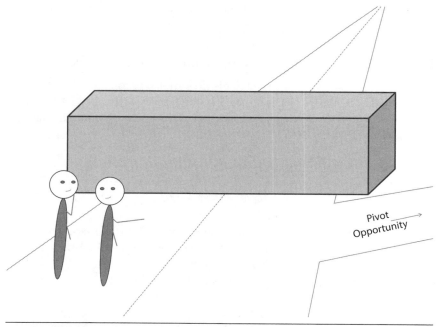

Figure 12.3   Roadblocks are simply pivot opportunities.

information you have, and understand where the overall industry is heading; doing so can keep you moving forward.

The challenge is being willing to change and to leave behind what you potentially have made a large investment in. Here are a few key considerations when you need to explore pivoting:

- Why is the current approach not working?
- What assumptions are not valid?
- Has anything fundamentally changed in the industry?
- Are other people having similar problems with this architectural approach?
- Does your vision need to change based on the realities that have been learned?
- What is different about the new approach that will enable success?
- How will the pivot affect your customers?

Once you are comfortable with making course adjustments and successfully navigating the detours and challenges you face, your overall confidence to jump in and take on whatever is thrown your way goes up dramatically. You realize it is okay for things to go wrong and just deal with it.

Learn by Doing (Making Mistakes), but Do It Cost-Effectively

In the world of software, there really is no better way to learn than to actually do what you desire to get done. You don't necessarily need to do everything, but you do need to play around with the software enough that you have a sense of

- What its capabilities are
- Where it is effective
- Where it doesn't work well
- What assumptions you have that don't hold up
- What new risks exist that you were previously unaware of
- What new dependencies exist that you were previously unaware of
- Where the software needs to be improved
- Whether what you hope to do is even possible

The first challenge of experiencing learning is to establish clear goals about what you are seeking to learn and determine how much time you are willing to invest. By time-boxing and financially boxing in a proof of concept or spike, you will be able to gain the key learnings that are needed with limited investment.

The second challenge is to secure the funding necessary to learn what you are seeking. This work may not be capitalizable due to its lack of size, and the business may not have planned on this effort as part of its capital planning. With clear objectives about risk to delivery and a little persistence, you can secure some portion of the budget to allow for these kinds of activities.

By taking the time to make mistakes, to learn, and to try again, you can mitigate the risks associated with a particular direction and help gain the business's confidence that this new way of approaching a problem is viable. This low-cost approach to eliminating risk and increasing the likelihood of delivery will help you have the staying power you need to inject innovation and entrepreneurship into your business.

Seek Feedback

One of the best ways to establish a route to your vision is to create a feedback loop (see Figure 12.4). You regularly need to get feedback about

- Where you are
- What has been completed
- Where you are going
- What is not working
- What is working
- How things could be improved

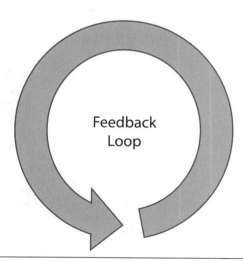

Figure 12.4   Feedback loops will keep you aligned with your goals even when they change.

This feedback can come from customers, vendors, and employees. Getting feedback from different perspectives can help ground your decision making. Make sure you electronically capture all of the feedback you receive so that it will be easy to find in the future.

You want to listen closely to what is being said, both positive and negative. By listening closely to feedback, you have the opportunity to use feedback like a GPS system and let it help guide you to your destination.

The challenge with a waterfall approach to development is that there really is no opportunity for feedback to occur and for incremental improvements to be a source of constant refinement and perfection of the solution.

As you use feedback loops to help with course corrections, keep your end state in mind to help avoid optimizations that don't move you toward your larger goals.

Seek Leverage

It is rare that any solution is completely new and that every component of the solution is a first-time build. The uniqueness and innovation come from the unique combination of the components of the solution (most of which previously existed) and adding only those things for which a solution did not previously exist. Leveraging gives you the opportunity to meet your business needs in a cost- and time-effective manner (see Figure 12.5).

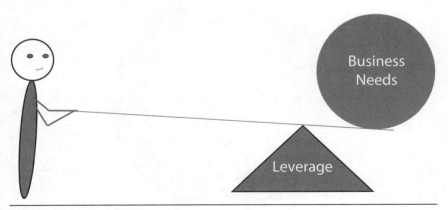

Figure 12.5   Leverage

Leveraging existing components, especially open-source and other commodities, can

- Significantly reduce your overall cost of ownership.
- Allow you to get to a working solution more quickly.
- Allow you to focus on the areas where you provide unique value.
- Leverage the work and experience of others. You can stand on their shoulders.
- Limit your potential set of solutions. You need to think about what you are giving up, what new risks you are introducing, and what new dependencies you are adding.

Leverage can be both good and bad (generally more on the good side). As with all decisions, you need to spend some time thinking through what you are gaining and losing in making this choice. Most decisions can be reversed later. However, if it is a core foundational piece of the architecture, swapping it out later may be a costly endeavor.

Sometimes you can isolate these types of components within the system so that changing them later does not negatively affect everything. Using these forms of indirection can be very powerful in an architecture. However, having too many levels of indirection can cause confusion and a general lack of understanding. Use indirection with caution.

ARCHITECTING WITH ENTREPRENEURIAL EXECUTION

"I don't know the key to success, but the key to failure is trying to please everybody."

—Bill Cosby

Architecting with entrepreneurial execution is fun and exciting. It does bring out naysayers as well. You need to pick the path that is right for your customers and for the business. The entrepreneurial principles can be a measuring stick for the decisions that need to be made and allow you to move forward in bringing new things into the architectural stack in a way that aligns well with the business and creates new capabilities to give you a competitive advantage in the marketplace.

SUMMARY

The road to entrepreneurial execution begins with

- Understanding the elements of entrepreneurial execution
  - Entrepreneurial spirit
  - Calculated risk taking
  - Delivering results
- Using entrepreneurial execution principles as guidance
  - Affordable Loss Principle
  - Lemonade Principle
  - Patchwork Quilt Principle
  - Bird-in-the-Hand Principle
  - Pilot-in-the-Plane Principle
  - Seize the moment
  - Follow your passion
  - Learn to pivot
  - Learn by doing and making mistakes
  - Seek feedback
  - Seek leverage
- Architecting with entrepreneurial execution

For me, working with new product development, innovating on new and improved products, and developing business-relevant architectures are challenging and exciting. Operating with an entrepreneurial spirit keeps the technology stack current and allows for areas of greenfield development that provide significant value to the business.

REFERENCES

Bank, Steve. 2012. *The Startup Owner's Manual: The Step-by-Step Guide for Building a Great Company*. K&S Ranch.

————. 2013. *The Four Steps to the Epiphany, Second Edition*. K&S Ranch.

Blekman, Thomas. 2011. *Corporate Effectuation: What Managers Should Learn from Entrepreneurs*. K&S Ranch.

Croll, Alistair, and Benjamin Yoskovitz. 2013. *Lean Analytics: Use Data to Build a Better Startup Faster*. O'Reilly Media.

Harvard Business Review. 2011. *Harvard Business Review on Succeeding as an Entrepreneur*. Harvard Business Review Press.

Holiday, Ryan. 2013. *Growth Hacker Marketing: A Primer on the Future of PR, Marketing, and Advertising*. Portfolio.

Johnson, Kevin D. 2013. *The Entrepreneur Mind: 100 Essential Beliefs, Characteristics, and Habits of Elite Entrepreneurs*. Johnson Media Inc.

Kuratko, Donald F. 2008. *Entrepreneurship: Theory, Process, and Practice*. Cengage Learning.

Ries, Eric. 2011. *The Lean Startup: How Today's Entrepreneurs Use Continuous Innovation to Create Radically Successful Businesses*. Crown Business.

Sarasvathy, Saras D. 2009. *Effectuation: Elements of Entrepreneurial Expertise*. Edward Elgar Publishing.

Siroker, Dan, and Pete Koomen. 2013. *A/B Testing: The Most Powerful Way to Turn Clicks into Customers*. Wiley.

Epilogue

BRINGING IT ALL TOGETHER

This book and my first book (*12 Essential Skills for Software Architects*) focus on the skills needed to become a successful software architect.

These skills can be thought of in two key dimensions:

- **Soft skills.** Soft skills are the ability to relate to people (the focus of my first book).
- **Technical skills.** Technical skills are the ability to contextually apply and drive technology (the focus of this book).

It is the combination of soft and technical skills that will enable you reach your architectural goals (see Figure E.1).

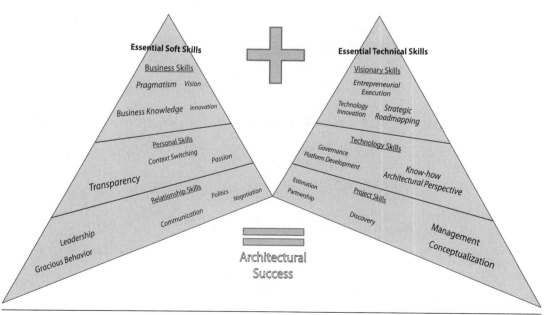

Figure E.1   Equation for architectural success

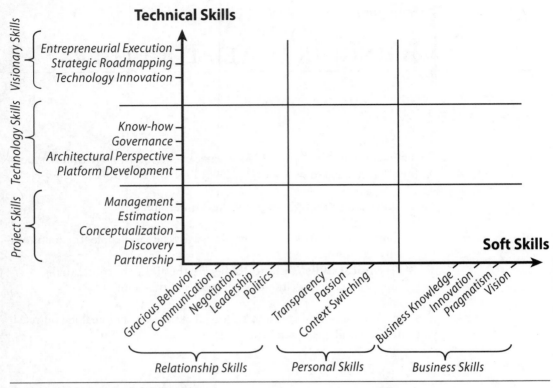

Figure E.2   Areas of skills development

THINKING ABOUT SKILL DEVELOPMENT

As you consider what areas of skill development to work on (as shown in Figure E.2), take time to think about the following:

- Where do your skills intersect?
- What are your strengths and weaknesses?
- In what areas have you received feedback from others?

When you are dealing with skill development, there is a tendency to focus on weaknesses. The focus should rather be on your natural strengths and only those areas of weakness that are major roadblocks to your moving forward in your career.

FINAL THOUGHT

Overall, it has been an interesting journey for me. I discovered that I enjoy writing—at least on topics that I am passionate about. This is something I could never have imagined in college, and I am sure my professors would agree with that sentiment.

These books have enabled me to connect with great new people, reconnect with old friends, and gain opportunities to do things that would never have surfaced otherwise.

My advice is to take chances, try new things, and you will be surprised at what you are able to accomplish.

Good luck and best wishes on your architectural endeavors!

INDEX

A

Acquisition projects, estimating, 86
Advisory boards, for platform development, 150–151
Affordable Loss Principle, 276
Agile development, and governance, 209–210
Alignment
    architecture review board, 10–11
    choosing partners, 7–9
    community review, 10–11
    decision making, 11
    influencers, 10
    shared vision, 11–12
    stakeholders, 8–9
    thought leaders, 9
    trusted advisers, 10
Alternative financing, 86–87
Ambiguity, dealing with, 217
API explorers, 154
APIs, designing, 147–148
Applications
    consolidating during platform development, 163
    vs. platforms, estimation, 93
Approach reviews, 206
Architectural approach to estimation. *See* Estimation, architectural approach
Architectural communication. *See also* Presentations
    context diagrams, 185
    domain models, 184
    executive overview diagrams, 187
    hardware environment diagrams, 187–188
    in the ideation and discovery phases, 184
    logical architecture diagrams, 186–187
    process diagrams, 184–185
    RAID (risks, assumptions, issues, dependencies), 188–191
    system boundaries, showing, 185
    system components, showing, 186–187
    user interface mock-ups, 186
    work flow, showing, 184–185

Architectural concerns
    availability, 178–179
    business continuity, 196–197
    changing the system, 182
    compatibility, 182
    disaster recovery, 196–198
    extensibility, 181–182
    maintenance windows, 179
    open-source licensing, 195–196
    power outages, 179
    repeatability, 182
    scalability, 180–181
    security, 201–202
    server failure, 179
    site loss, 179
    site outages, 179
    software compatibility issues, 179
    storage failure, 179
    storage full, 178–179
    sustainability, 182–183
    third-party integration, 182–183
Architectural elevator speech, 126
Architectural overviews, platform development, 154
Architectural perspectives. *See also specific perspectives*
    definition, 170
    overview, 171
Architectural principles
    cost of delay, 176–177
    KISS (Keep It Simple, Stupid), 175–176
    Law of Demeter, 172
    meeting user expectations, 170–172
    minimizing dependencies, 172
    narrowly defining services, 175
    Occam's Razor, 175–176
    Principle of Feedback, 177
    Principle of Last Responsible Moment, 176–177
    Principle of Least Effort, 172–173
    Principle of Least Knowledge, 172
    Principle of Least Surprise, 170–172
    Principle of Natural Intuition, 171

Architectural principles (*continued*)
    Principle of Opportunity Cost, 173–175
    Principle of Parsimony, 175–176
    Principle of Single Responsibility, 175
    solving immediate problems, 172–173
    Zipf's Law, 172–173
Architecture review board, 10–11
Architecture reviews
    approach, 206
    development, 207
    enterprise, 207
    executive, 206–207
    governance areas, 206–207
    hardware, 207
    peer, 207
Assumptions
    establishing, 68–69
    RAID (risks, assumptions, issues, dependencies),
        68–69
Automation, governance principles, 203
Availability, architectural concerns, 178–179

B

Bargaining, in estimation, 101
BCPs (business continuity plans), 197–198
Big data trends, 252–253
Bird-in-the-Hand Principle, 277
Blogging, 225
Building, governance area, 208–209
Business case estimate, 82
Business case validation estimates, 82
Business continuity, architectural concerns, 196–197
Business continuity planning, governance prin-
    ciples, 196–198
Business discovery, 52
Business goals
    aligning research with, 245
    discovery of your business, 52
    platform development ecosystems, 153
    strategic roadmapping principles, 262
Business unit driven research, 246

C

Calculated risk taking, 275–276
Capabilities
    APIs, designing, 147–148
    conceptual models, 147
    defining, 146
    defining objectives, 145–146
    definition, 144
    establishing, 69–70
    leveraging, 146–147
Captive customers, 242–243
Caving in
    decision making, 124
    in estimation, 101
    resolving issues, 124
Changing the system, architectural concerns, 182
Checklists for estimation, 99
Cloud capability trends, 241
Code names, strategic roadmapping, 258
Coding, governance areas, 208–209
Collaboration
    becoming a mentor, 22–23
    bringing value to the table, 22
    giving feedback, 23
    moving toward ideation, 24
    seeking a mentor, 23–24
    as a source of opportunity, 24
    strategic roadmapping, 258
    strengthening partnerships, 24–25
Commitment
    concept formation, 62–63
    overcommitment, 13–15
    time management, 127–128
Communication. *See* Architectural communica-
    tion; Documentation; Presentations; Visual
    models
Community review, 10–11
Company assets, consolidating during platform
    development, 157–158
Compatibility, architectural concerns, 182
Competition, studying, 48–50
Complexity, reducing, 72–73
Concept evolution
    adjacent opportunities, 75
    conceptual integrity, 73–75
    history of the concept, 71–72
    multiple perspectives, 72–73
    reducing complexity, 72–73
Concept formation
    conceptual diagrams, 64
    context diagrams, 64
    customer involvement, 65–66
    domain models, 59, 61
    early involvement, 65

identifying main concepts, 60
listening to the customer, 65–66
making a commitment, 62–63
problem scope, 60–62
saying no, 62–63
speaking the customer's language, 59–60
visual models, 63–67
Concept life cycle, 58
Concept reification
assumptions, establishing, 68–69
customer involvement, 70–71
customer pain points, 70
customer roles, establishing, 69–70
definition, 67
essential capabilities, establishing, 69–70
experimentation, 68
MVPs (minimum viable products), 67
POCs (proofs of concept), 68–69
reevaluating the product concept, 69–70
Conceptual diagrams, 64
Conceptual integrity, 73–75
Conceptual models for platform capabilities, 147
Conceptualization. See also Ideation
concept life cycle, 58. See also specific stages
early involvement, 57
overview, 55
Concerns. See Architectural concerns
Conferences
attending, 220
presenting at, 223
for professional development, 132–133
trends, 240
Configurability vs. hard coding, 165
Consolidating
applications during platform development, 163
company assets during platform development, 157–158
Context
business, 17
contributing to your partner's success, 20–21
for decision making, 52
guarding relationships, 20
safety in numbers, 21
technical decisions, 18–19
when presenting information, 19–20
Context diagrams, 64, 185
Contractors
in leadership positions, 119
for platform development, 158

Contractual relationships vs. partnerships, in estimation, 88–89
Corporate innovation labs, 247
Cost estimation. See Estimation
Costs
of delay, architectural principle, 176–177
of disruption, governance principles, 196–198
platform development, 161–162
saving money, 228
Credibility, 275
Customer feedback
analyzing, 243
getting, 242–243
Customer inquiries, trend analysis, 242
Customer involvement
concept formation, 65–66
concept reification, 70–71
Customer pain points, 70
Customer roles, establishing, 69–70
Customers. See also Discovery, of customers; Users of platforms
captives, 242–243
fans, 242
followers, 243
interaction with during platform development, 153
perspective of, 35–37
as platform users, 148, 153
themes, identifying, 50–51
training courses. studying, 37
utilitarians, 242
value, identifying, 47–48
Customers' competitive knowledge trends, 241
Customer's language
concept formation, 59–60
learning, 42
NPD (new product development), 34

D

Dashboards, 226–227
Data centers, 114–115
Data lock-in, governance principles, 203
Data portability, governance principles, 203
Deadlines, time management, 130
Decision making
alignment, 11
business context for, 52
consistency, 122–124
knowing when to cave, 124

Decision making (*continued*)
    with limited data and time, 130
    role of alignment, 11
    standing your ground, 125
    technical decisions as political decisions, 18–19
Delegation, 130–131
Delivering projects
    areas of responsibility for architects, 119–120
    concentrating on problem areas, 118
    contractors in leadership positions, 119
    eliminating dependencies, 116
    managing by walking around, 120–121
    managing expectations, 116–117
    mastering the development process, 117
    nontransparency, 118–119
    partnering with project managers, 116
Delivering results, 276
Demos, platform development, 154
Dependencies
    eliminating, 116
    minimizing, 172
    RAID (risks, assumptions, issues, dependencies), 116
Dependency awareness, strategic roadmapping, 257
Deployment
    governance areas, 208–209
    platform development, 159–160
Design reviews, 208
Development process, mastering, 117
Development reviews, 207
Development staff. *See* Teams
Diagrams
    conceptual, 64
    context, 64, 185
    executive overview, 187
    hardware environment, 187–188
    logical architecture, 186–187
    process, 184–185
    simplifying, 126
Disagreement, voicing, 125
Disaster recovery
    architectural concerns, 196–198
    governance principles, 196–198
Discovery. *See also* Strategic research
    definition, 30
    keys to, 30, 31. *See also specific keys*
Discovery, of customers
    accessing products, 36
    customer's language, 34, 42

    customer's perspective, 35–37
    interviewing key people, 36
    marketing department, 32–37
    meeting with customers, guidelines for, 37–43
    NDAs (nondisclosure agreements), 38
    NPD (new product development), 34–35
    partnering with customers, 32–37
    sales department, 32–37
    studying marketing materials, 35–36
    support calls, 36
    techniques for, 35–37
    training courses, 37
Discovery, of the market
    customer themes, 50–51
    customer values, 47–48
    guidelines, 43–46
    studying the competition, 48–50
    [the]customer's customer, 46–47
Discovery, of your business
    business context for decision making, 52
    goals and strategies, 52
Divestitures, platform development, 158
Documentation, platform development, 159. *See also* Presentations
Domain models
    architectural communication, 184
    concept formation, 59, 61
Drive-by estimation, 80–81

E

Ecosystems, platform development
    advisory boards, 150–151
    aligning with company goals, 153
    conflicting requirements, 153
    consolidating applications, 163
    consolidating company assets, 157–158
    contractors for, 158
    costs, 161–162
    definition, 144
    deployment, 159–160
    divestitures, 158
    documentation, 159
    funding, 149–150
    grooming the right team, 158–161
    intellectual property management, 160–161
    interaction with end customers, 153
    leveraging common assets, 163
    leveraging other platforms, 163

mergers and acquisitions, 157
mobile support, 163–164
on-boarding new partners, 153–154
oversight, 150–151
platform awareness and acceptance, 154–155
platform integration, 162–164
platform management, 155–158
platform ownership, 148–155
platform users, 148, 153
political issues, 150–151
pre-engagement materials, 152
quality management, 162. *See also* Technology
    excellence
requirements management, 152–153, 159
steering committees, 150–151
timely feedback, 153
type of integration, 163
user interface, 163
Education. *See* Enhancing your skill set;
    Know-how
E-mail, time management, 131
E-mail alerts, trends, 241
Enhancing your skill set. *See also* Know-how
becoming an expert, 135
doing technical things every day, 134–135
local conferences and user groups, 132–133
mastering the development process, 117
mentorship programs, 131–132
sitting with other architects, 134
stretching your comfort zone, 135
technology forums, 132
Enterprise reviews, 207
Entrepreneurial execution
architecting with, 282–283
calculated risk taking, 275–276
credibility, 275
definition, 272
delivering results, 276
depth of knowledge, 274
elements of, 273–276
focus, 274
innovation, 274
optimism, 274
passion, 274
thriving on adversity, 274
trusting your gut, 274
Entrepreneurial execution, principles
Affordable Loss Principle, 276
Bird-in-the-Hand Principle, 277

following your passion, 278–279
learning by doing, 280
Lemonade Principle, 276–277
Patchwork Quilt Principle, 277
Pilot-in-the-Plane Principle, 277
pivoting, 279–280
seeking feedback, 281–282
seeking leverage, 282–283
seizing the moment, 278
shiny object syndrome, 277
Entrepreneurship, definition, 272
Estimation
business case estimate, 82
business case validation, 82
drive-by, 80–81
governance areas, 204–205
level of detail, 80–82
overview, 80–84
project context, 82
purpose of, 80–82
quick sizing effort, 80–81
rough order of magnitude, 81
Estimation, architectural approach
business rationale, 89
external research, 96
issues to consider, 92
leverageable components, 96–97
marketing approach, 89–90
organizational structure, 95–96
overview, 82–84
partnerships *vs.* contractual relationships,
    88–89
platforms *vs.* applications, 93
repeat estimates, 90–91
re-platforming, 93–94
risk management, 91–93
technologies involved, 94–95
Estimation principles
avoiding negativity, 100
bargaining, 101
beware of external estimates, 101
caving in, 101
flexibility in design decisions, 100
knowing the hard problem, 100
knowing the targeted price, 101–102
opportunities to say yes, 100–101
providing options, 100
scheduling, 100, 102
trusting your gut, 101

Estimation process
  for acquisition projects, 86
  alternative financing, 86–87
  engaging executives, 103–104
  financing, business process, 87–88
  for integration projects, 86
  leverage points, 103
  for maintenance projects, 85
  for migration projects, 85
  for new/enhancement projects, 85–86
  personnel involved, 102
  pipeline process, 84–85
  project centric financing, 87
  reviewing estimates with executives, 126
  selling the estimate, 104–106
  spending envelope financing, 86–87
  timeline, 102
  types of projects, 85–86
  validating the estimate, 105–106
  visual presentation, 103
Estimation strategies
  concentrating on the critical, 98
  developing checklists, 99
  estimation feedback loops, 98
  executive and organizational buy-in, 99
  organization coupling and cohesion, 98
  planning for unknowns and challenges, 97
  PowerPoint presentations, 99
  realistic expectations, 98
Executive overview diagrams, 187
Executive reviews, 206–207
Executives. *See also* Management
  engaging in the estimation process, 103–104
  estimation buy-in, 99
Experimentation, 68
Extensibility, architectural concerns, 181–182
External partnerships, 26

F

Fans, 242
FAQs, platform development, 152
Feedback
  giving, 23
  during platform development, 153
  seeking, 281–282
Feedback, from customers
  analyzing, 243
  getting, 242–243

Feedback loops
  for estimation, 98
  technology innovation principles, 250
Financing
  alternatives, 86–87
  business process, 87–88
  governance areas, 206
  platform development, 149–150
  project centric, 87
  spending envelope, 86–87
  technology innovation principles, 247–248
Follower customers, 243
Funding. *See* Financing
Fuzzy front end. *See* Conceptualization

G

Goals, business
  aligning research with, 245
  discovery of your business, 52
  platform development ecosystems, 153
  strategic roadmapping principles, 262
Goals, quality, 164
Governance
  and agile development, 209–210
  definition, 194
Governance areas
  architecture reviews, 206–207
  building, 208–209
  coding, 208–209
  deploying, 208–209
  estimates, 204–205
  finance, 206
  integrating, 208–209
  IT compliance, 206
  legal compliance, 206
  management concerns, 205–206
  monitoring, 208–209
  overview, 204
  portfolio management, 205
  procurement, 205
  product lines, 205–206
  regulatory compliance, 206
  testing, 208–209
Governance principles
  automation, 203
  business continuity planning, 196–198
  cost of disruption, 196–198
  data lock-in, 203

data portability, 203
disaster recovery, 196–198
IAM (identity and access management),
    202–203
integration, 203
leveraging common capabilities, 199–200
loose coupling between business units, 198–199
open-source usage, 195–196
Principle of Least Authority, 202
Principle of Least Privilege, 202
regulatory compliance, 200–201
security, 201–202
vendor lock-in, 194–195
Grooming technical talent. *See also* Mentoring
    hiring the best people, 133–134
    local conferences and user groups, 132–133
    mentorship programs, 131–132
    technology forums, 132
Guiding principles, platform development
    configurability *vs.* hard coding, 165
    definition, 144
    leverageability, 165
    linear scalability, 166
    operational excellence, 165
    platform entanglement, 166
    platform sprawl, 166
    quality goals, 164
    redundant architecture, 166
    technical debt, 165
    upgrading to current technologies, 166

H

Hack-a-thons, attending/hosting, 221
Hard coding *vs.* configurability, 165
Hardware capability trends, 241
Hardware environment diagrams, 187–188
Hardware reviews, 207
Hiring the best people, 133–134

I

IAM (identity and access management), 202–203
Ideation phase. *See also* Conceptualization
    architectural communication, 184
    definition, 56
    in partnerships, 57
-ilities. *See* Architectural concerns
Industry trends, 239–240

Influencers, 10
Innovation, entrepreneurial execution, 274
Instrumentation, 226–227
Integration
    governance areas, 208–209
    governance principles, 203
    platform development, 162–164
    types of, 163
Integration projects, estimation, 86
Intellectual property
    management, 160–161
    trends, 241
Introducing new technologies, 250–251
IT compliance, 206

K

KISS (Keep It Simple, Stupid), 175–176
Know-how. *See also* Enhancing your skill set
    applying to your domain, 215–217
    blogging, 225
    conferences, attending, 220
    conferences, presenting at, 223
    currency, 214, 218–221
    dealing with ambiguity, 217
    definition, 214
    developing a model, 217
    excellence, 214, 221–229
    hack-a-thons, attending/hosting, 221
    instrumentation, 226–227
    leveraging online resources, 221
    online communities, 225–226
    open-source projects, 225–226
    performance tuning, 227–228
    POCs (proofs of concept), 220, 222
    project management, 228–229
    relevance, 214, 215–218
    saving money, 228
    scaling, 227–228
    selling, 217–218
    software construction process, 229
    teach a class, 224
    user groups, as resources, 222–223
    vetting, 217–218
    writing a book, 224–225
Know-how, technology knowledge
    acquiring, 218–221
    evaluating technologies, 215–217
Know-how-driven architecture, 230–231

L

Lab areas, 249–250
Law of Demeter, 172
Learning by doing, 280
Legal compliance, 206
Lemonade Principle, 276–277
Leverage, seeking, 282–283
Leverageability, platform development, 165
Leverageable components, in estimation, 96–97
Leveraging
    capabilities, 146–147
    common assets, 163
    common capabilities, 199–200
    online resources, 221
    other platforms, 163
    solutions, 115
Live demos
    acquiring know-how, 223
    platform development, 154
Logical architecture diagrams, 186–187
Loose coupling between business units, 198–199

M

Maintenance projects, estimating, 85
Maintenance windows, architectural concerns, 179
Making small bets, 248
Management. *See also* Executives
    definition, 110
    key areas of responsibility, 110. *See also*
        specific areas
Management concerns, governance areas, 205–206
Managing by walking around, 120–121
Managing expectations, 116–117
Managing your time. *See also* Time allocation
    avoiding e-mail, 131
    defining your role, 128
    delegating, 130–131
    limit meeting attendance, 130
    limiting commitments, 128
    making decisions under constraints, 130
    meeting in person, 131
    prioritizing, 128–130
    setting deadlines, 130
Market, discovery of
    customer themes, 50–51
    customer values, 47–48
    guidelines, 43–46
    studying the competition, 48–50
    [the]customer's customer, 46–47
Marketing approach to estimation, 89–90
Marketing materials, discovery of customers,
    35–36
Measuring strategic roadmapping, 259
Meetings
    with customers, guidelines for, 37–43
    limiting your attendance, 130
    time management, 130
Mentoring, 22–23. *See also* Grooming technical
    talent
Mentorship programs, 131–132
Mergers and acquisitions, platform development,
    157
Migration projects, estimating, 85
Mobile support, platform development, 163–164
Mobile trends, 253
Modeling concepts. *See* Visual models
Models, developing, 217
Monitoring, governance areas, 208–209
MVPs (minimum viable products), 67

N

NDAs (nondisclosure agreements), 38
Negativity in estimation, 100
Networked platforms, trends, 253
New/enhancement projects, estimating, 85–86
NPD (new product development), 33–35

O

Objectives, defining, 145–146
Occam's Razor, 175–176
On-boarding new partners, 153–154
Online communities, source of know-how, 225–226
Online resources, leveraging, 221
Open disclosure, 12–13
Open innovation challenges, 247
Open-source licensing, architectural concerns,
    195–196
Open-source projects, source of know-how, 225–226
Open-source tools, trends, 240
Open-source usage, governance principles, 195–196
Operational excellence, 165
Operations support, 114–115
Optimism, 274

Organizational structure, and estimation, 95–96
Organizations
    coupling and cohesion, 98
    estimation buy-in, 99
Overcommitment
    avoiding, 13–14
    coping with, 14–15
Oversight, platform development, 150–151
Ownership, platforms, 148–155

P

Partnering with executives
    avoid interrupting, 127
    confidence, 127
    having your boss's back, 127
    managing risk through transparency, 125–126
    reviewing estimates, 126
    simplifying presentation diagrams, 126
Partnerships. *See also* Relationships
    choosing partners, 7–9
    conceptualization, 57
    context, 17
    vs. contractual relationships in estimation,
        88–89
    contributing to your partner's success, 20–21
    with customers, 32–37
    definition, 6
    external, 26
    having your partner's back, 20
    ideation, 57
    key aspects, 6. *See also specific aspects*
    moving toward ideation, 24
    on-boarding new partners, 153–154
    political decisions, 19
    with project managers, 116
    safety in numbers, 21
    as a source of opportunity, 24
    strengthening, 24–25
    technical decisions, 18–19
    with universities, 246–247
Passion, 274, 278–279
Patchwork Quilt Principle, 277
Patent searches, 114
Peer reviews, 207
Performance tuning, 227–228
Perspective. *See* Architectural perspective
Pilot-in-the-Plane Principle, 277

Pipeline estimation process, 84–85
Pivoting, 279–280
Platform, definition, 143
Platform development
    consolidating company assets, 157–158
    contractors for, 158
    definition, 144
    key elements, 144–145. *See also specific elements*
Platform entanglement, 166
Platform sprawl, 166
Platforms
    vs. applications, estimation, 93
    awareness and acceptance, 154–155
    integration, 162–164
    managing, 155–158
    ownership, 148–155
    users, 148, 153
POCs (proofs of concept)
    calculated risk taking, 275
    concept reification, 68–69
    developing know-how currency, 220
    developing know-how excellence, 222
Political issues
    platform development, 150–151
    technical decisions, 18–19
Portfolio management, governance areas, 205
Power outages, architectural concerns, 179
PowerPoint presentations, for estimates, 99
Pre-engagement materials, platform development,
    152
Prerecorded product overviews, platform develop-
    ment, 152
Presentations. *See also* Architectural communica-
    tion; Documentation; Strategic roadmapping;
    Visual models
    architectural overviews, 154
    estimates, 99, 103
    FAQs, 152
    on-boarding new partners, 153–154
    PowerPoint, 99
    pre-engagement materials, 152
    prerecorded product overviews, 152
    scripted live demos, 154
    simplifying diagrams, 126
    white papers, 152
Principle of
    Feedback, 177
    Last Responsible Moment, 176–177

Principle of (*continued*)
    Least Authority, 202
    Least Effort, 172–173
    Least Knowledge, 172
    Least Privilege, 202
    Least Surprise, 170–172
    Natural Intuition, 171
    Opportunity Cost, 173–175
    Parsimony, 175–176
    Single Responsibility, 175
Principles of
    architecture. *See* Architectural principles
    cost estimation. *See* Estimation principles
    entrepreneurial execution. *See* Entrepreneurial
        execution, principles
    governance. *See* Governance principles
    platform development. *See* Guiding principles,
        platform development
    roadmapping. *See* Strategic roadmapping,
        principles
    technology innovation. *See* Technology innova-
        tion, principles
Prioritization
    strategic research, 245–246
    strategic roadmapping, 259
    time management, 128–130
Problem resolution. *See* Resolving issues
Process diagrams, 184–185
Procurement, governance areas, 205
Product lines, governance areas, 205–206
Professional development. *See* Enhancing your skill
    set; Know-how
Project centric financing, 87
Project life cycle diagram, 3. *See also specific
    stages*
Project management know-how, 228–229
Project skills, 1–3. *See also specific skills*
Projects, delivering
    areas of responsibility for architects, 119–120
    concentrating on problem areas, 118
    contractors in leadership positions, 119
    eliminating dependencies, 116
    managing by walking around, 120–121
    managing expectations, 116–117
    mastering the development process, 117
    nontransparency, 118–119
    partnering with project managers, 116

Proofs of concept (POCs). *See* POCs (proofs of
    concept)
Publishing strategic roadmaps, 259

Q

Quality goals, platform development, 164
Quality management, platform development, 162.
    See also Technology excellence

R

RAID (risks, assumptions, issues, dependencies),
    188–191
Rapid experimentation, 250
R&D approach to research, 246
Redundant architecture, 166
Reevaluating the product concept, 69–70
Refactoring code, 35
Regulatory compliance
    governance areas, 206
    governance principles, 200–201
    trends, 241
Reification. *See* Concept reification
Relationships. *See also* Partnerships
    dealing with caustic people, 26–27
    external partnerships, 26
    give-and-take, 25–26
    overcoming bad experiences, 26
    purpose of, 25
Repeatability, architectural concerns, 182
Re-platforming, estimation, 93–94
Report-out mechanism, strategic research, 246
Requirements management
    conflicting requirements, 153
    platform development, 152–153, 159
Research. *See* Discovery; Strategic research
Resolving issues
    asking the tough questions, 121
    being consistent in your decisions, 122–124
    head-on, 124
    knowing what is not your problem, 125
    knowing when to cave, 124
    in the moment, 121–122
    RAID (risks, assumptions, issues, dependencies),
        188–191
    saying no, with options, 122

standing your ground, 125
voicing disagreement, 125
Reviews
design validation, 208
estimates, 126
Reviews, architecture
approach, 206
development, 207
enterprise, 207
executive, 206–207
hardware, 207
peer, 207
review board, 10–11
Risk management
A/B testing, 275
calculated risk taking, 275–276
estimation, 91–93
minimizing investments, 275
RAID (risks, assumptions, issues, dependencies), 188–191
Risks, assumptions, issues, dependencies (RAID), 188–191
Roadmapping. See Strategic roadmapping
Rough order of magnitude estimation, 81

S

Saying no
concept formation, 62–63
importance of, 15–16
resolving issues, 122
Saying yes, in estimation, 100–101
Scalability
architectural concerns, 180–181
linear, 166
Scaling, know-how, 227–228
SCQA (situation, complication, question, answer). See SCRAP (situation, complication, resolution, action, politeness)
SCRAP (situation, complication, resolution, action, politeness), 19–20
Scripted live demos, 154
Security. See also Disaster recovery
architectural concerns, 201–202
governance principles, 201–202
Seizing the moment, 278
Selling know-how, 217–218

Server failure, architectural concerns, 179
Shared vision, 11–12
Shiny object syndrome, 277
Site loss, architectural concerns, 179
Site outages, architectural concerns, 179
Skill development, 287–288. See also Enhancing your skill set; Grooming technical talent; Know-how; Mentoring
Skills. See Project skills; Technology skills; Visionary skills
Soft skills, 287–288
Software compatibility issues, architectural concerns, 179
Software construction process, 229
Spending envelope financing, 86–87
Stakeholders, identifying, 8–9
Steering committees for platform development, 150–151
Sticky notes, strategic roadmapping, 260
Storage failure, architectural concerns, 179
Storage full, architectural concerns, 178–179
Strategic research. See also Discovery
alignment with business goals, 245
approaches, 246–247
business unit driven approach, 246
corporate innovation labs, 247
external, 96
open innovation challenges, 247
prioritization, 245
purpose of, 246
R&D approach, 246
report-out mechanism, 246
time and resource allocation, 246
university partnerships, 246–247
Strategic roadmapping
architect's role, 265–266
considerations, 266–267
definition, 256
finding what energizes you, 265
key milestones, 264–265, 269
socialization, 268–269
uses for, 266
visual representation, 258
visualizing, 256
Strategic roadmapping, elements of
code names, 258
collaboration, 258

Strategic roadmapping, elements of (*continued*)
    context dependency, 258
    dependency awareness, 257
    iteration, 259
    measuring, 259
    multidisciplinary, 258
    personalization, 258
    prioritization, 259
    publishing, 259
    specialization, 258
    strategic focus, 257
    swim lanes, 257
    time sequencing, 257
    updating, 259
    visual representation, 258
Strategic roadmapping, principles
    finding what energizes you, 265
    focus on the destination, 264–265
    getting started, 262
    having fun, 262
    keeping it simple, 261–262
    key milestones, 264–265
    partnering with the business, 262
    setting goals, 262
    skill and knowledge gaps, identifying, 263
    taking a new route, 263–264
    target areas, identifying, 263
    timing flexibility, 263
Strategic roadmapping, strategies
    capturing underlying principles, 261
    roadmapping as a project, 261
    sticky notes, 260
    whiteboarding, 260
    working backward, 260
    workshops, 260–261
Strategic solutions, 115
Striving toward technology excellence
    data centers and operations support, 114–115
    dealing with technical debt, 112
    establishing a vision, 112
    generalizing solutions, 115
    keeping technical staff engaged, 113
    leveraging solutions, 115
    patent searches, 114
    strategic solutions, 115
Support calls, discovery of customers, 36–37
Sustainability, architectural concerns, 182–183

Swim lanes, strategic roadmaps, 257
System boundaries, showing, 185
System components, showing, 186–187

T

Teaching classes, 224
Teams. *See also* Grooming technical talent
    hiring the best people, 133–134
    for platform development, 158–161
Technical debt, 112, 165
Technical skills, 287–288
Technologies involved in estimation, 94–95
Technology excellence. *See also* Quality
    management
    data centers and operations support,
        114–115
    dealing with technical debt, 112
    establishing a vision, 112
    generalizing solutions, 115
    keeping technical staff engaged, 113
    leveraging solutions, 115
    patent searches, 114
    strategic solutions, 115
Technology forums, 132
Technology innovation
    definition, 238
    pragmatic, 252–253
Technology innovation, business alignment
    customer feedback, 242–243
    trend analysis, 243–245
    trends on customer inquiries, 242
Technology innovation, principles
    feedback loops, 250
    introducing new technologies, 250–251
    lab areas, 249–250
    making small bets, 248
    rapid experimentation, 250
    time and funding, 247–248
    trend scouting, 248–249
Technology innovation, strategic research
    alignment with business goals, 245
    approaches, 246–247
    business unit driven approach, 246
    corporate innovation labs, 247
    open innovation challenges, 247
    prioritization, 245

purpose of, 246
R&D approach, 246
report-out mechanism, 246
time and resource allocation, 246
university partnerships, 246–247
Technology innovation, trend awareness
applying, 241–242
big data trend, 252–253
cloud capabilities, 241
conferences, 240
customers' competitive knowledge, 241
e-mail alerts, 241
hardware capabilities, 241
industry, 240
intellectual property, 241
mobile trend, 253
networked platform trend, 253
open-source tools, 240
regulatory compliance, 241
university research, 240
vendor capabilities, 241
Technology knowledge management, 141. *See also* Know-how
Technology leverage, 141. *See also* Platform development
Technology oversight, 141. *See also* Governance
Technology skills. *See also specific skills*
dimensions of, 141
overview, 139–140
Testing, governance areas, 208–209
Third-party integration, architectural concerns, 182–183
Thought leaders, 9
Time allocation. *See also* Managing your time
strategic research, 245–246
technology innovation principles, 247–248
Training. *See* Enhancing your skill set; Know-how
Transparency
delivering projects, 118–119
in partnerships, 16–17
risk management, 125–126
Trend analysis, 243–245
Trend awareness
applying, 241–242
big data, 252–253
cloud capabilities, 241
conferences, 240

customer inquiries, 242
customers' competitive knowledge, 241
e-mail alerts, 241
hardware capabilities, 241
industry, 240
intellectual property, 241
mobile, 253
networked platforms, 253
open-source tools, 240
regulatory compliance, 241
trend analysis, 243–245
trend scouting, 248–249
university research, 240
vendor capabilities, 241
Trend scouting, 248–249
Trust
establishing, 12
learning to say no, 15–16
open disclosure, 12–13
overcommitting, 13–15
transparency, 16–17
Trusted advisers, 10
Trusting your gut
entrepreneurial execution, 274
estimation, 101

U

University partnerships, strategic research, 246–247
University research trends, 240
Upgrading to current technologies, 166
User groups
for professional development, 132–133
as resources, 222–223
User interface
mock-ups, 186
platform development, 163
Principle of Least Effort, 172–173
Users of platforms, 148, 153. *See also* Customers
Utilitarian customers, 242

V

Validating estimates, 82, 105–106
Vendor capability trends, 241
Vendor lock-in, governance principles, 194–195
Vetting know-how, 217–218

Vision, establishing, 112
Visionary skills, 233–235. *See also specific skills*
Visual models
    concept formation, 63–67
    conceptual diagrams, 64
    context diagrams, 64

W

White papers, platform development, 152

Whiteboarding, strategic roadmapping,
    260
Work flow, showing, 184–185
Workshops, strategic roadmapping,
    260–261
Writing a book, 224–225

Z

Zipf's Law, 172–173

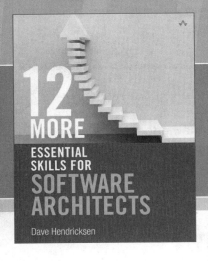

12 MORE ESSENTIAL SKILLS FOR SOFTWARE ARCHITECTS

Dave Hendricksen

FREE
Online Edition

Safari
Books Online

Your purchase of *12 More Essential Skills for Software Architects* includes access to a free online edition for 45 days through the **Safari Books Online** subscription service. Nearly every Addison-Wesley Professional book is available online through **Safari Books Online**, along with thousands of books and videos from publishers such as Cisco Press, Exam Cram, IBM Press, O'Reilly Media, Prentice Hall, Que, Sams, and VMware Press.

Safari Books Online is a digital library providing searchable, on-demand access to thousands of technology, digital media, and professional development books and videos from leading publishers. With one monthly or yearly subscription price, you get unlimited access to learning tools and information on topics including mobile app and software development, tips and tricks on using your favorite gadgets, networking, project management, graphic design, and much more.

Activate your FREE Online Edition at
informit.com/safarifree

STEP 1: Enter the coupon code: XNWIPXA.

STEP 2: New Safari users, complete the brief registration form.
Safari subscribers, just log in.

If you have difficulty registering on Safari or accessing the online edition,
please e-mail customer-service@safaribooksonline.com

Addison Wesley · Adobe Press · ALPHA · Cisco Press · FT Press · IBM Press · Microsoft Press · New Riders · O'REILLY

Peachpit Press · Prentice Hall · que · Redbooks · SAMS · SAS · vmware PRESS · WILEY · wrox